D0776613

NAPOLEON'S GLANCE
·THE SECRET OF STRATEGY·

ALSO BY WILLIAM DUGGAN

The Great Thirst
Lovers of the African Night
The Art of What Works

NAPOLEON'S GLANCE: THE SECRET OF STRATEGY
Copyright © 2002 William Duggan

First Nation Books edition 2002
First Nation Books trade paperback edition 2004

Published by
Nation Books
An Imprint of Avalon Publishing Group Incorporated
245 W. 17th St., 11th Floor
New York, NY 10011

Nation Books is a co-publishing venture of the Nation Institute and Avalon Publishing Group Incorporated.

All rights reserved. No part of this publication may be reproduced or transmitted in any form or by any means, electronic or mechanical, including photocopy, recording, or any information storage and retrieval system now known or to be invented, without permission in writing from the publisher, except by a reviewer who wishes to quote brief passages in connection with a review written for inclusion in a magazine, newspaper, or broadcast.

Library of Congress Cataloging-in-Publication Data
Duggan, William R.
  Napoleon's glance: the secret of strategy / William Duggan.
  p. cm.
  Includes bibliographical references.
  ISBN 1-56025-457-2
  1. Strategy—Case studies. I. Title.
U162 .D84 2003
355.4—dc21   2002075071

Book design by Simon M. Sullivan

Distributed by Publishers Group West

NAPOLEON'S GLANCE

·THE SECRET OF STRATEGY·

WILLIAM DUGGAN

Thunder's Mouth Press • Nation Books
New York

CONTENTS

✝ ✝ ✝

For Lynn and Emmaline

NAPOLEON'S GLANCE
·THE SECRET OF STRATEGY·

1
+ + +
# IN SEARCH OF STRATEGY

T ake a close look at great heroes of history and you see that they're all very different, except for one thing: They're all great strategists.

A great strategy beats the odds: In the face of uncertainty, obstacles, and risk, you decide what course of action leads to success. So then we ask: What is great strategy? How do you know what path to take, what course to follow, what means will lead to your end?

To answer the question "What is great strategy?" let's first define our terms. By "great" we mean successful. As for "strategy," the dictionary tells us the word comes from ancient Greece. A *strategos* was an army general, and his post was a *strategia*, the way a president's post is a presidency. Over time, *strategia* came to mean the craft of generalship instead of just the job. *Strategia* spread to French as *stratégie*, and then to English as "strategy" in 1810.

That all seems clear enough. There's nothing surprising, except for the date. It took a long time for the word to reach the English language. Was it just a matter of gradual spread from Greek to French to English, or was there something special about 1810?

As it turns out, the year 1810 was the height of success for the most successful general in history: Napoleon Bonaparte. His enemies studied his method to learn how to defeat him. That led to a great discovery: the secret of strategy.

Napoleon's glance.

It was a Prussian officer, Carl von Clausewitz, who made the discovery. He fought against Napoleon, and lost. In 1810, von Clausewitz joined the faculty of the new Prussian War College in Berlin, where he spent the next twenty years struggling to pin down on paper the genius of Napoleon. Von Clausewitz was never satisfied, and never finished. In 1831, on a routine tour of duty in Poland, he died of cholera. His beloved wife, Marie, took up his great work. She polished up and published the first volume as *On War* in 1832.

In Chapter Six, "The Genius of War," we find Napoleon's glance. Von Clausewitz calls it *coup d'oeil* (pronounced koo-DOY). In French, *coup* means "stroke" and *oeil* means "eye": So *coup d'oeil* means a stroke of the eye, or "glance." To von Clausewitz, *coup d'oeil* is sudden insight that shows you what course of action to take. It comes from knowledge of the past: You draw on what worked in other situations, in a new combination that fits the problem at hand.

Coup d'oeil was the secret of Napoleon's success. He made no innovations himself: Instead, he studied in detail the winning campaigns of the great generals who came before him, all the way back to Alexander the Great more than two thousand years before. Napoleon imitated their tactics but always in a new combination that fit the present situation. He put his army in motion with no particular destination, until he saw in a *coup d'oeil* a chance to win a battle. The place and time were completely unpredictable, and he passed up more battles than he fought.

Napoleon began his career as an ordinary lieutenant in the French army at the time of the Revolution. In less than a decade, he was emperor of Europe. He conquered more territory, faster, than the Roman Empire of ancient times or the Holy Roman Empire of the Middle Ages. No wonder his enemies scrambled to learn how he did it, and so invented the new science of "strategy."

This book tells how ten great strategists of history owe their success to *coup d'oeil*. All ten of them applied it with great effort and risk and with no guarantee it would work. You can't know whether you've chosen the right battle, or drawn on the right combination of past tactics, until the battle is over. But there is no other way to win, except through blind luck.

In case after case, we find the same story. How American women won the right to vote. How General Patton became the most successful Allied general on the Western Front of World War II. How Joan of Arc saved France from certain conquest by England. How in one generation Japan went from a peasant backwater to an industrial giant. How Picasso became the leading artist of the twentieth century. The American civil rights movement, Africa's greatest empire: You can pick up the newspaper and find a new case every day. With your eye out for *coup d'oeil*, you start to see it everywhere.

In only one case—General Patton—does our strategist look to von Clausewitz or Napoleon. The rest of them either lived centuries before or knew nothing of military strategy. All the same, they owed their success to *coup d'oeil*. In some cases, you can pin down the moment the *coup d'oeil* struck, but mostly you just find the year or maybe the month. But always, you have to hunt. Sometimes, like in the Patton story, we can track down direct evidence for *coup d'oeil* in written records. Other times we have only hints and traces to go on.

For example, the African empire of Mali arose in the thirteenth century and lasted two hundred years without any written records. A clan of poets, the *griots*, passed down the story of the empire's founding in oral form. "The Epic of Sundiata" tells the tale of Sundiata Keita, Mali's first emperor. This poem remains the main source of information on Mali's early days. You might know the story, but with animals instead of people: *The Lion King*. It doesn't come through in the Disney version, but the Lion King owed his success to *coup d'oeil*.

In telling these stories, this book might suffer from "confirmation bias": That is, you find what you're looking for and ignore everything else. For example, if we look for red hats in a crowd, we'll probably find them. But that doesn't tell us what color hats most people wear, because we ignored all the other colors. To the charge of confirmation bias, we can only plead guilty. But the aim here is a modest one: only to show that red hats exist. That Napoleon's glance is real.

Also, science supports it.

In a key passage, von Clausewitz describes *coup d'oeil* as "the rapid discovery of a truth which to the ordinary mind is not visible at all or only becomes so after long examination and reflection." So *coup d'oeil* is an act of the mind: Some minds do it, and some don't. This leads us to modern-day "mind research," a wild frontier of psychology that studies *coup d'oeil* from many different angles: brain scans, master chess-players, Zen philosophy, firefighters, emergency room nurses, and artificial intelligence.

We find that modern science has its own name for *coup d'oeil*: expert intuition. Psychologists see it as a form of déjà vu, a sixth sense based not on dreamy visions but on solid knowledge and past experience. Research on expert intuition makes the star of von Clausewitz glow only brighter: A century and a half later, science confirms the power of Napoleon's glance.

As expert intuition, Napoleon's glance might sound like the "great man" theory, where a single individual—the expert— changes the course of history. But the opposite is the case. In a *coup d'oeil*, the strategist draws on what other people achieved before in similar situations. It is an act of humility, not hubris. You don't impose your will on the world: Your will conforms to what the world imposes on you.

Such is the secret of strategy as our ten stories reveal.

2

+ + +

NAPOLEON VS. THE NOBLES

Tell me how the Germans have trained you to fight Bonaparte by this new science you call strategy.

—Prince Bolkonsky to his son, Andrei, in *War and Peace* by Leo Tolstoy

I n late March of 1796, General Napoleon Bonaparte went to Nice in the south of France to take up his first command. The country was under attack.

It was the seventh year since the French Revolution deposed the king, and the fourth year since the new government beheaded him. There was no turning back. The Revolution overthrew everything, from noble privilege to the days and months of the year: March 1796 was Floréal IV in the new regime. In response, the nobles of Europe banded together in a great coalition to mount armies and invade France, to stamp out the Revolution before it spread to overthrow them too.

Napoleon was twenty-six years old. That was too young for a general in ordinary times, but during the Revolution the older generals of France had fled the country. Most of them came from the high nobility, with everything to lose in the new regime. To replace them, the army promoted young officers like Napoleon. Most of the young officers were commoners, or poor nobles with nothing to lose, like Napoleon.

Napoleon's command was a contingent of the army in the south of France. They faced a much larger coalition force of Italians and Austrians across the border in Italy. Napoleon arrived at headquarters in Nice to find his troops hungry, unpaid, in ragged uniforms and worn-out shoes. They were short on cavalry and artillery. He started off with a speech, but instead of a rally to revolution, he spoke to their empty stomachs: "Soldiers! You are ill-fed and almost naked. The government owes you a great deal but it can do nothing for you. . . . I shall lead you into the most fertile plains on earth. There you will find great cities and rich provinces. There you will find honor, glory, riches. . . . "

This was a call to conquest, pure and simple, for the age-old prize of plunder. But could Napoleon deliver? His poor noble birth had at least gained him entry to military school, and he earned a reputation as a good artillery officer, but he arrived at the front with no experience leading an army in battle. At five foot two, he was smaller than almost all of his men. They did not even consider him French, for he came from Corsica, an Italian island that had become part of France only recently, in 1769, three months before Napoleon was born.

But even in his Corsican accent, Napoleon spoke with great confidence and quickly organized his troops for battle. They were one of three French armies fighting. The other two were farther north, in Holland and Germany, where they held the enemy at a standstill. But they could not hold out for long. France was collapsing. The Revolution had succeeded in overthrowing the nobility, but it could not run a government or supply an army. So Napoleon was right—his troops were on their own. It was up to them to win or lose, to conquer or be conquered, for their own sake and for the survival of the Revolution.

As Napoleon's ragtag army crossed the border into Italy, the coalition forces divided in two. The Italians spread out in an arc to defend the city of Turin. The Austrians spread out to defend Milan. But instead of heading for one or the other, Napoleon went between them.

This confused the enemy to no end. Where was Napoleon going?

The Italians sent out troops to find him. Napoleon picked them off in a series of quick battles near the towns of Montenotte, Millesimo, Dego, and Mondovi. These locations had no importance at all except that they happened to be where Napoleon saw a chance to meet the enemy and win.

In shock and dismay, the Italians gave up. The Austrians fell back, closer to defend Milan. But again Napoleon surprised them. He kept on going and bypassed Milan completely.

The Austrians panicked. They feared he was on his way to invade Austria instead, so they left their defenses and rushed off after him. When they moved close to the Adda River, Napoleon saw they would have to cross at the town of Lodi. So he quickly set up artillery facing the bridge in the middle of town. Sure enough, the enemy appeared. Napoleon's artillery opened fire.

At the start of the campaign, Napoleon had stayed in the rear of his army, with his maps and a comfortable tent, like most generals of the day. But with each battle, he moved closer to the front. Now at Lodi, he went right to the bridge and directed the artillery himself. In the smoke and thunder of the cannons, his men saw their young commander moving from cannon to cannon, calling out orders to the gunners and pointing to adjust their range and aim. Sweat and powder streaked his face. It was a job for a corporal, not a general, so there and then Napoleon's men named him the "Little Corporal."

The artillery held off the Austrians across the river. Then Napoleon called up his infantry, arranged them in attack formation, and sent them across the bridge. The Austrians fell back, and then broke rank. They turned and ran.

And so ended Napoleon's first campaign. He won five swift victories in less than a month, against troops much greater in number and better equipped. His triumph at the Lodi bridge showed him the future: "From that moment, I foresaw what I might be. Already I felt the earth flee from beneath me, as if I were being carried into the sky."

Over the next twenty years, Napoleon repeated the same formula of success from his first campaign, in fifty-five battles across Europe. His victories made him the ruler of France in 1799 and then emperor of Europe in 1804. His enemies scrambled to study his methods, to learn his secrets and defeat him. They founded military colleges and drew arrows on maps. Bookshelves filled with volumes of theory, principles, and detailed descriptions of the Little Corporal's every move.

And so was born a new science: strategy.

It is easy to forget the impact of Napoleon. For Americans especially, he is mostly a cartoon figure of fun, a little man with a big hat shaped like a boat upside-down, barking out orders, with one hand mysteriously clutching his chest underneath his coat. But in Europe, they remember.

Most of France's modern institutions began under Napoleon, especially the government administration and the legal and education systems. Germany's great war machine, which wreaked so much terror in the twentieth century, first arose to atone for dozens of humiliating defeats at Napoleon's hand. Even in the modern European Community, the leaders of France and Germany continue a rivalry that brings back the memory of Napoleon: He was the first head of state since Charlemagne to use the term "Europe" for the lands he ruled.

In Russia, once a year they still re-create the battle that turned the tide of Napoleon's invasion, marking the country's passage from a clumsy giant to a powerful nation. And Napoleon is the dominant character in what many authorities consider the greatest novel ever written, and certainly the greatest Russian novel—Leo Tolstoy's *War and Peace*. Throughout the book, Tolstoy puzzles over the secret of Napoleon's success, and what that success means for the future of Russia.

In England, we even find Napoleon in the great children's novel *Peter Pan* by James M. Barrie, published in 1911. At the time, the English still knew Napoleon as the most brilliant strategist in history. Barrie tells us how the girl Wendy sees that her kind but unremarkable father "got all of" her magnificent mother, except for a kiss in the corner of her mother's mouth. Barrie writes: " . . . and in time he gave up trying for the kiss. Wendy thought Napoleon could have got it . . . "

During Napoleon's time, the English press portrayed him as not just a brilliant strategist, but an evil force out to do them in. Nannies scared children: "Be good or Boney will get you!" The English hated and feared Napoleon because of his battlefield success and because of what he wanted to do to them: topple their beloved king. It was Napoleon versus the nobles, but the English kings—and queens, princes and princesses—managed to stay on their throne even to this day.

The English royal family might seem quaint and colorful now—especially to many Americans, who worship them from afar. But in Napoleon's time, Europe made its first great strides to free itself from the grip of its nobles. The French Revolution made a spark, but it was Napoleon who made a fire. The modern democracies of Europe owe their existence more to Napoleon than to any other individual in history.

Once Napoleon used his strategy to defeat an enemy's army, he used another weapon against its nobles: the Napoleonic Code. The code came from the Declaration of the Rights of Man, which stated the basic principles of the French Revolution in 1789. The new government started converting the declaration into law in 1793, and in 1800 Napoleon set up a commission to complete the work. The result was the Napoleonic Code. Its most basic feature—and greatest threat to the nobles—was equality before the law.

Napoleon imposed the code on his conquests. He set up his family members and loyal generals as kings of lands he conquered, and then set about dismantling the local nobility. He wrote to his brother Jerome in Germany:

What the peoples of Germany desire most impatiently is that talented commoners should have the same right to your esteem and to public employments as the nobles, that any trace of serfdom and of an intermediate hierarchy between the sovereign and the lowest class of the people should be completely abolished. The benefits of the Napoleonic Code, the publicity of judicial procedures, the creation of juries, must be so many distinguishing marks on your monarchy . . . What nation would wish to return to the arbitrary Prussian government once it had tasted the benefit of a wise and liberal administration?

This was Napoleon's version of the French Revolution, exported. He declared, "Liberty means a good civil code" and "My motto has always been: a career open to all talents, without distinctions of birth." And: "The annexed territories must be just like France, and if you went on annexing everything as far as Gibraltar and Kamchatka, the laws of France would have to spread there, too. I am pleading the cause of the humble folk; the others never lack good dinners and brilliant drawing rooms that will plead for them."

So Napoleon's noble enemies studied his strategy not just to defeat him in battle but to save their way of life. The feudal system had lasted a millennium—from A.D. 800, when the emperor Charlemagne united French and German lands, and confiscated farmland and gave it to his loyal generals. The peasants on those farms now tilled the estates and fought in the armies of their noble lords. The feudal system spread throughout Europe and hardened into the "absolutist" states where kings claimed authority directly from God. It seemed like the natural order of life. Then came the French Revolution, and Napoleon.

No single individual did more to end monarchy than Napoleon Bonaparte—yet today the debate over his legacy continues. For example, in June 2002 we find a *New York Times Book Review* cover article on two new biographies of Napoleon. We learn that there are more books about Napoleon than about any other historical figure except for Christ. One biographer, Paul Johnson, sees a vicious tyrant who helped set the stage for Hitler and Stalin. The other biographer, Frank McLynn, sees a tormented soul obsessed with his mother. The reviewer, Mark Mazower, points out how both authors downplay Napoleon's worthy fight against monarchy. Mazower cites the "positive verdict" of Theodore Kolokotronis, a national hero who fought for Greece in the 1820s:

> *The French Revolution and the doings of Napoleon opened the eyes of the world . . . The nations knew nothing before and the people thought that kings were gods upon the earth . . . Through this present change it is more difficult to rule the people.*

Yet not even Mazower mentions the source of Napoleon's success: his military strategy. Napoleon himself knew very well where his power came from:

> *My power proceeds from my reputation, and my reputation from the victories I have won. My power would fail if I were not to support it with more glory and more victories. Conquest has made me what I am; only conquest can maintain me.*

Napoleon won battles. That was the key to his success. But how did he win them? What was the secret of his strategy?

The first popular book on Napoleon's strategy was *Summary of the Art of War* by Antoine Jomini, a Swiss. Jomini claimed inside knowledge, for he served on Napoleon's staff for more than a decade. In 1813, Jomini switched sides and joined the enemy. He founded Russia's first military academy in 1830 and his book came out eight years later, to immediate success. Jomini was an arrogant dandy know-it-all, and a traitor to boot. But he wrote well, in elegant French, so his book was easy to read and simple to follow.

Jomini presents Napoleon as a chessboard planner: "Strategy is the art of making war upon the map." You identify a strategic objective and then concentrate your forces to seize or defend it. From Jomini, generals learned to plan massive battles on maps in great detail, deploying their troops like pieces on a chessboard, from the safety of headquarters far behind the lines. Jomini's ideas became so popular that both sides of the American Civil War and World War I followed them closely, in the belief that they were imitating Napoleon. The result was static fronts, massive battles of mutual slaughter, and tragedy on a monumental scale.

We can see that Jomini was wrong just from Napoleon's first campaign. The Italians and Austrians identified Turin and Milan as strategic objectives. So that was where they concentrated their forces. But Napoleon had no strategic objectives. Instead, he set his army in motion with no definite destination, and then looked for opportunities where he could win a battle. The place and time were completely unpredictable, and he passed up more battles than he fought.

This mobile view of Napoleon's strategy comes from Jomini's leading competitor, Carl von Clausewitz. A shy, intense, studious, and patriotic Prussian, von Clausewitz fought on the losing side in some of Napoleon's greatest battles. Then he spent twenty years on the faculty of the new Berlin War College, where he struggled to capture the essence of Napoleon's strategy and pass it on to his countrymen. He never finished. After von Clausewitz's death, his wife published his disorganized writings as *On War* in 1832.

It took many years for *On War* to develop a following outside Prussia. Soldiers from other countries, especially England, studied French to read Jomini, for after all, that was the language of Napoleon himself. No one studied German just to read von Clausewitz. And *On War* was much harder to read than Jomini's book. Von Clausewitz wrote in the heavy, abstract philosophical style of German philosophers like Hegel and Kant. But also, von Clausewitz had a harder time writing because he looked deeper than Jomini. Von Clausewitz worked and worked at the question of how Napoleon decided just when and where to fight a battle. That is, how did he know that the Austrians were headed for the Lodi bridge, and then how did he know he could beat them?

It takes von Clausewitz hundreds of pages to answer this elusive question. Reading *On War*, you get the feeling that through all the underbrush of ponderous prose, von Clausewitz is chasing a rabbit. He hears a rustle over there and sets off after it. Then a rustle over here, and he goes back where he started. To and fro von Clausewitz thrashes, page after page after page. But in the end, he catches the rabbit. He tells you the essence of strategy. There, in a chapter titled "The Genius for War," we find the secret of Napoleon's success.

Napoleon saw when and where to fight in a sudden flash of insight. Von Clausewitz called it *coup d'oeil*, using the French term for "glance." *Coup d'oeil* is "the rapid discovery of a truth which to the ordinary mind is not visible at all or only becomes so after long examination and reflection." It comes from "those combinations which military history can furnish." After *coup d'oeil* comes "resolution," which is "the office of removing the torments of doubt, and the dangers of delay, when there are no sufficient motives for guidance." To stay prepared for *coup d'oeil*, you must expect the unexpected through "presence of mind," for war "is indeed nothing but a great conquest over the unexpected."

So for von Clausewitz, the secret of Napoleon's strategy boils down to four key elements: the *coup d'oeil*, combinations from history, resolution, and presence of mind. We understand now why Napoleon's battles took place in such odd locations: He did not know where he would fight until the *coup d'oeil* came. Then he rode his horse into the thick of the fighting, for more *coups d'oeil* until the battle was won. That was why he led from the front, as at the Lodi bridge, the better to see in a glance the battle unfolding and make adjustments along the way.

Napoleon made no military innovations himself. Instead, his *coups d'oeil* repeated the achievements of great generals who came before him. Before he fought his first battle, Napoleon had studied their campaigns so thoroughly that he could draw on their successful tactics at a glance, like arrows in a quiver, and bring them to bear on the matter at hand. In Napoleon's Italian campaign, he especially borrowed from Frederick the Great of Prussia in the Seven Years War, half a century before.

In Napoleon's own writings and sayings, he gives many clues to support von Clausewitz:

> *The principles of warfare are those that guided the great captains whose high deeds history has transmitted to us—Alexander, Hannibal, Caesar, Gustavus Adolphus, Turenne, Eugene of Savoy, Frederick the Great . . . The history of their eighty-three campaigns would constitute a complete treatise on the art of war.*

> *The art of war consists, with a numerically inferior army, in always having larger forces than the enemy at the point which is to be attacked or defended . . . it is an intuitive way of acting which properly constitutes the genius of war.*

> *The issue of a battle is the result of a single instant, a single thought . . . the decisive moment appears; a psychological spark makes the decision; and a few reserve troops are enough to carry it out.*

> *Tactics can be learned from treatises, somewhat like geometry, and so can the various evolutions of the science of the engineer and the gunner; but knowledge of the grand principles of warfare can be acquired only through the study of military history and of the battles of the great captains and through experience.*

> *I never truly was my own master but was always ruled by circumstances.*

To every circumstance its own law.

The greater one is, the less will he must have. He depends on events and circumstances.

I had few really definite ideas, and the reason for this was that, instead of obstinately seeking to control circumstances, I obeyed them ... Thus it happened that most of the time, to tell the truth, I had no definite plans but only projects.

The fact was that I was not a master of my actions, because I was not so insane as to attempt to bend events to conform to my policies. On the contrary, I bent my policies to accord with the unforeseen shape of the events.

A battle is my plan of campaign, and success is my whole policy.

In many of these quotes, Napoleon stresses how he never tried to impose his will on circumstances. Rather, he yielded to them. This seems completely contrary to his nature and achievement: After all, he conquered Europe. Wasn't that imposing his will? The answer is no. He had no plans to speak of. Instead, he struck whenever he saw a way to combine tactics from the past to suit the immediate moment. You cannot force *coup d'oeil*. It comes or it doesn't. If you don't see a battle to win, keep moving until you do.

But one time, Napoleon forgot *coup d'oeil*. He made the mistake of telling his enemies exactly where he was going.

It was 1812, when Napoleon ruled all of continental Europe. That left only England and Russia against him. He knew he could not cross the English Channel to fight on English soil, so he tried to weaken England by blocking its trade to the continent and Russia.

Since Napoleon ruled the continent, that part was easy. Stopping England's trade with Russia was something else. So he mounted his largest army ever, more than 600,000 soldiers drawn from all the countries he conquered, and headed for Moscow.

In March 1812, Napoleon declared: "Barbarian nations are superstitious and have simple ideas. A single blow delivered at the heart of the Russian empire, at Moscow the Great, Moscow the Holy, will in a single instant put this whole blind and apathetic mass at my mercy. "

Here we have Napoleon following Jomini, not von Clausewitz. Napoleon set a strategic objective—Moscow—and then concentrated his forces to take it. He saw nothing blocking his way: Russia's "barbarian" army was poorly trained and led, and its extreme form of feudalism—serfdom—meant that the Russian masses would never come to the aid of their nobles.

Or so thought Napoleon on the eve of his greatest campaign. On his way to Russia, he stopped in Dresden, Germany, where he held court to receive the conquered nobles and their armies. Again, he told the world where he was going.

On the second day of summer, June 23, Napoleon's army crossed into Russia.

From the point of view of von Clausewitz, Napoleon made a terrible mistake before he started: "When Bonaparte marched to Moscow in 1812, all depended on whether the taking of the capital, and the events which preceded the capture, would force the Emperor Alexander to make peace . . . we cannot regard the firmness of Alexander as something unpredictable . . . What can be more natural than to say that in the years 1805, 1807, 1809, Bonaparte judged his opponents correctly, and that in 1812 he erred in that point?"

Why was the firmness of Alexander predictable? Because Napoleon did not defeat the Russian army in battle, which was the basis of all his previous success. Alexander was willing to give up

Moscow as long as his army remained intact. During the whole long march across Russia, for the first time in Napoleon's career everyone knew where he was going. He was on his way to Moscow. He was not on his way to defeat the Russian army. He thought that if he took Moscow, the army would give up. It was pure Jomini, and the exact opposite of Napoleon's previous method.

Why did Napoleon change strategy? We don't know. Perhaps at the height of his success, with all of Europe at his command, at the head of the largest army the continent had seen in centuries— he finally felt invincible. After all, he had met the Russian army once before, at Austerlitz in 1805, where he routed them completely. So in 1812, Napoleon lost his "presence of mind," where you expect the unexpected and so stay ready for *coup d'oeil*, where you see how to combine elements from the past in a new combination and follow through with resolution. In Russia, he thought he knew what to expect.

Of Napoleon's 600,000 troops, some 150,000 took up positions along and behind the border. That left 450,000 in the main force to march on Moscow. The Russian army totaled 400,000, with 150,000 in reserve positions, leaving 250,000 to face Napoleon. For the first time, Napoleon's army greatly outnumbered his foe. But it was three times greater than any army he had ever commanded before. With such a massive force, he lost mobility. That meant if his strategy started to fail, he lacked the ability to change it.

For two months, through July and August, Napoleon marched his force across the great Russian steppes. The summer took its toll: Heat and thirst weakened the troops, who fell sick and dropped behind in larger and larger numbers. The Russian army retreated in fear and disarray, stopping here and there to fight or mounting hit-and-run raids.

By early September, Napoleon was seventy miles from Moscow. His main force was down to 130,000 troops. The Russians finally threw themselves in his way, with 120,000 soldiers. It was a lucky break for Napoleon: Despite his mistake of aiming for Moscow, here was a chance to defeat the Russian army in battle.

The battle took place on September 7 at a bend in the Moskva River, near the village of Borodino. As usual, there was nothing special about the location, except that Napoleon saw a way to win there. But on the eve of the battle, he fell sick. He was unable to mount his horse and ride into the fighting to follow up his first *coup d'oeil* with smaller *coups d'oeil* as the battle unfolded. Instead, Napoleon's generals came back and forth to his tent behind the lines to report what was happening and receive new instructions.

Napoleon's doctor described his illness: "persistent dry cough, difficult irregular breathing, his urine came only in drops and with pain and was thick with sediment . . . his legs and feet were oedematous, the pulse febrile in type and intermittent every twelve beats." So Napoleon, too, suffered from his months in the cruel Russian summer.

At a high point in the battle, Napoleon's generals implored him to send in the reserves for a final blow. He replied, "Before I commit my reserves I must be able to see more clearly on my chessboard." The *coup d'oeil* did not strike, and Napoleon knew he could not force it. But he was too far away from the action, so the whole battle passed without the final *coup d'oeil* to win the day.

In late afternoon, the Russians withdrew from the field. So technically it was a French victory, although the actual fighting came out a draw: Each side lost more than 30,000 troops. Napoleon now faced a choice: pursue the Russian army for a final defeat, or continue his march on Moscow.

Von Clausewitz reports:

> *The victory which he had just gained gave him nearly a certainty of taking that capital, for that the Russians would be in a condition to fight a second battle within eight days seemed in the highest degree improbable; and in Moscow he hoped to*

find peace. No doubt the complete dispersion of the Russian Army would have made this peace much more certain; but still the first consideration was to get to Moscow . . .

And so Napoleon pursued his "first consideration"—Moscow—instead of the Russian army.

On September 15, he entered the Russian capital.

It was empty.

There was no army, no merchants, no royal court, no bankers, no factories running. A few stragglers hid in their houses, but most of the population had fled the city. They had plenty of time to pack, because Napoleon had told the world exactly where he was going.

Now Napoleon was really in trouble. He was not ready for the unexpected: He had expected a thriving, bustling Moscow, where he could order up food and clothing and all the other supplies his troops needed. Instead, he found a ghost town.

And then it burned down.

No one knows how the fire started—perhaps careless looters, or arson by the Russians—but a city of wood burns fast. By the time Napoleon's troops put the fire out, even the scraps left behind were gone.

Napoleon wrote to the czar to demand surrender, and added in fury:

How is it possible to destroy one of the most beautiful cities in the world and the labor of centuries for so small an aim? . . . Since the Russian army had left Moscow unprotected, common humanity and Your Majesty's own interests required that this city be entrusted to my safekeeping. The administration, the magistrates, and the militia should have been left here. It was thus that things were done in Vienna, on two occasions, in Berlin, and in Madrid . . .

But in Vienna, Berlin, and Madrid, Napoleon had defeated the enemy army first.

The czar never replied to Napoleon's demand for surrender. Weeks passed. Napoleon knew he could not survive the winter in the burned remains of a ghost town. So on October 19, Napoleon began his retreat.

Two weeks later, on November 3, the first snow fell.

Over the next six weeks, the Russian winter, the Russian army, and bands of Russian peasants attacked Napoleon's army. His army left Moscow with 100,000 troops: Only 10,000 made it back to the border, in mid-December.

Napoleon made it back to France and raised another army. But his conquests now turned against him and joined the Russians. It took another year of fighting, but in March 1814, the royal armies of Europe entered Paris. They sent Napoleon into exile and put a new French king on the throne. The French nobles returned from exile to reclaim their estates.

And so the French Revolution was over. It had taken twenty-five years of struggle, from the fall of the Bastille in 1789, but the nobles of Europe were safe again.

Or were they?

Napoleon's place of exile was the island of Elba off the southern coast of France. On February 26, 1815, he escaped.

Napoleon landed near Cannes and headed north. As he made his way, army units flocked to join him. On March 19, the French king fled with his court. The next day, Napoleon entered Paris.

Right away, Napoleon had a *coup d'oeil*. He saw in a flash a chance to defeat the enemy army.

On March 25, England, Austria, Prussia, and Russia formed a new coalition against Napoleon. Austria and Russia had disbanded their troops, so they needed time to muster them up again. England and Prussia were ready with troops in the field. So Napoleon set out to defeat them one by one: first England, then Prussia, then Austria and Russia later as they brought their troops to battle.

It was yet one more variation of Napoleon's original Italian campaign, the same strategy that won him so many battles before. Now in his first stroke, instead of Italians and Austrians, he faced English and Prussians. But he did the same thing. Instead of attacking one or the other, he went between them, with no particular destination.

The English commander was the Duke of Wellington. His army included Dutch, Belgian, and German troops, for a total of 110,000. The Prussians under Marshal Blucher had the same number, bringing the total to 220,000. Napoleon had 125,000. Just like in the Italian campaign, Napoleon faced larger total forces but set out to beat them one at a time.

Wellington's base was Brussels, the capital of Belgium. On the morning of June 15, Napoleon's troops crossed the border into Belgium. The news reached Wellington in the afternoon. Instead of rushing to battle, he kept his engagement to attend a lavish ball that evening at the mansion of the Duchess of Richmond. The next morning, Wellington joined his army.

So Napoleon gained a full day of maneuver against the English. Also, Wellington set off in the wrong direction. He assumed that Napoleon was trying to cut him off from the ports of the coast to prevent the arrival of English supplies and reinforcements. So Wellington sent his army to defend the ports. It was a typical Jomini mistake: Ports were strategic objectives. Wellington thought that Napoleon was aiming to take them. But no: Napoleon was looking for a chance to defeat the enemy army in battle.

In moving toward the sea, Wellington's troops moved away from Blucher's Prussians. So it opened up a hole between the two allies. It was just like the Italians and Austrians pulling back to Turin and Milan instead of sticking together. Once again, Napoleon rushed between them.

Another day passed before Wellington saw his mistake. He switched direction and moved back toward Blucher. On June 17, Napoleon almost trapped Wellington, but in late afternoon a thunderstorm struck. In just a few moments the ground turned to mud. So both sides retired for the night, to fight the next day, at Waterloo.

All was in Napoleon's favor; except for the rain. Years later he wrote:

> During the whole night of June 17–18 the weather was horrible, and the terrain was impracticable until 9 AM. This loss of five hours (from dawn to 9 AM) was entirely in the enemy's favor . . . if the weather had permitted the French army to maneuver on its terrain beginning at 4 AM, the Anglo-Dutch army would have been cut up and scattered before 7 AM . . . there would have been ample time in the evening to go meet Marshal Blucher and to inflict a similar fate on him.

So Napoleon waited for the rain to stop. Otherwise all would sink in the mud: the feet of soldiers, the hoofs of horses, the wheels of cannons. When the ground finally dried out enough, Napoleon started moving. Toward noon he attacked. But it was too late. A few hours after, the Prussians arrived and joined the battle.

As evening fell, the French gave up. They turned and ran. That was the end of Napoleon.

The coalition occupied Paris a second time. Again they restored the French king and sent Napoleon into exile, this time on the remote island of Saint Helena in the middle of the Atlantic Ocean. He died there in 1821, at the age of fifty-two.

The kings of Europe remained in power for decades after. But the movements that finally overthrew them drew inspiration from the French Revolution and its great champion, Napoleon. For example, Tolstoy's first idea that led to *War and Peace* was a novel about the Decembrists, a group of liberal Russian nobles who had wanted Napoleon to depose the czar. They staged their own rebellion in 1825. It failed completely. For most of Europe the key year was 1848, when dozens of nations and territories revolted against their kings, including France. These revolutions of 1848 all aimed for the end of noble privilege, in direct descent from Napoleon.

At the start of it all, at the very heart of Napoleon's success, we find *coup d'oeil.* Even his two great losses, in Russia and at Waterloo, confirm the genius of Napoleon's strategy. In Russia, he lost his presence of mind and fought the Jomini way. At Waterloo, Napoleon fought like von Clausewitz said, but the weather did him in. So even when you do everything right, you still might lose. *Coup d'oeil* does not guarantee victory. It only makes it more likely.

Perhaps the most telling clue to Napoleon's strategy lies at the foot of his tomb. After twenty-five years in a plain grave on Saint Helena, his body was returned to France for burial. The tomb is a popular tourist attraction today, in a magnificent chapel on the grounds of the Military Hospital in the heart of Paris.

Napoleon's massive coffin of dark stone sits beneath an ornate rotunda. On the walls are the usual accounts of his glorious deeds, including a carving of Napoleon as Moses delivering the Code Napoleon. But for strategy, look down.

There's a circle on the floor around the tomb. The circle is made of words, a mosaic of stone. The words spell out Napoleon's greatest victories. They are all in odd locations, like Rivoli, Wagram, Marengo, and Austerlitz. These places had no strategic value, except at a particular moment when Napoleon's *coup d'oeil* showed him the chance to win a battle there.

Etched in the floor, for all to see, is the secret of Napoleon's glance.

3

✛ ✛ ✛

PICASSO FINDS HIS STYLE

If I told him would he like it. Would he like it if I told him.
Would he like it would Napoleon would Napoleon would he like it.
If Napoleon if I told him if I told him if Napoleon. Would he like it if I told
him if I told him if Napoleon. Would he like it if Napoleon if Napoleon if I
told him. If I told him if Napoleon if Napoleon if I told him . . .
Who came first Napoleon at first. Who came first Napoleon the first. Who
came first, Napoleon first . . .
Let me recite what history teaches. History teaches.

— Gertrude Stein, *If I Told Him: A Completed Portrait of Picasso*

P ablo Picasso, the most famous artist of the twentieth century, reminded Gertrude Stein of Napoleon. We're never sure exactly why. Perhaps it was Picasso's early success—in 1906, when he first won fame, Picasso was twenty-five years old, a year younger than Napoleon when he won his first campaigns.

Or maybe it was the scale of Picasso's achievement: His fame lasted until his death at the ripe old age of ninety-two, in 1973. He kept painting right to the end. It was during his long career that "modern" art surpassed "classical" art in the eyes of the public and among artists themselves. The modern movement owes much to Picasso, its greatest star.

So how did he do it? What happened back in 1906? How did he find his winning style?

Stein was closer than she ever imagined: Picasso owed his success to Napoleon's glance.

Picasso was born in Malaga, Spain, in 1881. His father was an art teacher and his mother was the granddaughter of Italian immigrants. At the age of sixteen, Picasso graduated from the School of Fine Arts in Barcelona to the Royal Academy in Madrid. Both schools taught realism in the classical style.

Realism was the hallmark of classical art in Europe, from the ancient Greeks to Picasso's time. You try to make the painting look like your subject. This is very hard to do. After the fall of the Roman Empire, during the Dark Ages of A.D. 600 to A.D. 1100, artists in Europe lost the skill of realism. It took centuries to learn it again, mostly by studying Greek and Roman antiques. Picasso mastered realism at a very young age, as you can see from his early drawings in various museum collections.

Picasso left the Royal Academy after less than a year. He returned to Barcelona to paint. In 1904, at the age of twenty-two, Picasso moved to Paris. It was the international center of art for three reasons. First, the French government sponsored the world's leading classical art academy and bought artworks for its many public buildings. Second, Paris itself was a prosperous, beautiful city where wealthy patrons spent money on beauty for themselves— lavish living quarters, sumptuous clothes, attractive consorts, and art. Third, a bohemian world of struggling artists grew up in the poorer quarters. Some bohemians struggled to break into the government academy, while others struggled to break with tradition and create a modern style.

Picasso joined the moderns. He moved into a cheap tenement filled with poor artists in the teeming neighborhood of Montmartre. With laundry hanging everywhere, the tenement earned the nickname Bateau Lavoir, or "washerwoman's boat"—that is, a laundry barge on the Seine River. Because their apartments had little heat in the winter or air in the summer, the artists spent a lot of time in the cafés of the neighborhood. Picasso's favorite haunt was the Lapin Agile, "agile rabbit," a fair description of himself.

When Picasso arrived in Paris, there were three major styles of the modern movement—impressionism, pointillism, and distortion. The artists who worked in these styles struggled for years to find a dealer to take their paintings, and then it took years for the dealer to sell the paintings for enough money to earn the artist a decent income. But young Picasso, new to the scene, had no desire to starve. Like an agile rabbit, he wanted quick success—but how?

Of the three modern styles, impressionism sold the best. It was the oldest of the three, so established dealers and their wealthy clients started to pay good prices for paintings in this style. But the field was crowded. The good prices went to the oldest masters, while scores of young imitators scrambled behind. There was not much room for a newcomer like Picasso.

Impressionism dated from the invention of the camera in the middle of the nineteenth century. Why bother with classical realism when a camera did better with just the click of a shutter? At the same time, advances in chemistry put paint in handy tubes rather than in the traditional pots you had to mix up in the studio and use right away. Tubes of paint made the artist mobile. So a new generation carried their paints into the countryside, to cafés, the circus, the beach. There they invented impressionism.

Instead of providing a realistic copy of a subject, impressionism broke a scene into small brush strokes of color. By varying the colors and the strokes, you could produce a wide range of moods—cheerful or sad, sensitive or brash, still or shimmering. By choosing different effects, artists gave their impressions of a scene instead of a camera view. There were precedents in earlier art through the ages, but Manet in the 1860s was the first to turn impressionism into a full style. Monet, Renoir, Degas, and many others followed.

Over the years, artists broke the patches of color into smaller and smaller strokes. In the 1880s, that led to pointillism. The pointillists filled the canvas with tiny dots of color. At the same time, some artists started distorting the shapes on the canvas instead. Cezanne led the way by giving the scene a blocky look. Gauguin and van Gogh followed by giving their shapes a primitive feel. In these two newer styles—pointillism and distortion—the field was less crowded. But the paintings did not sell as well as impressionism. Fewer painters chased fewer buyers, so it still meant years of struggle.

Strokes of color, dots of color, distortions of shape—Picasso avoided them all. Instead, his first Paris paintings seem almost classical. His figures look like ancient Greek sculpture, but as common folk at the circus or the beach. We might call this presence of mind: He did not just pick a modern style. He waited for a style of his own.

In those early years, Picasso sold a few paintings but could not find a dealer willing to buy his work on a regular basis. Instead, he found Matisse.

Henri Matisse was twelve years older than Picasso. He came from a textile town in northeast France, where he turned down a career in the family business to take up the life of an artist. For twelve years, he starved. Like Picasso, Matisse had a solid classical training. Unlike Picasso, he tried all three modern styles—impressionism, pointillism, and the distortions of Cezanne, Gauguin, and van Gogh.

By 1905, Matisse had worked his way up from the tenement studios of Paris to a decent income, enough to support a wife and three children in a little apartment in the university quarter. He was active, too, in the modern movement: a co-founder of the two modern salons of Paris, the Salon of the Independents in 1899 and the Autumn Salon in 1903. A "salon" was an annual show that selected paintings from different artists for display in one place for a month or so. These modern salons imitated the two great classical salons sponsored by the French government: the Salon of French Artists and the National Salon.

In 1905, Matisse spent the summer at Collioure in the south of France with a fellow painter, André Derain. There, after years of searching, Matisse arrived at his breakthrough. He returned to Paris just in time to enter a Collioure painting—*Woman in a Hat*—in that year's Autumn Salon.

The picture caused a sensation. Crowds flocked to see it, some to jeer and some to admire. The leading magazine of modern art in Paris, *Illustrations,* reproduced seven of the Autumn Salon paintings in a two-page spread: Two of the paintings were *Woman in a Hat* and another Matisse from Collioure, *The Open Window.* The *Illustrations* article quoted a critic who called Matisse a fauve, meaning "wild beast." Others picked up the word and called the style "fauvism."

Matisse called it "expressionism." He distorted both color and shape but in larger blocks, which expressed the artist's feeling about a scene. So *Woman in a Hat* was made up of patches of color that included green and blue in her face. Matisse talked freely about what he did and how he came to do it, through interviews, at an open house once a week in his studio, and in an essay, "Notes of a Painter:"

What I am after, above all, is expression ... The chief function of color should be to serve expression as well as possible ...

The entire arrangement of my picture is expressive ...

Composition is the art of arranging in a decorative manner the diverse elements at the painter's command to express his feelings ...

I have never avoided the influence of others ...

The influence of Gauguin, and van Gogh, were felt then too (Collioure summer) ...
... the Italian Primitives and especially the Orientals had made color a means of expression ...

From Delacroix to van Gogh and especially Gauguin, through the Impressionists who cleared the way, and Cezanne, who gives the definitive impulse and introduces colored volumes, one can follow this rehabilitation of the role of color ...

One square centimeter of any blue is not as blue as a square meter of the same blue ...

In Collioure, Matisse had a *coup d'oeil.* The impressionists and then the pointillists had broken color down into smaller and smaller units—Matisse suddenly saw a way to build it back up again, in "volumes of color" that he found here and there in work by artists that came before him, from "Italian Primitives" and "Orientals" through van Gogh, Gauguin, and the "definitive impulse" of Cezanne.

In his great discovery, Matisse tried to give equal credit to André Derain, his friend and fellow painter in the Collioure summer. Yet Derain never came close to Matisse in style or quality. But someone else did.

The agile rabbit, Picasso.

Many scholars of modern art point out the great similarity in the works of Matisse and Picasso after 1905. Pierre Daix, a friend of Picasso's in his later years, explains in his book *Picasso—Life and Art:* "Picasso found in Matisse's work a style of drawing whose vehemence and simplifications, deliberately anticlassic, created a savage, gestural expressiveness." The discovery of Matisse came as a "shock" that "profoundly affected" Picasso.

Yet Picasso never quite admitted the influence of Matisse. The closest he came was a comment to Daix in the 1960s, a decade after Matisse's death. Picasso said: "You've got to be able to put together everything Matisse and I were doing at the time. No one had ever looked at Matisse's painting more carefully than I; and no one has looked at mine more carefully than he."

In his comment to Daix, Picasso presents a mutual influence between himself and Matisse. A recent study, *Matisse and Picasso* by Yves-Alain Bois, does what Picasso suggests: Bois puts the Matisse and Picasso paintings side by side. We see a strong similarity, but especially in the early years the influence flows one way, from Matisse to Picasso. Matisse, who proudly cited his sources, never mentioned Picasso among them. So

Matisse drew on painters who came before him, and Picasso drew on Matisse.

We know that Picasso visited the Autumn Salon and saw *Woman in a Hat*. But we have no direct quote from him about what he saw. In a recent biography of Picasso, John Richardson reports two reactions. First: "Picasso was envious . . . *Succès de scandale* put Matisse very much ahead." For a struggling painter, there was no such thing as bad publicity. Second: "Matisse . . . would draw on Cezanne, van Gogh, and Gauguin, the same sources that Picasso drew on . . . Picasso . . . realized that Matisse's grasp of color was instinctive as well as analytical and in both respects way ahead of his own."

After his first encounter with the new Matisse, Picasso resumed painting in his previous style, except for part of one picture. He started a portrait but could not finish the face. Everything else was normal, in his usual style—the body, the room around. But the empty face stared up from the easel like a ghost, calling out for Picasso to make his own breakthrough, just like Matisse at Collioure.

The missing face was American: Gertrude Stein.

Stein had moved to Paris in 1903, the same year as Picasso. She came with her brothers, Leo and Michael, and Michael's wife, Sarah. The Steins collected modern paintings, from an apartment in the prosperous neighborhood around the Luxembourg Gardens. In October 1905, when the Autumn Salon ended, Leo bought *Woman in a Hat* and hung it in the Stein apartment. A few days later, Leo bought his first Picasso through a dealer named Sagot. It was a recent study of three figures, mostly in the classical style.

Gertrude hated the Picasso. But through the picture, Gertrude met the painter. At first, she liked him much more than his painting: She described Picasso as "thin, dark, alive with big pools of eyes and a violent but not a rough way." They became fast friends. Picasso brought his gang of bohemians to Gertrude's intellectual soirees at the Stein apartment—where *Woman in a Hat* gazed down on him from the wall. In turn, Gertrude visited Picasso's dingy studio. And then, in the immortal tradition of struggling painters meeting wealthy collectors—he asked to paint her portrait.

Gertrude Stein sat for Picasso ninety times. He started in his usual style, but the face eluded him. Richardson reports: "It is probably no coincidence that Picasso's dissatisfaction with the Stein portrait coincides with his first meeting with Matisse—the only other artist Picasso would ever acknowledge as a rival and ultimately accept as an equal."

Picasso called Matisse a "rival" and "equal"—not an influence. But in the beginning, Matisse was hardly an equal: He was far ahead of Picasso. Yet Picasso could not just finish the Stein face with the face of the *Woman in a Hat*. He was far too proud and ambitious for that. Picasso did not want to imitate Matisse's style— he wanted to match Matisse's breakthrough with a breakthrough of his own.

The two painters met for the first time through the Steins, during the next modern show, the Salon of the Independents in the spring of 1906. There Matisse displayed his first major painting since the Collioure summer: *The Happiness of Life*. It created another sensation and won him a place with a top dealer, Eugène Druet.

All we know of the first meeting of Picasso and Matisse is that Gertrude, Leo, and Sarah Stein took Matisse and his daughter, Marguerite, to Picasso's studio in the Bateau Lavoir. We have no record of what the two painters said to each other, or Picasso's reaction to Matisse's new painting.

Picasso's response came after. He stopped working on Gertrude's portrait. For part of the summer he returned to Spain to paint, and then came back to work in the Bateau Lavoir. Richardson reports: "Now that he had been able to assess his adversary face to face, the competitive Picasso, who had recently taken up boxing, went, as it were, into training; he could no longer allow Matisse's supremacy to go unchallenged."

In the early fall of 1906, Picasso and Matisse met again at the Stein apartment. Derain was there too. Both Matisse and Derain brought African sculptures. Matisse had bought his from a dealer. It was an angular, distorted sculpture. Derain's came from a fellow painter, Vlaminck. It was a smooth, almost abstract mask.

This was Picasso's first direct look at African art. Over the previous decades, as European powers conquered Africa, a stream of African sculpture made its way into European museums. Art collectors started to buy it, too, and so dealers started to deal in it. And then painters started to study it, like Vlaminck and now Matisse and Derain.

And Picasso. Whether or not he had known about African sculpture before, here Picasso saw it in the hands of Matisse. If Matisse found a statue worth studying, then Picasso did too. Hilary Spurling, a biographer of Matisse, gives this account:

> *Picasso reacted fast. He dined with the Matisses, refusing to be parted all evening from the statue, and staying up afterwards in his studio in the Bateau Lavoir, where Max Jacob found him next morning surrounded by drawings of a one-eyed, four-eared, square-mouthed monster which he claimed was the image of his mistress.*

That was it.
Coup d'oeil.

Picasso quickly finished the face of Gertrude Stein. He made it a smooth mask, like Derain's African carving. Then he began a painting that combined *The Happiness of Life* by Matisse and Matisse's more angular African statue. Many art experts consider it Picasso's greatest work. Richardson again: "No twentieth-century painting has attracted more attention than Picasso's great brothel composition of 1907, *Les Desmoiselles d'Avignon*."

While Picasso worked on *Desmoiselles*, Matisse created a third sensation, *Blue Nude*, at the Salon of the Independents in March 1907. Picasso replied with the angular *Nude on Drapery*, right after *Desmoiselles*. Richardson reports: "The scandal caused by Matisse's *Blue Nude* at the Indépendants had evidently spurred Picasso into going one better, and this standing/sleeping figure is the result."

So: *Desmoiselles d'Avignon* by Picasso came from *The Happiness of Life* by Matisse and African sculpture. *Nude on Drapery* by Picasso came from *Blue Nude* by Matisse and African sculpture. Picasso's *coup d'oeil* was this: to put Matisse and African sculpture together.

Picasso failed to cite Matisse as a source, but he did cite African sculpture. Derain took him to see the African carvings at the Ethnographic Museum in Paris—Richardson dates it March 1907, some six months after Picasso saw the carvings of Matisse and Derain. The writer André Malraux reports that Picasso told him: "The masks weren't just like any other pieces of sculpture. Not at all. They were magic things . . . *Les Desmoiselles d'Avignon* must have come to me that very day, but not at all because of the forms; because it was my first exorcism painting."

As usual, Picasso covers his trail. He claims that the African masks struck him for their "magic," not for their "forms." But of course, he goes on to put those forms in his paintings. But Picasso always spoke of his method in mystical terms, except for his one comment to Daix about Matisse, and this one well-known quote: *I do not seek. I find.*

That is Napoleon's glance: He found African sculpture and Matisse.

After 1907, Matisse and Picasso both went on to fame and fortune. Bois shows, painting by painting, how alike Matisse and Picasso remained throughout their long careers. The core elements of their common style remained: blocks of color in expressive shapes, half real and half abstract. Matisse put in more decoration, in the form of tapestries, tablecloths, wallpaper, and leafy plants that recalled the patterns of textiles from his hometown. Picasso tended to straighter lines, harsher angles, and more distorted shapes, in the style of African sculpture.

In 1946, Picasso finally painted a thank-you note to Matisse: *The Joy of Life*. Put beside *The Happiness of Life*, it makes you laugh. Picasso took Matisse's calm, lovely, romantic scene and turned it into a cheerful circus of bouncing shapes and colors.

Picasso never admitted in words his debt to Matisse—but there it is on canvas, plain as day, for all the world to see.

4

✠   ✠   ✠

A BOLT FROM THE BLUE:
SAINT PAUL ON THE ROAD TO DAMASCUS

T he most famous case of Napoleon's glance is St. Paul the Apostle.

As Jesus founded the Christian faith, it was Paul who founded the Christian church. After the death of Jesus, Paul turned the scattered groups of early Christians into a formal religion. If not for Paul, their creed would have died out, like hundreds of forgotten cults through the centuries. Instead, Christianity became the most successful religion in history in numbers of members and spread throughout the world.

How did Paul do it?

He started as an enemy of the Christians named Saul. His job was to stamp them out. Then, on the road to Damascus, a revelation knocked him off his horse. It was a sign from heaven, a bolt from the blue of blinding force. He changed his name to Paul and switched from a persecutor of Christians to become their greatest champion, their leader, the greatest of all the Apostles.

Nearly twenty centuries later, we recognize that bolt from the blue: *coup d'oeil*. It showed Paul the way ahead to found the Christian church.

The key to the *coup d'oeil* that struck Paul is the religious tradition he grew up in: Paul was a Pharisee.

The Pharisees were a sect of Jewish rabbis. In the Christian Bible, they do not appear in the Old Testament, which tells the story of the Jewish people up to about 450 B.C. The Pharisees arise later, around 200 B.C. They go on to play a key role in the

New Testament, which picks up the story again two centuries later with the birth of Jesus.

The New Testament starts with the Gospel of Matthew. The Pharisees first show up in Chapter 3:

> *In those days came John the Baptist, preaching in the wilder-*
> *ness of Judea, and saying repent ye: for the kingdom of heaven*
> *is at hand ... Then went out to him Jerusalem, and all Judea,*
> *and all the region about Jordan, and were baptized of him in*
> *Jordan, confessing their sins. But when he saw many of the*
> *Pharisees and Sadducees come to his baptism, he said unto*
> *them, O generation of vipers, who hath warned you to flee*
> *from the wrath to come?*

In this passage and in many others of the New Testament, the Pharisees and Sadducees appear together. The Sadducees were another Jewish sect, about a century older than the Pharisees. We see that John hates them both. But he does baptize them. Then he baptizes Jesus, who goes into the wilderness to pray and comes back to preach himself.

By the time of Jesus, the Pharisees and Sadducees dominate Jewish life. But the two are very different: In some passages, the Pharisees are "lawyers," and the Sadducees are "scribes." The Pharisees tell you how to follow Jewish laws, while the Sadducees enforce them, plus the decrees of the Roman rulers. It was the job of the Sadducees to keep the Jews loyal to Rome.

The Sadducees opposed Jesus. Some Pharisees opposed him, some remained neutral, and some supported him. Some scholars even say that Jesus was a Pharisee himself. He drew his teachings from the Old Testament, just like they did. There were Pharisees who made things complicated, and there were Pharisees who made things simple, like Jesus. There were rich Pharisees, and there were poor Pharisees, like Jesus. The Pharisee movement thrived on debate and diversity, not orthodox rules from a central authority. The Pharisees had no authority to impose their views. It was the Sadducees who made things official, who had the power to stamp out threats to their own position and to Roman rule.

One thing makes Jesus stand out from other Pharisee preachers of his time: success. We don't know how many followers he had, but they number enough to draw the attention of the Sadducees and the Romans. Jesus came from Galilee, a hundred miles north of Jerusalem, so that is where he starts preaching. A few Sadducees and Pharisees come to hear him, but still it is safe enough for a time. Then, as a pious Jew, Jesus joins the annual Passover pilgrimage to Jerusalem. Some Pharisees try to warn him. Jesus goes anyway, to meet his enemies face-to-face.

In Jerusalem, Jesus goes to the Temple and out-debates first the Sadducees, then the Pharisees. Matthew again:

> But when the Pharisees had heard that he had put the Sadducees to silence, they were gathered together . . . . Then one of them . . . asked him a question . . . Master, which is the great commandment in the law? Jesus said unto him, Thou shalt love the Lord thy God with all thy heart, and with all thy soul, and with all thy mind. This is the first and great commandment. And the second is like unto it, Thou shalt love thy neighbor as thyself. On these two commandments hang all the law and the prophets.

Here we see the essence of Jesus's teaching: two simple rules, completely in line with Jewish "law and prophets." Jesus cut to the heart of Jewish law with a simple message of love for God and neighbor. It appealed especially to the poor and illiterate. In contrast, here is a typical Pharisee debate of the day, cited by Hans Lietzmann, a noted German scholar of the early Christian church:

> In the time of Jesus, there were two famous rabbis, Shammai

and Hillel, and their disciples disputed whether the evening prayer was to be offered in a standing posture or lying in bed; what was the appropriate order for prayers after a meal; whether the towel used for drying one's hand was to be placed upon the table or upon the cushion used as a seat.

In fairness to the Pharisees: It was a difficult age. Jerusalem stood astride major trade routes from the Egyptian, Roman, and Greek worlds to the north and west, Arabia to the south and east, and dozens of Asian kingdoms farther east and north. All traditions met in Jerusalem. So Jews ran into countless "gentile"—that is, non-Jewish—customs. They asked the Pharisees which gentile customs they were allowed to follow and which they must resist.

This led to lively debates. For example, the law of Moses barred Jews from eating pork, shellfish, or meat slaughtered by a gentile butcher. And Jews could not sit through gentile prayers at the table. But could you come in after the gentiles prayed, and bring your own meat, while the gentiles ate their gentile food? The Pharisees debated that one too.

In Jerusalem, Jesus goes from debating in the temple to preaching in public. He draws a huge crowd and makes a long speech:

The Sadducees and the Pharisees sit in Moses' seat: All therefore whatsoever they bid you observe, that observe and do; but do not yet after their works: for they say, and do not. For they bind heavy burdens and grievous to be borne, and lay them on men's shoulders; but they themselves will not move them with one finger. But all their works they do for to be seen of men: they make broad their phylacteries, and enlarge the borders of their garments, And love the uppermost rooms at feasts, and the chief seats in the synagogues ... Woe unto you, scribes and Pharisees, hypocrites! for ye devour widows' houses, and for a pretense make long prayer: therefore ye shall receive the greater damnation . . .

Jesus goes on to recite a long list of evil deeds that the Sadducees and Pharisees commit. Note that he does not dispute their religious authority: They "sit in Moses' seat." He tells the people to obey them. But Jesus goes on to accuse the Sadducees and Pharisees of hypocrisy. For example, they wear expensive clothes and overcharge widows for their husbands' funerals. Jesus, in contrast, wears the clothes of a pauper and charges nothing for his prayers.

This is the speech that leads to his arrest. While some Pharisees support Jesus, the Sadducees and some other Pharisees realize that if Jesus succeeds, he will put them out of business. So the Sadducee ruling council, the sanhedrin, decides to arrest him. But on what grounds?

Not blasphemy. Jesus told the crowd to follow Jewish law. According to Hans Lietzmann:

> . . . we can say, with some certainty, that the sanhedrin came to no legal condemnation on the count of blasphemy, for then they would have had to execute Jesus on their own authority by stoning.

The Sadducees did not dare lay a hand on Jesus themselves. As Matthew reports: "But when they sought to arrest him, they feared the multitude, because they took him for a prophet." The crowd might turn on them instead. So they "delivered him to Pontius Pilate, the governor." Roman soldiers, not the Sadducee police, arrested Jesus.

The Romans stayed out of religious disputes: All they wanted to know was if Jesus was a threat to Rome. There was another Jewish sect of the day, the Zealots, who preached that Roman rule violated Jewish law. Revolts broke out all the time: When Jesus was six years old, the Romans crucified four thousand Jews who refused to pay their taxes. Jesus never spoke against the Romans, but some of his followers did. They hoped he would rise to "King of the Jews" and throw the Romans out.

When the Romans conquered the Jewish lands in 64 B.C., they defeated a Jewish king. In the hundred years since, they knew that the people expected a messiah to come, declare himself king, and throw the Romans out. Matthew:

And Jesus stood before the governor: and the governor asked him, saying, Art thou the King of the Jews? And Jesus said unto him, You say so.

These are the only words Jesus spoke to the Romans. His followers called him the Messiah, so that did make him their king. Jesus never spoke a word against Rome, but he was still very young, only thirty-three years old. If he preached for another decade or two, he might stir up the entire Jewish nation. He might gain the power to revolt against Rome.

So just to be safe, the Romans put Jesus to death. Like the four thousand tax rebels of previous years, they crucify him. As usual, the Romans write the criminal's crime on the top of the cross. Matthew reports:

The soldiers of the governor . . . set up over his head his accusation written, This is Jesus, King of the Jews.

His family and disciples bury him. Two days later, on Passover, they find his tomb empty. He appears to them alive. He tells them to spread his teaching to "all nations:"

Teaching them to observe all things whatsoever I have commanded you: and, lo, I am with you always, even unto the end of the earth.

So ends the story of Jesus.

And begins the story of Paul.

The first books of the New Testament are the four Gospels of Matthew, Mark, Luke, and John. They all recount the life of Jesus. The next book is the Acts of the Apostles, also written by Luke. The Acts have twenty-eight chapters. In the first six, the main character is Peter. In the other twenty-two chapters, the main character is Paul.

Peter is the first disciple of Jesus that the Gospels mention: Jesus meets Peter and his brother Andrew fishing in the Sea of Galilee. At the time, Peter's name is Simon. Before his fateful trip to Jerusalem, Jesus says to Simon: "You are Peter, and upon this rock I will build my church."

So Jesus changes Peter's name and makes him the lead disciple. At the start of the Acts of the Apostles, the leader of the church is Peter. At the end, it is Paul. How did Paul make the switch?

Under Peter, the followers of Jesus were a Jewish sect like many others, with their own synagogues and preachers. They were known as "Nazarenes," because Jesus came from Nazareth. The Nazarenes follow the law of Moses and preach among fellow Jews. Without their great preacher, Jesus, they pose no threat to the ruling order. The Sadducees leave them alone.

Until the trial of Stephen. This takes place in Jerusalem, starting in the sixth chapter of Acts:

> *Then there arose certain of the synagogue, which is called the synagogue of the Freedmen, and Cyrenians, and Alexandrians, and of them of Cilicia and of Asia, disputing with Stephen . . . We have heard him speak blasphemous words against Moses, and against God. And they stirred up the people, and the elders, and the scribes, and came upon him, and caught him, and brought him to the council . . . This man ceaseth not to speak blasphemous words against this holy*

place, and the law: For we have heard him say, that this Jesus of Nazareth shall destroy this place, and shall change the customs which Moses delivered us.

Stephen was not an original disciple of Jesus, but "a man filled with faith." But what was his faith—exactly?

At his trial, Stephen describes Moses not as a giver of law but a prophet of the true word of God against idols: "And they made a calf in those days, and offered sacrifice unto the idol, and rejoiced in the works of their own hands." Moses won over the Jews with a true "tabernacle of witness in the wilderness," which came down "with Jesus into the hands of the Gentiles." The Sadducees who rule the temple today have no claim to Moses, for "the most High dwelleth not in temples made with hands."

Here Stephen says that the temple where the Sadducees rule is the same as the calf that Moses opposed: They are both idols "made with hands." Jesus does not need a temple: "Heaven is my throne . . . saith the Lord . . . Ye stiff-necked and uncircumcised in heart and ears, ye do always resist the Holy Ghost: as your fathers did, so do ye."

Stephen preaches that Jesus, not the Sadducees, descend from Moses. Their temple is irrelevant, and their law of Moses is irrelevant. Jesus inherited from Moses not a set of laws but a "tabernacle of witness"—that is, true faith in God. Stephen told Jews in the "synagogue of the Freedmen, and Cyrenians, and Alexandrians, and of them of Cilicia and of Asia" to abandon Jewish law and follow Jesus instead.

This is blasphemy.

Guilty as charged.

The Sadducees condemn him to death by stoning.

And so Stephen becomes the first Christian martyr. But more: He was the first Christian.

It is Stephen who first claims that the law of Moses conflicts with faith in Christ. Peter and the Nazarenes follow the law of

Moses. They see no conflict. Jesus himself never preached against the law of Moses. On the contrary, he said his teaching conformed to it.

Starting with Stephen, the Christians break off from the Nazarenes. But Stephen is dead. Who carries on after him?

Enter Paul.

Still known as Saul, Paul is there at Stephen's trial:

> . . . and the witnesses laid down their coats at a young man's feet, whose name was Saul. And they stoned Stephen, calling upon God, and saying, Lord Jesus, receive my spirit . . . And Saul was consenting unto his death. And at that time there was a great persecution against the church which was at Jerusalem . . . As for Saul, he made havoc of the church, entering into every house, and hailing men and women committed them to prison.

Paul did not take part in the stoning—he kept on his coat—but he presided over it as an official of the Sadducees. After, he went after Stephen's followers too. The Nazarenes he left alone, so they kept on preaching in peace.

The followers of Stephen fled north, out of the Jewish heartland. Paul took up the chase.

To Damascus.

On the way: *coup d'oeil.*

Damascus is one hundred fifty miles from Jerusalem. So along the way, Paul passed through mostly gentile territory. It must have seemed familiar: He came from gentile territory himself.

Paul was a native of Tarsus, eight hundred miles north of Jerusalem. Northern Jews spoke Greek—like Stephen. In fact, all the Christian heretics spoke Greek. They fled north because that was where they came from.

Back in Jerusalem, the Nazarenes spoke Aramaic, the language of the Jewish heartland. Stephen probably knew Aramaic as a second language. Jesus himself spoke Aramaic only. When he called Peter his "rock," the name he actually spoke was "Cephas," which means "rock" in Aramaic. In later translations of the Gospel, Cephas became Peter, which means "rock" in Latin.

As for Hebrew, it was the ancient language of sacred texts that only Sadducees and Pharisees knew. Jesus himself spoke no Hebrew. As a Pharisee, Paul spoke Hebrew, but not very well. Like Stephen, Paul spoke Greek first and Aramaic as a second language. Paul's later writings show that he knew his Old Testament from Greek translations, not the Hebrew original.

In Jerusalem, you had to know Hebrew well to succeed as a Pharisee scholar. Paul failed to make the grade. Instead, he wound up a hitman for the Sadducees.

Among Pharisees, Paul was not at all unusual. It was common for Jews in the north to know other languages. That was how they made converts, by preaching to the gentiles. Thanks to Pharisee preachers, millions of gentiles converted to the Jewish faith. So Jews made up about seven percent of the Roman empire at the time of Jesus—a much higher percentage than they ever reached in Europe in later ages.

When gentiles converted, the Pharisees baptized them in water. That was where John the Baptist got the idea. And the Pharisees had a special status for half-converts who followed only part of Jewish law: "God-fearers." They declared Noah the chief prophet of the God-fearing half-Jews, the way Moses was the chief prophet of the full Jews.

Some scholars think that Paul himself was born a gentile or a half-Jewish God-fearer. They cannot trace his exact ancestry, or how he gained his Pharisee training. Whatever the details, on his way to Damascus one thing is certain: Paul was more like the Christians he pursued than like the Sadducees who sent him.

Damascus lay beyond Roman rule, in the realm of an Arab king. The Sadducees of Jerusalem had no jurisdiction there. Acts tells us that Paul asked for letters of introduction to the Arab king and the local Jews:

> *And Saul, yet breathing out threatenings and slaughter against the disciples of the Lord, went unto the high priest, and desired of him letters to Damascus to the synagogues, that if he found any of this way, whether they were men or women, he might bring them bound unto Jerusalem.*

This passage shows Paul eager to stamp out the Christians as he set out for Damascus. But along the way, he had plenty of time to think. As a Greek-speaking northerner, he would know how to track down his prey. But we know from his later career that Paul was at heart a holy man: Presiding over the death of Stephen must have come as a grisly shock. And now Paul was on his way to Damascus for more, "whether they were men or women."

From the arrests he made in Jerusalem, and from the trial of Stephen, Paul knew that the heretics would not give up their heresy. They spoke of Jesus as someone they knew. Many said he appeared to them: They saw him in the flesh. Gentile converts especially found the teaching of Jesus easier to grasp than even the God-fearing half-Jewish status. Among Greek-speaking northerners, the Christian faith was catching on. It was Paul's job to crush it. On his way to Damascus, he knew that a bloodbath lay ahead of him.

Then:

> *And as he journeyed, he came near Damascus: and suddenly there shined round about him a light from heaven: And he fell to earth, and heard a voice saying unto him, Saul, Saul, why persecutest thou me? And he said, Who art thou, Lord? And*

the Lord said, I am Jesus whom thou persecutest: it is hard for thee to kick against the pricks. And he trembling and aston-ished said, Lord, what wilt thou have me do? And the Lord said unto him, Arise, and go into the city, and it shall be told thee what thou must do. And the men which journeyed with him stood speechless, hearing a voice, but seeing no man.

In other words: *coup d'oeil.*

From then on, Paul became a Christian Pharisee.

All the elements of the Christian church were in place. It just needed a lawyer—a Pharisee—to put them in order. Paul knew how the Jewish Pharisees did it for the Jewish faith; now he saw a way to do the same thing for the Christian faith.

He gave up his Hebrew name, Saul, in favor of Paul, a Roman name. Right away we see a switch in audience; from the seven per-cent of the Roman empire that was Jewish to the ninety-three per-cent that was not. The voice in Paul's revelation says, "It is hard for thee to kick against the pricks." That is, there are little pockets of Christians everywhere: One big blow in Damascus—one "kick"—would not be enough. Perhaps Paul had even run into villages of these gentile Christians along the Damascus road.

Paul had a long, vicious campaign ahead to stamp out the Christian faith in the Greek-speaking north. Instead, he saw in a flash a way to make it as strong as the Jewish faith in the south.

In his later writings, Paul gives this account of his *coup d'oeil*:

You have heard what manner of life was when I was still a practicing Jew: how savagely I persecuted the church of God, and tried to destroy it; and how in the practice of our national religion I was outstripping many of my Jewish contemporaries in my boundless devotion to the traditions of my ancestors. But then in his good pleasure God, who had set me apart from

birth and called me through his grace, chose to reveal his Son
to me and through me, in order that I might proclaim him
among the Gentiles.

This event took place within a year of the death of Jesus. When Paul reached Damascus, he spent "certain days" with the Christians there and "preached Christ in the synagogues." Then he goes into the wilderness—like Jesus himself—and comes back to preach. For two years he preaches from Damascus among the gentiles. Then he visits Jerusalem to learn about Jesus firsthand from Peter and the other Apostles.

For the next thirteen years, Paul preaches among the northern gentiles. He avoids the Nazarenes—the Jewish followers of Jesus. For the first few years, his base is his hometown of Tarsus, far to the north. Then in A.D. 43, ten years after the death of Jesus, Paul makes Antioch his base. Antioch is six hundred miles from Jerusalem: like Tarsus, far beyond the reach of the Sadducees. Antioch was the old Greek capital of the Syrian empire, which had lasted more than two hundred years, from the days of Alexander the Great to the Roman conquest. It was still a great Greek-speaking city, even under the Romans.

The Acts tell us:

And the disciples were called Christians first in Antioch.

So thanks to Paul, the non-Jewish followers of Jesus became a separate religion. Each local Christian church ran its own affairs, like Jewish synagogues. Paul moved among them explaining the law of the church, like a Pharisee. After fifteen years, his converts were so far-flung that he started writing them letters too—like the written laws of Moses.

The fourteen Letters of Saint Paul are the third part of the New Testament, after the Gospels and the Acts. Then come three Letters from Peter, two from John, and one from Jude. The last part of the New Testament is Revelation, a dream of the future, or "Apocalypse," by John. Paul's Letters are the oldest part of the New Testament. Then his disciple, Mark, wrote the first Gospel. The other three Gospel-writers drew from Mark. One of them, Luke, was also a disciple of Paul. And Luke wrote the Acts.

So the New Testament was largely a creation of Paul and his followers, Mark and Luke. None of them ever met Jesus in person. The other four authors—Matthew, John, Peter, and Jude—were original Apostles and Nazarenes, who did know Jesus directly. The New Testament first appeared as just the four Gospels and the Acts, known as "The Gospel and the Apostle." The "Apostle" is Paul. The word "Apostle" never appears in the Gospels: Luke uses the word in the Acts to make Paul the equal of the Nazarenes who knew Jesus personally.

Paul's New Testament had a very successful model to follow: the Old Testament. The first five books of the Old Testament are known as the "Law" or "Books of Moses." The New Testament was also a "Law" or "Books of Paul"—Paul is the Apostle of Jesus, the way Moses was the Apostle of Yahweh, the God of the Jews. But instead of ancient Hebrew, the New Testament was all in Greek, the language of gentile converts.

In his new church, Paul made sure to stay loyal to the Romans. Some modern scholars say he skewed the text of the New Testament in favor of the Romans and against the Jews. For example, he lumps the Sadducees, Pharisees, and ordinary Jews together, when it was the Sadducees who denounced Jesus to the Romans and killed Stephen.

And Paul denies in his Letters that Christ's teaching fits squarely in the Pharisee tradition—whereas Jesus said it did fit. Paul made Christians choose between "Abraham and Jesus"—the founder the Jewish faith versus the founder of the Christian faith. He did that to attract the gentiles: He wanted them to become Christians, not Jews, so he exaggerated the difference between the two. Yet even that was not his idea; Stephen had it first. Paul saw the appeal it had among the Greek-speaking converts, so he made the idea his own.

So, too, with baptism, the sign of Christian conversion. That was an old Pharisee custom for gentile converts, while John the Baptist and then Jesus baptized both gentiles and Jews. And Paul made Sunday the sabbath, complete with a sabbath meal, in imitation of the Jewish Saturday. The Jews fasted on Thursday, so Christians fasted on Friday, the day Jesus died. Passover became Easter. And so on through the content of all Paul's Letters: There is nothing new in his Christian laws.

Even as Paul became the Apostle of the gentiles, Acts gives credit to Peter for the first gentile conversion. But if we look closely, we see that the gentile in question—Cornelius, a Roman soldier—was not a gentile but a God-fearer half-Jew. Acts calls him "a devout man, and one that feared God with all his house, which gave much alms to the people, and prayed to God always." Peter and the Nazarenes made converts among the half-Jews around Jerusalem. It was Paul who brought in the true gentiles, from the great Roman empire beyond.

When he was fifty-nine, Paul moved to Rome. He went there to work among the Greek-speaking Christians, who had come from Antioch a few years before. With Paul, the center of Christianity shifted to Rome. It has stayed there ever since.

When Paul was in his sixties, safe in Rome, the Jewish revolt finally broke out in Jerusalem. It lasted from A.D. 66 to 70. The Romans destroyed the temple. That was the end of the Sadducees. As for the Pharisees, they continue to this day as the dominant tradition of Jewish rabbis.

There is some dispute about Paul's death. A popular Christian tradition says he died on the same day as the Apostle Peter: They were both martyrs at the hands of the Roman emperor Nero. What a coincidence: Jesus named Peter his chief Apostle, but Paul made himself chief Apostle instead. Now Peter and Paul die together?

Not very likely. It was just a way for Paul or his disciples to link him to Peter. Paul had no right to call himself an Apostle, for he never met Jesus. Yet the Acts of the Apostles are mostly about Paul.

Some modern scholars think Paul did die a martyr, if not on the same day as Peter. The Roman empire did turn against the Christians sometime near the end of Paul's life. But in the end, the whole empire converted and spread the Christian faith through Europe.

Other scholars think that Paul lived to a ripe old age. The Acts do not tell us one way or the other. They end with Paul in Rome, still very much alive:

> *Preaching the kingdom of God, and teaching those things which concern the Lord Jesus Christ, with all confidence, no man forbidding him.*

Paul owed his success to his great *coup d'oeil* on the road to Damascus. He drew together past achievements—from the Pharisees, Jesus, and Stephen—in one great flash of insight. And his resolution carried him on through thirty-five years of founding the Christian church.

The only thing missing was presence of mind: Here is a rare case of Napoleon's glance where the strategist fails completely to expect the unexpected.

Perhaps that explains the force of Paul's revelation. Maybe it really did knock him off his horse.

5

✢ ✢ ✢

THE LION KING OF OLD MALI

I n 1960, the African colony of French Soudan became an independent country. The new nation took the name Mali, after a great empire of the Middle Ages that once covered the region. In the old days, Mali stretched fifteen hundred miles, from Africa's western tip to the deep heart of the continent. It was Africa's largest empire, and the first to stand up to a new religion that threatened to conquer the land: Islam.

The Mali empire lasted two hundred fifty years. Through the ages, it inspired legends of lost cities and boundless treasure. There is an old phrase, "for all the gold in Timbuktu." There really was a Timbuktu—in old Mali. The founder of Mali both secured the faith of his people and turned them into mighty rulers of a vast and splendid realm. He started out as a minor prince of a small kingdom, much like Napoleon started out as a simple lieutenant. And instead of nobles against the French Revolution, it was Islam against African religion. In both cases, a defensive battle turned into conquest that founded an empire.

The founder of Mali was Sogolon Diata. Over time his name became So'on-Diata, and then Sundiata. Sogolon was his mother's name, and his father's name was Diata. In the Manding language of Mali, Diata means "lion." So Emperor Sundiata was known as the Lion King.

The Mali Empire left no written records. We know about the Lion King through bits and pieces that modern historians put together with delicate care, like shards of an antique bowl. Meanwhile, a clan of local poets, the *griots*, passed down his story in oral form. In 1960, an African historian, Djibril Niane, took down the words of one of the *griots*, Djeliba Koro. Niane translated the story from Manding into French. Then a British scholar, G. D. Pickett, translated the French into English, as *Sundiata: An Epic of Old Mali*.

The word "griot" has made its way into the English language. The Oxford English Dictionary gives this definition: "A member of a class of traveling poets, musicians, and entertainers in North and West Africa, whose duties include the recitation of tribal and family histories; an oral folk-historian or village story-teller, a praise-singer." And Niane tells us: "Formerly griots were the counselors of kings, they conserved the constitutions of kingdoms by memory work alone; each princely family had its griots appointed to preserve tradition; it was from among the griots that kings used to choose the tutors for young princes."

Sure enough, a griot figures in the epic of Sundiata, as the Lion King's loyal adviser. His name was Balla Fasséké, and his instrument was a *balafon*, a kind of guitar with hollow gourds for the body. As Sundiata's griot, Balla was likely the author of the original tale, the first to tell the Lion King's story.

Handed down through the centuries, from Balla to Koro, and then in translation, from Koro to Niane to Pickett—surely the story changed. But even today we can see within it the essence of Sundiata's success. We see how he did it.

Napoleon's glance.

As Balla the Griot tells us, one day when Sundiata was seven, his father pulled him aside:

I am growing old and soon I shall be no more among you, but before death takes me off I am going to give you the present each king gives his successor. In Mali every prince has his own griot. Doua's father was my father's griot, Doua is mine, and the son of Doua, Balla Fasséké, will be your griot. Be inseparable friends from this day forward. From his mouth you will hear the history of your ancestors, you will learn the art of governing Mali according to the principles which our ancestors have bequeathed to us . . . May your destiny be accomplished, but never forget that Niani is your capital and Mali is the cradle of your ancestors.

In this scene, Balla the Griot rewrites history. Sundiata's father was not the king of Mali, and Sundiata was not his successor. Niani was only one of many minor Manding kingdoms, and Sundiata's mother was one of the king's many minor wives. And when Sundiata founded the Mali empire, he governed it not "according to the principles which our ancestors bequeathed to us," but in a new way that solved the problem of Islam.

So why this scene? Because in Africa, as in royal Europe, kingship passed from father to son. When Sundiata took power, Balla the Griot invented a lineage that made the new king legitimate. Imagine a French poet writing a song that made Napoleon's father the king of France, who passed on to the boy at the age of seven the destiny of the French people. Balla the Griot wrote such a song for Sundiata, and for centuries, it worked.

The major kingdom of the region was Sosso, not Niani. Balla the Griot tells us about Sosso and its king, Soumaoro:

With his powerful army of smiths the king of Sosso had quickly imposed his power on everybody . . . Soumaoro was descended from the line of smiths called the Diarisso who first harnessed fire and taught men how to work iron, but for a long time Sosso had remained a little village of no significance. The powerful king of Ghana was the master of the country. Little by little the kingdom of Sosso had grown at the expense of Ghana and now . . . dominated their old masters.

Ghana was the first great African empire, starting from about

A.D. 800. Like "Mali," the British colony of the Gold Coast took the name "Ghana" when it became an independent country in 1957. The old Ghana empire lived by protecting and taxing the trade in gold from the forests farther south. Berber caravans from the north crossed the Sahara to buy the gold in the Ghana capital, between the forest and the desert. The Berbers were light-skinned natives of Morocco who converted to Islam when the Arabs invaded around A.D. 700. In 1076, a Berber army invaded Ghana to convert the country to Islam and take over the whole trade.

They succeeded in destroying the Ghana capital, but that was all. Trade dried up. The African kingdoms that made up the empire declared their independence. The Ghana empire fell apart. Some of the Berbers stayed on to trade as best they could, but most returned to Morocco.

After the fall of the Ghana empire, the Sosso kingdom grew in its place. Balla the Griot describes Soumaoro, the Sosso king:

> Like all masters of fire, Soumaoro Kante was a great sorcerer. His fetishes had a terrible power and it was because of them that all kings trembled before him, for he could deal a swift death to whomever he pleased. He had fortified Sosso with a triple curtain wall and in the middle of the town loomed his palace, towering over the thatched huts of the village. He had had an immense seven-story tower built for himself and he lived on the seventh floor in the midst of his fetishes. This is why he was called "The Untouchable King."

Pickett offers this explanation for Soumaoro's conquests: "One of the most important castes was that of smiths who, in an iron age society, had the power to make the best weapons and use them to their own advantage." A smith was a sorcerer, who made iron by magic. That is, the smiths kept the secret of forging iron among themselves. Soumaoro also used "fetishes:" carvings of ancestors and other spirits. Islam forbade such carvings. Like Abraham before him, the Prophet Mohammed swept away idols in favor of a single, invisible God. So Soumaoro of Sosso, the Sorcerer Smith, defended African religion against the threat of Islam.

As part of his conquests Soumaoro occupied nearby Niani, the home of Sundiata. In some accounts, Soumaoro also took over the Ghana capital, like the Berber army more than a century before. Balla the Griot tells us the Sosso "dominated their old masters," the kings of Ghana. We know that Ghana managed to build back a minor trade, and that Soumaoro was not yet close enough to stamp out the trade completely. So when Sundiata fled Niani, he made his way to Ghana.

There, sometime around the year 1230, the Lion King had a *coup d'oeil.*

According to Balla the Griot, Sundiata was lame until the age of seven. Then his father died. Sundiata's mother was the second wife—now the first wife and her son took power in Niani. They insulted Sundiata's mother for having a lame child. Balla the Griot said to the boy: "Arise, young lion, roar, and may the bush know that from henceforth it has a master."

Sundiata rose and walked. A crowd came to watch. Balla says: "His first steps were those of a giant." Balla sang to the crowd:

Room, room, make room!
The lion has walked
Hide antelopes
Get out of his way

Now the boy grew up. Balla the Griot "gave the child education and instruction according to Manding rules of conduct." In Balla's account, "Manding" refers to Mali, the way "French" refers to

France. Sundiata "liked hunting best of all," and "was quite young when he received the title of Simbon, or master hunter, which is conferred only on great hunters who have proved themselves."

Balla the Griot also told the boy "the history of the kings." Sundiata was "enraptured" by the story of Alexander the Great, "whose sun shone over quite half the world." The story of Alexander leads directly to the royal family of Ghana:

> Formerly the Cissés of Ghana were the most powerful of princes. They were descended from Alexander the Great, the king of gold and silver . . . At the time of Sundiata, the descendants of Alexander were paying tribute to the king of Sosso.

We do not know whether Balla the Griot invented the connection between Greece and Ghana, or if the legend dated from earlier times. We do know why Balla mentions it. He proclaims at the start of the whole tale:

> By my mouth you will get to know the story of the ancestor of great Mali, the story of him who, by his exploits, surpassed even Alexander the Great, he who, from the East, shed his rays upon all the countries of the West.

Sundiata outshines even Alexander. Even if Alexander never came close to Ghana or Mali, he "shed his rays" upon them. Alexander conquered the eastern Mediterranean, the Persian empire, and western India more than a thousand years before the founding of Ghana, and fifteen hundred years before Mali. But his example carried over to both.

Balla tells us that Sundiata became so much like a young Alexander that the new king of Niani grew jealous and banished him from the kingdom. Sundiata and his mother wandered for a while, until Ghana took them in. Another Manding legend says that Sundiata fled when Soumaoro of Sosso conquered Niani and murdered eleven sons of the king. The twelfth escaped: Sundiata.

Balla the Griot stayed behind. Soumaoro held him captive. Then:

> *One day when the king was away, Balla The Griot managed to get right into the most secret chamber of the palace where Soumaoro safeguarded his fetishes. When he had pushed the door open he was transfixed with amazement at what he saw. The walls of the chamber were tapestried with human skins and there was one in the middle of the room on which the king sat; around an earthenware jar nine heads formed a circle; when Balla had opened the door the water had become disturbed and a monstrous snake had raised its head. Balla The Griot, who was also well versed in sorcery, recited some formulas and everything in the room fell quiet, so he continued his inspection.*

Here Balla reveals Soumaoro as not just a defender of African religion, but a ghoul. Sorcery was fine—Balla himself practiced it—but Soumaoro went too far.

As Balla continued his inspection, he heard "hurried steps in the corridor and Soumaoro bounded into the room, sword in hand." Balla grabbed a *balafon* and started to play and sing. That saved his life: "Balla sang and his voice, which was beautiful, delighted the king of Sosso." Soumaoro declared: "Balla the Griot, you will nevermore return to Mali for from today you are my griot."

Balla concludes the scene: "Thus . . . the king of Sosso . . . stole the precious griot . . . In this way war between Sundiata and Soumaoro became inevitable."

But we wonder: Did Balla stay with Soumaoro as a captive, or did Balla switch to the winning side and join Soumaoro willingly? We don't know. By the way Balla tells it, he was an innocent victim.

And his captivity allowed him to study Soumaoro's secrets, for later use by Sundiata.

Sundiata arrived in Ghana with his mother and a few followers on a trading caravan from the south. What did he find?

> The town was surrounded with enormous walls, very badly maintained. The travelers noticed that there were a lot of white traders . . . and many encampments were to be seen all around the town. Tethered camels were everywhere.

The "white" traders were Berbers, who stayed on after their army destroyed the Ghana empire. They crossed the desert back and forth, from Morocco to Ghana, but from there south, from Ghana to the forest, the people of Ghana took over:

> Ghana was the land of the Soninke, and the people there did not speak Manding any more, but nevertheless there were many people who understood it, for the Soninke travel a lot. They are great traders. Their donkey caravans came heavily laden to Niani every dry season. They would set themselves up behind the town and the inhabitants would come out to barter.

Note how Balla says the Soninke "did not speak Manding any more." So in the future, when they became part of Mali, Sundiata did not impose a foreign culture on them but brought back something they lost. But the real situation was something else. It was more like France at the time of the Revolution, when only a quarter of the country spoke French as a first language. Instead, they spoke German, Breton, Dutch, Italian, Catalan, Basque, Provençal, or, like Napoleon, Corsican. Napoleon ordered the French language taught in all schools, and that made everyone French.

So, too, in Mali. Under Sundiata, other people became Manding, starting with the Soninke of Ghana.

But at the beginning, Sundiata just looked. He saw his first Berbers. But it was not his first brush with Muslims:

> *There were also a lot of mosques in this city, but that did not astonish Sundiata in the least, for he knew that the Cissés were very religious; at Niani there was only one mosque.*

Now we learn there were Muslims in Niani before Sundiata left it, and that the royal family of Ghana were "very religious" Muslims. The Muslims of Niani had to be Manding, unless the Soninke traders of Ghana who "set themselves up behind the town" in the dry season managed to build a mosque there. In either case, we know that Islam penetrated the African kingdoms south of Ghana. That helps explain the ferocity of Soumaoro of Sosso, the Sorcerer Smith, in fighting against it.

As Balla reminds us:

> *At the time when Sundiata was preparing to assert his claim over the kingdom of his fathers, Soumaoro was the king of kings, the most powerful king in the land of the setting sun. The fortified town of Sosso was the bulwark of fetishism against the word of Allah.*

Sundiata spent only a short time in Ghana. His mother, Sogolon, fell sick. The king of Ghana sent her to the court of his cousin at Mema, "a great kingdom on the Niger . . . Doubtless the air which blew from the river would be able to restore Sogolon's health." Sundiata and his followers went along.

We can figure another reason for Sundiata going to Mema: The caravan trade was there. The decline of Ghana and the rise of Sosso pushed the center of the trade farther east, to the banks of the great Niger River.

On the map of Africa, the Sahara stretches in a wide band from east to west across the northern half of the continent. In the west, the Niger River curves north to the edge of the desert and then south to the ocean. At the bend, where the river touches the sand, was Mema. It was the first of several river towns that thrived there, including Timbuktu. When Sundiata arrived, Mema was far enough from Sosso to keep its independence. So the caravan traders moved there to escape their enemy, Soumaoro.

To get to Mema, Sundiata and his entourage joined a caravan from Ghana:

> It was a large caravan and the journey was done by camel . . . Always keen to learn, Sundiata asked the caravaneers many questions. They were very well-informed people and told Sundiata a lot of things. He was told about the countries beyond Ghana; the land of the Arabs; the Hejaz, cradle of Islam . . . He learnt many things about Alexander the Great, too, but it was with terror that the merchants spoke of Soumaoro, the sorcerer-king, the plunderer who would rob the merchants of everything when he was in a bad mood.

Alexander again! But also Sundiata found out about the Arab conquerors from Hejaz in Arabia, where Islam began. And he learned firsthand that Soumaoro plundered the caravans, while the kings of Ghana and Mema gave them protection.

Sundiata arrived while the king of Mema was away fighting a neighbor. The king's sister received Sundiata instead. Then the king came back:

> The city of Mema gave a triumphal welcome to its king. Moussa Tounkara, richly dressed, was riding on a magnificent

horse while his formidable cavalry made an impressive escort.
The infantry marched in ranks carrying on their heads the
booty taken from the enemy.

That was it.
Coup d'oeil.

We do not know the moment, exactly. But we do know this: When
Sundiata saw the Mema cavalry, it was the last of the elements from
past achievement to make up his future strategy.

One of those elements was the example of the Mema king.
When Sundiata turned eighteen, he became the king's "viceroy."
That was the title that Sundiata kept for the rest of his days, and so
did all future emperors of Mali. The Mema king was himself a
vassal of the Ghana king. So through Mema, Sundiata ruled in the
name of the Ghana king. Mema was richer and stronger by far than
Ghana, but the Mema king was happy to bow to his poor but illus-
trious kin. That way Mema, and then Sundiata, traced the line of
their rule back to Alexander the Great.

And so when Sundiata came to rule the new Mali empire, he
claimed he was only restoring the old Ghana empire. Mali was twice
the size of Ghana, but no matter. The trade of old Ghana reached deep
into the forest of the south, so wasn't that part of the Ghana empire?
Sundiata welcomed the forest kingdoms back into the fold—or else.
But most of the kingdoms gave in without a fight. They were happy
to go with Sundiata instead of his enemy, Soumaoro of Sosso.

But why? Soumaoro defended African religion against Islam.
What did Sundiata do to solve the religious problem?

In Mema, Sundiata saw Islam and African religion side by side,
at peace. The thriving caravan trade mixed Muslim Berbers and
Africans together. Many of the African traders were converts to
Islam, including the royal family of Ghana. Islam had many commercial advantages: writing and numbers in Arabic, and a standard

set of weights and measures. There were Muslim warriors who tried to spread Islam by force—like the Berber army that ruined Ghana—but mostly Islam moved into Africa by the steady spread of trade.

In Balla the Griot's whole tale, we never hear that Sundiata converted to Islam. But Balla gives him a Muslim descent: Bilali Bounama was one of the Prophet Mohammed's closest followers, and Balla makes him an ancestor of Sundiata's father. Whether or not Sundiata became a Muslim himself, he became the protector of Muslim traders, just like Ghana and Mema. And he did it the way Manding society already handled experts in a particular skill, like smiths or griots: through a caste, the Dyula.

Some accounts report Dyula in the old Ghana empire. Most often, we hear they started under Sundiata. The Dyula were Manding-speaking Muslim traders. In the same way the Berbers traded in every corner of the Sahara, the Dyula spread out to trade in every corner of what became the Mali empire. The two groups of traders met between, in Mema or later Timbuktu.

Sundiata allowed the people he conquered to keep their religion. The Dyula were not missionaries. Quite the opposite: They kept writing and numbers in Arabic as a secret among themselves—just like Soumaoro's smiths. The Dyula made money as sorcerors too: For example, they wrote you a blessing of sacred Muslim words in the sand, spoke the words, and then wiped the sand clean. Or they sold you an amulet with sacred words on a slip of paper inside, to wear around your neck or waist.

Under Sundiata, Islam posed no threat to African religion. If you wanted to convert, fine. But no one tried to force you. That meant the people of Mali could trade freely with the Dyula without fear of losing their way of life. It was the opposite strategy from Soumaoro, who tried to stamp out Islam completely. Sundiata found a way to have both, Islam and African religion, by combining elements he encountered in his travels.

But what about Soumaoro's army?

That's where the cavalry comes in.

A few horses probably crossed the Sahara with caravans from the beginning of the Ghana empire. But they were useless for trade: Balla told us that donkeys carried goods from Niani to Ghana and camels carried them on to Morocco. The Berber army that defeated Ghana in 1076 rode horses. At the time, the Ghana army had a small cavalry at best, because they put up so little resistance. Most of the Berber horses returned to Morocco with their riders, but some probably stayed behind and ended up in African hands.

When Sundiata arrived, the Ghana capital had a small cavalry. Mema had a big one, safely out of reach of Sosso.

Now wonder:

Sundiata, growing up in Niani, hears about the glories of the old Ghana empire from the Muslim traders who come every year to camp outside the town. He sees the traders write and count in Arabic. The traders themselves or Niani converts go to their mosque without disturbing the Manding religion of everyone else. The traders tell Sundiata about Ghana's sorry state and Mema's thriving commerce and cavalry. And they tell him how Soumaoro of Sosso, the Sorcerer Smith, is conquering all the kingdoms around, to drive out the Muslims and stamp out their trade.

This is the start of Sundiata's *coup d'oeil*. Before Soumaoro conquers Niani, or even right after, Sundiata sets out for Ghana and Mema to see for himself what he learned from the traders. Step by step, he figures out exactly how each element works, and puts together a way to combine them. The last piece of the puzzle is the Mema cavalry. Sundiata hears the war drums. The king is back. Sundiata joins the crowd to watch.

Now the *coup d'oeil* is complete.

Or this:

A minor prince from a southern kingdom becomes a caravan trader. His travels take him to the trading town of Mema. He joins the cavalry there and impresses the king with his skill. The king makes him a general. The general has a *coup d'oeil*, to combine all the elements he's seen in his travels to restore the Ghana empire. He sets off on a campaign of conquest to do it.

There is some hint of this "general" story in Balla the Griot's tale. Once in Mema, Sundiata joined the army. The army fought neighboring kingdoms. Sundiata excelled:

> ... The youth sowed panic among the enemy. He had remark-
> able presence of mind, struck right and left and opened up for
> himself a glorious path ... From that day Sundiata did not leave
> the king any more. He eclipsed all the young princes and was the
> friend of the whole army ... Men were even more surprised by
> the lucidity of his mind. In the camp he had an answer to every-
> thing and the most puzzling situations resolved themselves in
> his presence ... After three years the king appointed Sundiata ...
> his Viceroy, and in the king's absence it was he who governed.

However it was that Sundiata made his way to the head of the Mema army, from there the story is clear. He set out to defeat Soumaoro of Sosso and restore the old Ghana empire.

Balla the Griot starts Sundiata off on campaign through a visit from relatives. They traveled from Niani to Mema to find Sundiata. Their leader said to him:

> Soumaoro Kante, the powerful king of Sosso, has heaped death
> and desolation upon Mali ... Whatever rank you may hold
> here, leave all these honors and come and deliver your father-
> land. The brave await you, come and restore rightful authority
> to Mali. Weeping mothers pray only in your name, the assem-
> bled kings await you, for your name alone inspires confidence
> in them. Son of Sogolon, your hour has come ... for you are the
> giant who will crush the giant Soumaoro.

The king of Mema protested at first:

Never did he think the son of Sogolon could leave him. What was he going to seek in Mali? Did he not live happy and respected by all at Mema? ... "Ungrateful creature," said the king.

So perhaps Sundiata was really an ambitious general, in conflict with his king. In any event, the Mema king gave Sundiata half of his army. And:

The most valiant came forward of their own free will to follow Sundiata in the great adventure. The cavalry of Mema, which he had fashioned himself, formed his iron squadron. Sundiata, dressed in the Muslim fashion of Mema, left the town at the head of his small but redoubtable army.

Sundiata stopped first at Ghana, where the king "gave Sundiata half of his cavalry and blessed his weapons." Sundiata's brother was now among his troops, and he asked Sundiata: "Do you think yourself able to face Soumaoro now?" Sundiata replied: "With my cavalry I shall clear myself a path to Mali."

The king of Ghana also gave Sundiata two "divines" for the campaign:

It was a forced march and during the halts the divines ... related to Sundiata the history of Alexander the Great and several other heroes, but of all of them Sundiata preferred Alexander, the king of gold and silver, who crossed the world from west to east. He wanted to outdo his prototype both in the extent of his territory and the wealth of his treasury.

Alexander, of course, used cavalry. There were many similarities in cavalry tactics between Alexander and Sundiata, including a core guard of expert troops that the commander led in person. And there were similarities in how the two generals administered their empires after conquest. We don't know whether these elements survived in the legends of Alexander down to Sundiata's day. Some of the elements were common to the Arab army, too, which Sundiata also heard much about.

Most likely, some of the Berber cavalry of 1076 who stayed on in the region taught their craft to their former victims. Mema had a cavalry when Sundiata arrived, and he then had years of practice commanding it.

Soumaoro of Sosso heard about Sundiata's advance from Mema. Soumaoro sent an army to stop him, led by his son:

> In the evening, after a long day's march, Sundiata arrived at the head of the great valley which led to Tabon. The valley was quite black with men . . . and some were positioned on the heights which dominated the way through. When Sundiata saw the layout of Soumaoro's son's men, he turned to his generals laughing.

The generals asked:

> "Why are you laughing, brother, you can see that the road is blocked."
> "Yes, but no mere infantrymen can halt my course towards Mali," replied Sundiata.

Sundiata had seen the same thing many times on a smaller scale in Mema: The neighboring armies of foot-soldiers were no match for cavalry. Now, facing the much larger infantry of Soumaoro's son, Sundiata knew what to do:

> The lightning that flashes across the sky is slower, the

thunderbolts less frightening and floodwaters less surprising
than Sundiata swooping down on Soumaoro's son and his
smiths. In a trice, Sundiata was in the middle of the Sossos
like a lion in a sheepfold . . . The horsemen of Mema wrought
a frightful slaughter and their long lances pierced flesh like a
knife sunk into a papaya.

After defeating Soumaoro's son, Sundiata made a pact with the
Manding kingdom of Tabon. This pact became the model for Sundiata's rule. The Tabon king remained on his throne. He paid tax to
Sundiata, supplied troops when needed, and allowed the Dyula
traders to come and go in peace. Everyone was free to practice
whatever religion they wished, African or Islam.

Sundiata made the same pact with twelve Manding kings. Their
twelve kingdoms formed the core of the Mali empire. As Mali grew
beyond the Manding, Sundiata offered the same pact to other
kings he conquered.

Including Soumaoro, the Sorcerer Smith of Sosso.

The two armies met at Kirina in 1235. On the eve of the battle,
Sundiata said to Soumaoro: "I am coming back, Soumaoro, to
recapture my kingdom. If you want peace, you will make amends
to my allies and return to Sosso, where you are the king."

Soumaoro replied: "I am the king of Mali by force of arms. My
rights have been established by conquest."

Sundiata: "Then I will take Mali from you by force of arms and
chase you from my kingdom."

Soumaoro: "Behave yourself, little boy, or you will burn your
foot, for I am the red-hot cinder."

Sundiata: "But me, I am the rain that extinguishes the cinder; I
am the boisterous torrent that will carry you off."

So Soumaoro rejected Sundiata's offer of peace, and the battle
began. Balla the Griot calls it "a rout." Many Sosso died, but
Soumaoro escaped. He was never heard from again.

Balla himself had slipped out of Sosso town just before the battle, and now after it, he led Sundiata to Soumaoro's "magic chamber:"

Sundiata had all Soumaoro's fetishes taken down . . . When everything was outside the town and all that there was to take had been taken out, Sundiata gave the order to complete its destruction . . . Sosso was razed to the ground. It has disappeared, the proud city of Soumaoro.

Note that Sundiata removed the "fetishes" before destroying Sosso town. And he had offered peace to Soumaoro on the eve of the battle. It was Balla the Griot who called Soumaoro an "evil demon"—Sundiata never said a word against him. Was Soumaoro's "fetish room" a chamber of horrors, as Balla paints it, or a typical shrine with carvings of ancestors that Sundiata made sure to respect? Sundiata did not seek to wipe out Soumaoro's African religion the way Soumaoro sought to wipe out Islam. Sundiata married the two.

Sundiata even took Soumaoro's "fetishes" back to Niani. Balla the Griot describes a triumphant march through Manding country to Sundiata's hometown:

Flocking from every corner of Mali, all the inhabitants were resolved to see their savior from close up. The women of Mali tried to create a sensation and they did not fail. At the entrance to each village they had carpeted the road with their multi-colored sarongs so that Sundiata's horse would not so much as dirty its feet entering their village. At the village exits the children, holding leafy branches in their hands, greeted Sundiata with cries of Wassa, Wassa, Ayé. Sundiata was leading the van. He had donned his costume of a hunter king—a plain smock, skin-tight trousers, and his bow slung across his back. At his side Balla the Griot was still wearing his festive garments gleaming with gold. Between Sundiata's general staff and the army Soumaoro's son had been placed, amid his father's fetishes.

For his triumphal procession, Sundiata copied the return of the Mema king he had witnessed years before. Note the "fetishes" as a prize of war. Most of Sundiata's audience had shrines of their own, with carvings of their ancestors. To fight, Sundiata dressed like a Berber warrior, but to bring his victory home, he dressed like an African hunter. He did not want the people to think he was there to convert them to Islam.

Meanwhile, Balla the Griot dressed like a king.

After the defeat of Soumaoro came "the great assembly ... which gave Sundiata's empire its constitution." Sundiata held it in Ka-ba, between Niani and Mema:

Even before Sundiata's arrival the delegations from all the conquered peoples had made their way to Ka-ba ... Sundiata had put on robes such as are worn by a great Muslim king. Balla the Griot, the high master of ceremonies, set the allies around Sundiata's great throne ... On Sundiata's right, Balla the Griot, holding his mighty spear, addressed the throng in this manner: "Peace reigns today in the whole country. May it always be thus ..."
"Amen," replied the crowd.

As usual, we hear more from Balla than from Sundiata himself. Balla goes on to give a long speech. Then:

... One by one, the twelve kings of the bright savanna country got up ... Twelve royal spears were stuck in the ground in front of the dais. Sundiata had become emperor.

Then one by one, Sundiata picked up each spear and handed it to its owner. To each king he said: "I give you back your kingdom." So:

One by one all the kings received their kingdoms from the very hands of Sundiata, and each one bowed before him . . . Sundiata pronounced all the prohibitions which still obtain in relations among the tribes.

In this gathering, Sundiata and each king repeated before the others the pact they had agreed to one by one. It was the Mali constitution, preserved in the future through annual meetings in Niani, and on through the centuries without being written down. Balla tells us:

In their new-found peace the villages knew prosperity again, for with Sundiata happiness had come into everyone's home. Vast fields of millet, rice, cotton, indigo, and fonio surrounded the villages . . . Each year long caravans carried the taxes in kind to Niani. You could go from village to village without fearing brigands . . . New villages and new towns sprang up in Mali and elsewhere. "Dyulas," or traders, became numerous and during the reign of Sundiata the world knew happiness.

Sundiata ruled for twenty years, until his death in 1255. Balla does not tell us how Sundiata died. And we have no other account.

The Mali empire lived on for centuries. A copycat empire, Songhai, replaced it. Then Songhai ended in 1591 when a Berber army crossed the desert again, this time with guns. Then came the French in the nineteenth century, and independence again in the 1960s. Still the name of Sundiata lives on in Manding country.

And now we know why. Sundiata had the presence of mind to

wait, as he learned each element from past achievement, to make an empire from old Ghana and Islam together, with cavalry. His *coup d'oeil* showed him how to combine them. His resolution carried through five years of battle, and twenty years of peace.

Balla the Griot ends his account by throwing us off the scent. We can never really understand the epic of Sundiata:

> *Mali keeps its secrets jealously. There are things which the uninitiated will never know, for the griots, their depositories, will never betray them ... Sundiata was unique. In his own time no one equaled him and after him no one had the ambition to surpass him ... Do not seek to know what is not to be known ... I took an oath to teach only what is to be taught and to conceal what is to be kept concealed.*

But in the end, Balla's own tale has revealed the magic of Sundiata's success: the secret of strategy—Napoleon's glance.

6

✦ ✦ ✦

MISS BAKER AND CIVIL RIGHTS

I have a dream . . .

Four little words—but they moved a nation.

These words come from one of American's most famous speeches, by Martin Luther King at the March on Washington for civil rights in August 1963. A quarter of a million marchers heard King speak:

> *I have a dream that one day this nation will rise up and live out the true meaning of its creed: "We hold these truths to be self-evident: that all men are created equal."*
>
> *I have a dream that one day on the red hills of Georgia the sons of former slaves and the sons of former slave-owners will be able to sit down together at a table of brotherhood.*
>
> *I have a dream that one day even the state of Mississippi, a desert state, sweltering with the heat of injustice and oppression, will be transformed into an oasis of freedom and justice.*
>
> *I have a dream that my four children will one day live in a nation where they will not be judged by the color of their skin but by the content of their character . . .*

Ten months later, in June 1964, Congress passed the Civil Rights Act, which made racial discrimination illegal in the United States. A year later, the 1965 Voting Rights Act made illegal the local Jim Crow laws in the South that kept blacks from voting. It was a tremendous victory for racial equality, perhaps the greatest since the Civil War era when Congress abolished slavery and gave black men the vote.

There was still much to do after 1964 to enforce the law throughout the land, but the Civil Rights Act itself was a major triumph, a milestone of victory. It ended a dramatic era of the civil rights movement that made Martin Luther King a national and international hero. His many honors include the 1964 Nobel Peace Prize and, currently, the only federal holiday dedicated to one person.

But—did King do it alone?

Of course not.

There were a quarter of a million marchers that day in Washington, and ten other speakers. Each speaker represented a different organization, and thousands of their members were there in the audience.

Who were the other ten speakers? They were all black men, like King himself. The audience was at least half women. Let's imagine that there were twelve speakers instead of eleven, and the twelfth speaker was a woman—who would she be?

Many deserved to speak, but one stands out above the others: Ella Baker.

She was active in the civil rights movement for the previous thirty-three years, and old enough to be the mother of most of the eleven speakers. Yet Ella Baker did not appear at the podium that day, for two reasons. First, she was a woman. Second, she worked behind the scenes.

Ella Baker was not a public figure who gave speeches and interviews and appeared on television. Ella Baker was a strategist.

Martin Luther King had a dream, but he also had a strategy.

Dreams show you a future, but a strategy shows you the path to get there. Without a winning strategy, dreams fade and die.

The winning strategy of the civil rights movement dates from 1956. The eleven men who spoke at the March on Washington all had a key role in that strategy—and so did Ella Baker. She was the leading female strategist of the heroic era of civil rights, from 1956 to 1964. While most of the men had other public roles to play, too, Baker had the luxury—or the curse, as a woman—to stay out of the spotlight. That made her a pure strategist.

The winning strategy of 1956 to 1964 was nonviolent civil disobedience. Like all successful strategies, the idea was nothing new. But to know when and where you can use it to win, like Napoleon choosing his battles—that made all the difference. Starting in 1956, civil rights activists started breaking segregation laws and going to jail. That was easy to do on your own, and no one would ever know. You would simply rot in prison. But to do it as a group, as a movement, and win—that takes strategy.

Ella Baker was a great strategist of nonviolent civil disobedience— and a master of Napoleon's glance.

There are many fine books about the civil rights movement, often with gripping titles. Some are: *Parting the Waters* by Taylor Branch, *Bearing the Cross* by David Garrow, *To Redeem the Soul* by Adam Fairclough, and *Keeping the Dream Alive* by Thomas Peake. These books mention Ella Baker, but not very much.

Our chief source is an excellent biography by Joanne Grant, *Ella Baker: Freedom Bound*. Grant's title is all too true: Ella Baker was always "bound"—by circumstance. She never had things her way. Her struggle for freedom—for herself and her people—was bound by the possibilities before her. Instead of dreaming, she had the presence of mind to wait for the unexpected moment, when success was in her reach.

And she waited a long time. Her career in civil rights began in 1930, at the age of twenty-six. Her greatest *coup d'oeil* came in 1960, thirty years later, when she was fifty-six.

Ella Baker grew up in the segregated South: Norfork, Virginia, where her father worked as a waiter on a long-distance ferry and her mother took in boarders, and rural North Carolina, on the thriving family farm of her grandparents, who were former slaves. Baker worked her way through Shaw College in Raleigh, North Carolina, to earn a B.A. in 1927. During her college years, she traveled to conferences of the Young Women's Christian Association in Indianapolis and New York City. She must have liked New York, because after graduation she went there to live, in Harlem.

It was the peak of the Harlem Renaissance, when the prosperity of the Roaring Twenties spread some money to black people too. The good times supported black musicians and writers like Duke Ellington, Langston Hughes, and Zora Neale Hurston. And all over New York City, it was the great era of speeches. Speakers of every political persuasion rented a meeting hall or stood on a soapbox in a city park to orate to anyone willing to listen. Baker listened:

Sometimes I was the only woman there; sometimes the only black person, but I didn't care. I was there to learn.

And she worked as a waitress in the middle of it all: Judson House, a community center attached to the Judson Memorial Church on Washington Square Park. There were many speakers at Judson and more across the street in the park. She also took college courses in sociology, spent hours in public libraries, spoke at churches, and made extra money organizing excursions from New York to the Chicago World's Fair.

It was a thrilling and varied education. After two years, it came to an end. The Great Depression of 1929 threw most of Harlem out of work. But the speeches only increased, as everyone had a different answer to bring the good times back.

In 1930, Baker signed on to her first political cause: the Young Negro Cooperative League (YNCL). The founder of the YNCL was George Schuyler, a black journalist eight years older than Baker.

The YNCL organized consumer education and cooperatives for blacks to save money by buying in bulk among themselves. Baker was a founding member of the YNCL and became its first national director, part-time, in 1931.

The YNCL never grew beyond a few dozen buying clubs and a few hundred members around the country. But Ella Baker grew. She went on a national YNCL organizing tour, won a scholarship to an organizing institute of the Cooperative League of America, wrote newspaper and magazine articles, worked as a librarian and teacher, and served as the publicity director of the founding meeting of the National Negro Congress (NNC) in 1935. The NNC lasted only until 1940, but it brought together all the leading black organizations at the time, including the NAACP.

The NAACP—National Association for the Advancement of Colored People—was the leading civil rights organization of the era. It was founded in 1909, when Baker was six years old, and came to specialize in lawsuits against segregation. In 1935 they won their first case, for a black student to enter the University of Maryland. Baker's first contact with the NAACP in 1935 led her to speak at their annual convention. She joined their staff in 1941, first as field secretary and then as director of branches.

It was Baker's first full-time job as an organizer. In her varied activities of the 1920s and 1930s, she never stopped learning, but also—was she searching? The NAACP job put her right in the thick of the civil rights movement. She was thirty-eight years old, and the movement's highest-ranking woman. Was this her chance? Was this her time?

I came to the Association because I felt that I could make a contribution to the struggle for human justice and equality. I am leaving because I feel that there must be some way to do this without further jeopardizing one's integrity and sense of fair play.

This is an excerpt from Ella Baker's resignation letter of 1946. She was happy in the field, visiting local NAACP branches around the country—it was largely her efforts that tripled NAACP membership to half a million during World War II. But she found the Baltimore headquarters a stifling bureaucracy of "demoralizing" staff relations, "espionage," "futility and frustration." Baker returned to New York. Yet she remained a faithful NAACP member, became president of its New York branch, and traveled occasionally to speak at other branches.

But also, the NAACP's main activity had little to do with the branches. In 1946 they won another major lawsuit, when the Supreme Court ruled that states cannot enforce segregation on interstate trains and buses. Lawsuits took money and lawyers, not a multitude of members scattered across the country. Ella Baker was ahead of her time—mass action for civil rights was still a decade away.

Back in New York, Baker worked part-time for the Urban League, Salvation Army, and Cancer Society, and as a volunteer for the National Association of Consumers, the Welfare Council of New York City, the Consumer Advisory Committee of the President's Council on Economics, the New York City Board of Education's Commission on Integration, and a Quaker Prayer Pilgrimage to Washington—in addition to her local NAACP work. And she helped start Parents in Action, a school desegregation organization.

Again, it seemed that Baker was searching. Then, through the Quakers, she met Bayard Rustin. He was America's first expert on nonviolent civil disobedience.

In some ways, Baker and Rustin were opposites. When they met in 1946, she was forty-three and he was thirty-four, so they were not far apart in age. But Baker was a serious, sober, straitlaced black woman, born and raised in the black South, while Rustin was a gay black man, a former professional singer and former Communist, the life of every party, with a put-on British West Indian accent, born and raised in the relative integration of Philadelphia. Baker lived a quiet family life with her husband and an adopted niece in the conservative heart of Harlem, while Rustin moved in the integrated circles of radical bohemia in Greenwich Village and the Upper West Side.

On the other hand, Baker and Rustin were not such a strange duo. Strategy, not friendship, brought them together. On strategy, they ended up very close indeed.

Bayard Rustin dropped out of college in Pennsylvania and into his bohemian New York life in 1937, when he was twenty-five years old. He joined the Quakers and then the Young Communist League. In 1941 he quit the Communists. Instead, he turned to Gandhi.

In the 1920s and 1930s, Mahatma Gandhi led a mass campaign of nonviolent civil disobedience that brought India to the brink of independence from Britain. When World War II broke out, Gandhi called a truce. Right after the war, in 1947, India became independent. Through the 1940s, Americans began to study Gandhi's methods through books on the subject by Gandhi's followers, especially *War Without Violence* by Krishnalal Shridharani. One organization adopted Gandhi wholesale: the Fellowship of Reconciliation, which Rustin joined in 1941.

The fellowship was a pacifist group started in 1914 by Protestant clergy from both sides of World War I. The American branch began in 1915. Its members over the years included Reinhold Niebuhr, an activist theologian whose work Martin Luther King studied for his doctoral dissertation. Niebuhr is author of one of the modern era's most famous prayers:

Grant me the serenity to accept the things I cannot change
The courage to change the things I can
And the wisdom to know the difference

This prayer describes Napoleon's glance. It tells you to fight only battles you see a way to win, like Napoleon. You can't control circumstances: You can only look within them for moments to apply what you know to the matter at hand for a chance at success. Serenity is "presence of mind." Courage is "resolution." Wisdom is "insight," or *coup d'oeil*.

Rustin looked for his moment to win again and again through the war years. In September 1941, he became one of the fellowship's three paid staff members. The other two were Chicago-based seminary students James Farmer and George Houser. Farmer was black, Houser white. A few months later, Farmer founded the Congress of Racial Equality (CORE), with help from Houser and Rustin. This threesome, working for the fellowship and CORE, set out to adapt Gandhi's methods to the United States.

They started with interracial workshops to teach the methods in northern cities—if they tried it in the South, they would go straight to jail, or worse. A few times a workshop led to action: For example, they picketed a downtown Chicago restaurant that refused to serve blacks, and staged a sit-in at a segregated Washington cafeteria. Sometimes they lost, sometimes they won. It was the North, so the police never came to arrest them.

Then Houser and Rustin went to jail for resisting the wartime draft. Rustin served twenty-eight months in prison. He practiced nonviolent action by integrating the prisoner lunchrooms and recreation areas, which were off limits to blacks. That meant he joined his white fellows there. Other prisoners beat Rustin up. Neither he nor his friends fought back. The attackers backed away, confused by their victims' lack of fight.

Rustin came out of jail in June 1946. That was the year the NAACP won its case on interstate travel, so Rustin and Houser planned a Journey of Reconciliation to test the new ruling. A multiracial group—eight blacks and eight whites—would travel by bus from Washington, D.C., through four southern states in April

1947. They expected arrest at least and probably attack too. It would be the first application of Gandhi's methods in the South. Before they left, Rustin led a workshop for the group in the techniques of nonviolence.

The NAACP offered its network of southern lawyers, but they did not join in on the Journey. Thurgood Marshall, the NAACP's winning lawyer in their major court cases of 1935 and 1946, denounced the trip outright:

> ...A disobedience movement on the part of Negroes and their white allies, if employed in the South, would result in wholesale slaughter with no good achieved...

Rustin and Houser planned the trip from New York, where Ella Baker joined in. She and two other women among the planners assumed that they would go too. After all, Baker's NAACP work gave her more experience traveling in the South than everyone else combined. But because of the danger, at the last minute the men decided to leave the women behind.

They made it as far as Chapel Hill, North Carolina. There, as the Journeyers boarded the bus for Greensboro, the police and a mob arrived. There was only one blow—a slug to the head of a white Journeyer—as the police arrested the black Journeyers for refusing to move to the back of the bus. The recent Supreme Court ruling made the arrest illegal, but it would take another major court case to overturn the local convictions. The Journeyers expected that media coverage of the event would create a public outcry for the local court to drop the charges.

The coverage never came. No outcry. No major court case.

Rustin served twenty-two days on a North Carolina chain gang.

So ended Ella Baker's first brush with nonviolent civil disobedience. She missed out on the action but came close enough for the method itself to stick. It was there in her quiver like a fine-feathered arrow: At any moment she could reach behind, pull it out, and let the arrow fly.

For the next few years, Baker worked away on her various causes but spent most of her time on New York schools. The NAACP put education first: It was the subject of their 1935 victory for college integration, and of their next big case for elementary and high school, *Brown v. Board of Education of Topeka, Kansas.* In 1954, the Supreme Court ruled in favor of Brown. That made segregation illegal in public schools across the country.

That was it. Everyone saw clearly what to do next: a national campaign to make schools enforce the ruling.

For the school campaign, Baker and Rustin came back together. In 1955 they founded In Friendship, to channel northern support to southern school integration. Rustin had spent the previous eight years writing articles and speaking across the country and in Europe, Asia, and Africa as an informal ambassador for the American civil rights movement. But the night after a speech in Pasadena, California, in January 1953, the police arrested him and two other men for "homosexual activity." All three went to jail for sixty days.

From then on, Rustin joined Baker in the backseat of the civil rights movement. The scandal of his arrest meant he, too, had to work behind the scenes. And so he did, starting with In Friendship.

There was a third founder of In Friendship, Stanley evison, a Jewish lawyer the same age as Rustin. Levison was born and raised in New York, and made a small fortune in real estate and other businesses instead of practicing law. In the 1940s, some of the causes he raised money for were communist organizations. Levison also raised money for the NAACP—that was how he met Baker. We don't know how he met Rustin, most likely from Rustin's early days as a Communist.

Baker, Rustin, Levison: Again, it was an odd team to come

together. Again, the glue was strategy, not friendship, despite the organization's name.

And then in July, Baker gave a workshop at the Highlander Center in rural Tennessee. Highlander was founded in 1932 to teach adults to read and write. Through the years it hosted workshops for civil rights. The workshop in 1955 was part of a new program run by Septima Clark, a black teacher in South Carolina who lost her job over *Brown* when the school district ordered her to quit the NAACP. Clark refused, and they fired her. Highlander hired her to teach civil rights.

Clark had worked as a teacher for thirty years. She was fifty-eight at the time of the July workshop. Baker was fifty-two. Attending the class was Rosa Parks, a seamstress from Montgomery, Alabama. Parks was forty-three, and a lifelong NAACP member. From Baker's days traveling the South for the NAACP, she knew Parks well.

Inspired by the workshop, back in Montgomery, on December 1, 1955 Rosa Parks refused to move to the back of the bus. Her arrest began the Montgomery bus boycott, the rise of Martin Luther King, and America's first mass movement of nonviolent civil disobedience for racial equality.

The first leader of the Montgomery bus boycott was E. D. Nixon, president of two local branches of national organizations: the NAACP, and the country's largest union of mostly black members, the Brotherhood of Sleeping Car Porters. It was Nixon who bailed Parks out of jail and proposed a boycott. But the city's black ministers quickly took over—their churches were the only place in Montgomery where large groups of black people could hold meetings. The ministers appointed their youngest, Martin Luther King, to take the lead.

Before Montgomery, no one expected black ministers to lead a civil rights movement. And no one thought that a bus boycott would start it. Everyone's eyes were on education, to follow up *Brown*. Rustin was one of the first to switch: He went to Montgomery in February 1956 to offer training in nonviolent civil disobedience. He arrived just in time: He found armed black men guarding the ministers' houses, and guns inside King's home.

King was twenty-six years old when the boycott started. He had studied Gandhi for his theology dissertation but had no direct experience of Gandhi's methods. One big problem was the fear of going to jail: The city of Montgomery declared the boycott illegal and issued arrest warrants for ninety people. Men especially faced the risk of beatings or other humiliations by the police. So Rustin taught them how to go to jail. You go to the station before the police come to get you, and tell the press, who thus serve as witnesses to any police misconduct and also provide publicity afterward. So they did that. It worked. A crowd came to the station to cheer, so the whole event became a celebration for the boycott.

Back in New York, In Friendship raised money. Levison used his usual contacts, while Baker organized a benefit rally for civil rights in Madison Square Garden. They sent half the money to Montgomery. It was the first time top entertainers joined in, like Sammy Davis Jr. and Pearl Bailey.

Back in Montgomery, the opposition found out about Rustin's past, so he skipped town, but only to nearby Birmingham. From there he continued to advise King by phone and visits. He traveled back to New York too. Meanwhile, Baker and Levison went to Montgomery to see for themselves. Here's what they saw: a completely black-led movement of thousands of ordinary people defying the law in nonviolent protest of segregation. The buses on black routes went empty as the protestors walked to work or pooled the few cars among them. They went to jail peaceably and did not react with violence when the opposition bombed the houses of King and Nixon.

The country had never seen anything like it—and the country

saw it night after night on television. In 1947, when the Journey of Reconciliation failed to make any waves, fewer than one percent of American homes had a television. By 1953, half of American homes had one. Thanks to the news programs, Martin Luther King's face and voice became known throughout the land. And newspapers and magazines across the country and around the world reported on the boycott.

The NAACP took on the boycott lawsuits. The Supreme Court agreed to hear the case right away. Baker, Rustin, and Levison started to discuss what to do if the boycott succeeded.

On November 13, the Supreme Court ruled in favor. The boycott was over. They had won.

In Friendship held a second fund-raising benefit in December, where the young singer Harry Belafonte started his long parallel career in support of civil rights. During the planning for the benefit, while talking in Levison's kitchen on the Upper West Side of Manhattan, Baker, Rustin, and Levison had a *coup d'oeil*: an organization to repeat the Montgomery bus boycott, again and again, throughout the South.

In a 1974 interview with Eugene Walker, Ella Baker looked back on the boycott:

> ... *The NAACP struggle had been one of legal action to a large extent. The 1954 decision culminated an effort on the part of the lawyers of the Association to raise the question of the constitutionality of racial segregation ... So that becomes an historical monument and to some people it almost was interpreted as being the end of the struggle ... So when the unthought-of Montgomery bus boycott ended successfully here you had a social phenomenon that had not taken place in the history of those of us who were around at that time, where hundreds of people and even thousands of people, ordinary*

people, had taken a position that . . . at least made life less comfortable for them—when they decided to walk rather than to ride the buses . . . And this was a mass action and a mass action that anybody who looked at the social scene would have to appreciate and wonder. Those of us who believed that mass and only through mass action are we going to eliminate certain things, would have to think in terms of how does this get carried on.

Baker knew about "mass" from her years working with dozens of NAACP chapters and thousands of members. Rustin knew the method of nonviolent civil disobedience. Levison knew how to get the money. Mass, method, money—and Montgomery.

Coup d'oeil.

Baker's comments show a classic case of a strategist changing course because something unforeseen worked out. Note the key moment she cites: when the "unthought-of Montgomery bus boycott" ended successfully. She had the presence of mind to expect the unexpected. It showed her the path ahead: to switch from schools to "carry on" instead the Montgomery achievement.

Baker, Rustin, and Levin were not the only ones who saw the boycott as a turning point. King, other Montgomery ministers, and ministers from other southern towns also talked about a mass movement to follow the boycott. But only Baker, Rustin, and Levison saw how to do it. They wrote up their *coup d'oeil* in working papers, and urged King to call together a conference to consider them.

The meeting took place in Atlanta on January 10 and 11, 1957, just a few weeks after the boycott succeeded. Joanne Grant gives this view from Baker:

At this meeting there were over 100 men present. I don't think that there were any women there except me. There may have been one or two others. And these men were willing to do something I had never seen Negro ministers do before: They were willing to analyze each of the papers we presented.

In Baker's words, we see hope but also a glimmer of doubt. Could ministers really organize a mass movement? On the one hand, the black church in the South was a mass movement all its own, so the ministers had plenty of experience leading people. But could they blend that success with the hard lessons of the civil rights movement up to that time? In particular, would they listen to three outsiders with more experience in mass organization, in the methods of nonviolence, and in raising money—a woman, a gay man, and a Jew from New York?

Yes and no.

The ministers took the most important advice from Baker, Rustin, and Levin—to create a new organization, which became the Southern Christian Leadership Conference (SCLC), with King as president. And the SCLC adopted the decentralized structure that the trio proposed: independent affiliates, modeled on the Montgomery boycott group, that sent delegates to the national body. But the SCLC's first major activity was to join with the NAACP for a Prayer Pilgrimage to Washington on May 17, 1957, the third anniversary of *Brown*, in support of a civil rights act. So instead of a campaign of nonviolent civil disobedience, the SCLC started with prayer.

The SCLC campaign for civil disobedience had trouble getting off the ground for another reason too: Repeating the Montgomery success proved easier than anyone imagined. Through the year 1957, forty-two copycat boycotts sprang up across the South. Most succeeded right away, as the city bus companies figured they could not win. Adam Fairclough, an SCLC historian, tells us that many of the boycotts lasted only one day: "Such, for example, was the Atlanta boycott, a decorous affair in which a group of black ministers had themselves arrested and then filed suit in federal court."

Sometimes the boycott failed. In Rock Hill, South Carolina, it knocked the bus company out of business. In Miami and Talla-hassee, Florida, and in Birmingham, Alabama, the authorities held out and won. For even these few cases, the SCLC did not have a program of support for nonviolent civil disobedience. First it was busy organizing the Prayer Pilgrimage. After that, it turned to voter registration instead of nonviolent civil disobedience.

The Prayer Pilgrimage to Washington of May 1957 had a poor turnout: about 25,000, or one-twentieth the size of the March on Washington seven years later. There was almost no press coverage. The Congress did pass a civil rights act that year, but a very weak one, to establish a federal commission to hear grievances.

To document such grievances, the SCLC now planned a voter registration drive, on the advice of Rustin and Levin.

But not Baker. She was out of the picture completely.

In the early days of the SCLC, Rustin and Levin became King's closest advisers. Rustin even earned $50 a week as King's executive assistant. They helped King to plan his travels, to write his speeches, to meet key politicians and supporters, and to figure out what to do at every turn. King always made the final decision, but with constant counsel from Rustin and Levin. And Baker? King ignored her.

Why?

Septima Clark, who moved from the Highlander Center to the SCLC in 1960, put it this way: "It's a man's organization, and I don't think women's words had any weight whatsoever." Grant quotes Baker herself: The problem was King's "cult of personality" versus a "mass movement . . . SCLC has a real opportunity to develop the mass action that we must have." But the SCLC in 1957 failed to develop into a real organization—they did not even have a head-quarters. So Baker went back to her New York activities.

The real answer was both. The civil rights movement needed a charismatic leader as well as effective mass action. Rustin and

Levin should help King, while Baker sets up an SCLC organization. Rustin and Levin said so to King. But he hesitated, until December 1957, when the NAACP held a two-day meeting in Atlanta—on SCLC home ground—to announce a voter registration drive across the South. With its network of existing branches everywhere, the NAACP was about to put the SCLC out of business.

So King agreed to hire Baker to run the SCLC. In January 1958, she moved to Atlanta.

For a second time in her life, Ella Baker became the highest-ranking woman of the civil rights movement. Twenty-seven years before, it was to work for the NAACP, and after five years she gave that up because of the lack of mass action. This time, it was for an organization she helped create, to take the mass action of the Montgomery bus boycott to scale across the South.

So we see that many people besides Ella Baker had a *coup d'oeil* from Montgomery: Rustin, Levin, King himself, the other ministers of the SCLC, and the people of the forty-two copycat boycotts. They all wanted to repeat Montgomery's success. But Baker was the only one with the resolution to carry it through. By the end of 1957, the SCLC was an empty shell. In the nick of time, like cavalry riding over the hill, Baker arrived to save the day.

David Garrow, another SCLC historian, describes Baker's first days:

> *Initially she worked out of a room in the Savoy Hotel on Auburn Avenue, and with no word from King. Then, Samuel Williams, the Morehouse professor and Atlanta pastor who was one of SCLC's officers, offered his help and found her office space. With a phone, a typewriter, and little more, Baker got to work making contacts in different southern cities.*

Her first task was the voter registration campaign. It was not of her choosing, but she dutifully tried to make it work. Yet wherever she went, the NAACP was already there. Garrow reports that "Baker found only modest enthusiasm in many of the cities she contacted. In some, the local NAACP representatives were attempting to sandbag SCLC's efforts." Garrow quotes an NAACP report from Jackson, Mississippi, on Baker's activities: "We have naturally discouraged, 'tactfully,' any such movement here in Jackson. It will be our design through the NAACP ... to control the present state of affairs."

Garrow concludes: "With allies like the NAACP, SCLC's efforts had little chance of success."

Meanwhile, the ministers insisted on hiring a man as executive director, for Baker to report to. But they could not find one to take the job. So Baker found one for them—John Tilley, a minister and old college friend, from the SCLC affiliate in Baltimore. Even if it meant working under him, she needed all the help she could get. But Tilley did not work out. He stayed in Baltimore and visited Atlanta only on weekends. When King published his autobiography, *Stride Toward Freedom*, Baker found herself handling his mail and promoting the sales of the book, with no time left for voter registration.

In April 1959, King and the SCLC board dismissed Tilley. Baker became "interim director," working alone again.

Over the next few months, all on her own, Baker came up with a way to return the SCLC to its Montgomery roots: mass action for civil disobedience. At the October board meeting, she presented her proposal:

End the voter registration campaign. Instead, support literacy classes for voters by Septima Clark at Highlander. After more voters know how to vote, a registration campaign might follow in later years. For now, that frees up the SCLC affiliates to form "action teams" for nonviolent civil disobedience, following the example of Montgomery. James Lawson, a black divinity student in Nashville, Tennessee, trains the teams.

Baker found Lawson through the local Nashville SCLC. Young SCLC members attended Lawson's workshops on nonviolence at Vanderbilt University. In addition to studying religion, Lawson served as a regional officer of the old Fellowship of Reconciliation that first introduced Bayard Rustin to nonviolence in the 1940s. Lawson started giving his workshops in 1958. Baker wanted to spread his teachings throughout the SCLC.

She proposed administrative changes too:

Cut board meetings from three per year to two, and the full-member conventions from two to one. Cut the administrative committee from thirteen to five. King resigns from his Montgomery church and moves to Atlanta full-time.

At their October meeting, the SCLC board accepted some of what Baker proposed and decided that the rest "merited study," as Fairclough reports it. For Baker, that was success: They didn't say no.

Baker also suggested that Wyatt T. Walker, a minister in Petersburg, Virginia, replace Tilley as SCLC executive director. That way Walker could do the publicity work for King and Baker could carry out her on-the-ground proposals. In January, King offered Walker the job. He said yes.

That was it, the last piece of the puzzle. Three years after the Montgomery bus boycott succeeded, Baker had the elements in place to turn that success into a mass movement for nonviolent civil disobedience.

In January 1960, Baker was fifty-six years old. Her move to Atlanta had meant separation from her husband back in New York. They remained apart thereafter. The niece she had raised was grown and gone. Baker never fit in with the ministers of the SCLC, and Wyatt T. Walker would not arrive for another few months. There in Atlanta, after thirty years in the civil rights movement, Ella Baker found herself completely alone. She saw a way to build a mass movement at last, but years of toil lay ahead. It would not get any easier. But once again, she just rolled up her sleeves and got to work.

On January 31, Martin Luther King attended a farewell celebration in Montgomery, for his move to Atlanta and the SCLC. Garrow quotes King's words as he left:

> *I have a sort of nagging conscience that someone will interpret my leaving Montgomery as a retreat from the civil rights struggle. Actually, I will be involved in it on a larger scale. I can't stop now. History has thrust something upon me from which I cannot turn away.*

It was another turning point in the American civil rights movement. Nonviolent civil disobedience had almost died out. King moved to Atlanta to help Baker revive it.

But the next day, February 1, everything changed. Something happened that threw all of Baker's plans out the window.

This time, she alone had the great *coup d'oeil* that took the movement to victory.

Remember Greensboro?

On the Journey of Reconciliation in 1947, the first major attempt at applying the method of nonviolent civil disobedience against segregation, the police arrested Bayard Rustin as he got on a bus for Greensboro. Thirteen years later, the method arrived in Greensboro at last: At the downtown Woolworth's, four black college students sat down at the "whites-only" lunch counter.

They were still teenagers, freshmen at the local North Carolina Agricultural and Technical College. None of them had any nonviolent training or any contact with any civil rights organization. But the Montgomery boycott and the protests that followed in 1957 had made their mark on the most impressionable citizens of all, the young.

To get rid of the students, the Woolworth store closed early that day. The "Greensboro Four" returned to their dormitory and told the leaders of various student organizations what they had done. At first, no one believed them. Then more and more students arrived to hear the story.

The next day, two more students joined the original four at the counter. The local television station sent a cameraman. The two local newspapers sent reporters. Over the next few days, as the news spread, dozens of black and white students from several colleges in and around Greensboro took turns sitting in at the counter.

The protest spread to other lunch counters in Greensboro—and then to other towns.

To Winston-Salem and Durham, both in North Carolina, on February 8.

To Hampton, Virginia, on February 10.

To Raleigh, North Carolina, on February 12, which led to the first arrests: forty-one students.

Then: wildfire.

Clayborne Carson, a historian of the student movement, tells us that by the end of February the sit-ins drew thousands of students in thirty towns in seven states. There were arrests, some violent opposition, and in some places, quick success. But the longer a sit-in took to succeed, the more publicity it received, and the more students joined in.

Ella Baker spent the month of February on the phone. Once she learned of the Greensboro sit-in, Baker called her contacts all over the South to help spread the word to other towns. Sometime during the month, the idea of a student conference struck her—to bring all the protesters together. It was her great *coup d'oeil*—but she revealed the details to no one. In the end, the details made all the difference in the fate of the civil rights movement.

She proposed to spend $800 of the SCLC's money on the student conference. She wrote an invitation letter cosigned by King and herself for a "Southwide Youth Leadership Conference," to "chart new goals and achieve a more unified sense of direction for training and action in Nonviolent Resistance."

Note the title: did "Conference" mean "meeting" or "organization"? The name sounded remarkably like the SCLC: Southern Christian Leadership Conference. Substitute "Southwide Youth" for "Southern Christian"—was Baker setting up a new organization?

In some ways, the student conference was just like the meeting in January 1957 that launched the SCLC: Following a success in nonviolent civil disobedience, its leaders met with a larger group to see how to do the same thing elsewhere. So the student conference of 1960 was based on past achievement, like any good *coup d'oeil*. But this time, Baker also saw a way to avoid the mistakes of the SCLC.

After the letter from King and herself went out, Baker followed it up with more mailings to the participants on her own. She worked first with a student leader from Durham and with James Lawson at Nashville, where one of the biggest sit-ins broke out. But over the weeks, she contacted participants directly. She scheduled the meeting over Easter weekend, April 15 to 17, and invited northern colleges too. Her first public press release came out on April 5, and made no mention of King.

The location was Baker's alma mater, Shaw University in Raleigh, North Carolina. She knew the administrators very well, so she was very much on home ground. In every detail, Baker controlled the meeting. In those two months, from mid-February to mid-April, she followed through on her *coup d'oeil* with rapid resolution. She worked everything out herself. By the time of the meeting, only James Lawson knew exactly what she was up to. But soon enough, everyone else found out.

On Friday, April 15, the students arrived at Shaw. Baker had made arrangements for a hundred to be accommodated. Twice that number showed up, from fifty-eight southern towns in twelve states and from nineteen northern colleges, mostly blacks, including Ezell Blair from the original Greensboro Four, but also whites. In addition, there were "Adult Freedom Fighters" from the SCLC and other organizations. They were there for "counsel and guidance," according to the official conference program.

King led the SCLC contingent. He was to give the main address on Saturday night. He and other SCLC officers urged Baker to give the opening address on Friday night, on behalf of the SCLC. She insisted that Lawson give the address instead—on behalf of no organization.

That was Friday night. Lawson gave a thrilling speech on the principles and practice of nonviolence. The next morning, Lawson led the first session. He broke the students into working groups to tell one another their experiences so far and to discuss how they should organize themselves in the future.

The Adult Freedom Fighters were shocked. The way Baker had structured the conference, the students were to decide for themselves what to do. The "adults" had agreed to that as a purpose for the meeting, but now it seemed that Baker actually meant it.

It was the first crisis of the sit-in movement. Joanne Grant made a documentary film on Baker in 1980, and there we find the most complete account of what happened next.

First, Baker's view:

When the kids began to sit in and sat, and sat, and took it, none of us who were older who had a streak of humanity could fail to find some way of identifying with it, because we knew it should take place, and my generation didn't have the nerve to do it, maybe, but they did . . . Having worked with and for older "leadership" and the contrast between how much what those young people gave, I developed a special appreciation for what those young people did. I suggested there should be some meeting in order for those that had been involved and those who were chafing at the bit as it were to be a part of it, to meet and to have some sense of direction.

Julian Bond, student, on what happened at the meeting:

She helped us resist pressure from the NAACP, who wanted us to become NAACP youth chapters at the various colleges where there were sit-in groups, from CORE, who wanted us to become CORE chapters at the various places where all these student sit-in groups were located, and from SCLC, who wanted us to become a youth wing of SCLC. She insisted that we had something special that was special to us, I think both because of our age, and because when these other groups had been relatively quiet with the exception of CORE, we had spontaneously broken out in protest in Greensboro, and in Nashville, and in Atlanta and Birmingham. And she impressed upon us the necessity to keep this special thing separate.

On Saturday morning, while the students met among themselves, the "adults" took action. Baker recounts:

The ministers from the Southern Christian Leadership Conference and some others, they felt sort of left out and they called a gathering at the home of the president of the university and I attended it. I don't know that they had planned for me to attend it, but naturally I felt that somebody ought to be there, because I didn't know what was going down.

The "ministers" included King, Wyatt T. Walker, and at least two others. Why did they go to the "president of the university"? Were they trying to stop the meeting? But Baker was on home ground— it must have been the president who alerted her to the gathering, in time for her to attend.

Baker continues:

They were more concerned about how they could literally

attach the young to them. They didn't want to lose them because this was something new. This was vitality, I suppose.

In her book, Grant reports:

Walker even admitted to Baker that his motives were personal— in an attempt to strengthen the leadership role he was about to assume, he wanted the students "delivered" to his organization.

The ministers even had a plan: They had loyal SCLC activists among the key contingents of Virginia, Georgia, and Alabama. They "began to divide up the delegations that each one would lobby," but "Baker dug in her heels."

She explains in the film *Fundi:*

I had always assumed that my role was to facilitate, which did not involve leadership. I did not have the need for being considered a leader. I think that got over to them in the original meeting, because they knew that the meeting came into being because I did it. But they also saw that I made no effort to become a leading figure in the meeting. And so they began to have that kind of confidence, so they felt they could trust me to maybe further the matter of their independence. This was difficult of course for some who had been accustomed to feeling that these are children of my church, and these are our children, and we are the older ones, and I told them that I would not be a party to that kind of bargaining.

Baker walked out.

She returned to the conference. King and the others gave up their plans to take it over. But in the afternoon session on Saturday, Baker and the ministers chimed in sometimes. In his biography of King, Taylor Branch reports:

Ella Baker and King wrangled briefly . . . In fact, the mild undercurrent of tension between Baker and King became a subject of wonder and gossip at Shaw. Some of the students were astonished to see a woman contradict a man of King's stature. Her character itself was a cultural revelation.

The SCLC ministers left the meeting early, on Saturday night.

The next day, Sunday, the students voted to form their own organization.

And so began the Student Non-Violent Coordinating Committee, or SNCC—pronounced "snick." After that first meeting, eleven representatives met again in May in Atlanta, where Baker offered the SCLC office as temporary headquarters. She recruited Jane Stembridge, a white student from Virginia at the Union Theological Seminary in New York, to staff SNCC. Over the summer, Baker found money for a separate office for SNCC and recruited another student volunteer: Bob Moses, a black SCLC worker from Harvard.

Then she quit the SCLC. Baker, Stembridge, and Moses got SNCC off the ground.

It took off like nothing before in the civil rights movement. The protests kept spreading across the South, and adults joined in— from SCLC, NAACP, CORE, and others. As Fairclough reports:

The difficulty of mobilizing black adults remained, but the demonstration in 1960 that black parents would rally behind their children pointed towards an answer. During the heyday of the civil rights movement, young people—teenagers and children—furnished the most numerous and eager volunteers for jail . . . SCLC soon learned that the surest way to mobilize adults was first to involve their children. Young people made up the initial phalanx, the entering wedge.

In 1964, the year of the Civil Rights Act, Howard Zinn wrote:

For the first time in our history a major social movement,
shaking the nation to its bones, is being led by youngsters . . .
These young rebels call themselves the Student Non-Violent
Coordinating Committee, but they are more a movement than
an organization, for no bureaucratized structure can contain
their spirit . . .

And Grant, on Baker's break with the SCLC:

Baker's departure signaled the beginning of a new phase for
the civil rights movement. It was no longer to be controlled by
a stodgy ministerial or bureaucratic presence. It was to be led
by a new force.

Baker encouraged the SNCC to work closely with other civil
rights organizations. And they did. SNCC was there at the March
on Washington, where their president, John Lewis, joined the
"adults" as one of the eleven speakers. Despite the defeat of the
SCLC takeover, King always worked closely with the students. In
fact, the night he left SNCC's founding conference early, he
appeared on a national news program, *Meet the Press*, where he
praised the students for all the world to hear.

In Grant's film, a former SNCC member, Timothy Jenkins,
describes how Baker helped them:

Our original approach was always to attack the ministers as
Uncle Toms, and sellouts and everything else. And I think one
of the major contributions she made was to help us see them
in some way that was a positive respect and some method by
which we could coordinate our efforts and be non-threatening
to them.

No one knew better than Baker how to work with the SCLC,

with the NAACP, and the other older civil rights organizations. Now she passed on that knowledge to the students. Other student interviews in Grant's film give further details on the methods Baker taught them. The students show their great loyalty to her, their respect and admiration.

Eleanor Holmes Norton:

She had too much talent to be accepted at that time among a bunch of preachers who were never used to any women in their inner council. Remember, she was a peer of theirs, she was about equal time, and they were not ready for that. She was about raising hard questions outside of their normal ambit, and you know, we ate it up.

Baker's *coup d'oeil* of February 1960 was a magnificent case of Napoleon's glance. It showed astounding presence of mind: After all, she had just succeeded in turning the SCLC around. And the SCLC was a product of her previous *coup d'oeil* of December 1956. She was still in the phase of resolution from that first strategy, which makes it ten times harder to expect the unexpected, to keep your eye open to something else. Yet somehow, she did it. Ella Baker was a genius of strategy, not once but twice, in the greatest social movement of twentieth-century America.

SNCC was firmly based on the past achievements of Greensboro and of other civil rights organizations that preceded it. Baker used her knowledge of the "ministerial" SCLC and the "bureaucratic" NAACP to advise SNCC to remain self-organizing—like the spontaneous sit-ins that began the student movement. After the first wave of sit-ins, she alone saw what to do—and it worked.

Howard Zinn especially gives credit to Baker. He describes her fondly as "middle-aged, dark-skinned, beautiful, with a deep-throated voice that seemed suited for the stage." He called his history of the SNCC *The New Abolitionists* and dedicated the book to

Baker, "who is more responsible than any other single individual for the birth of the new abolitionists as an organized group, and who remains the most tireless, the most modest, and the wisest activist I know in the struggle for human rights today."

The members of SNCC called one another by their first names. But their mentor, Ella Baker, was old enough to be their grandmother. So what did they call her?

Miss Baker.

For the students, it was a sign of respect, the way Martin Luther King was "Dr. King." Their beloved Miss Baker accompanied them through the highs and lows of their great nonviolent movement, through the violent opposition that beat some and killed others. But in only five years, they won.

Miss Baker died in 1986, at the age of eighty-three. Grant's film is called *Fundi,* which means "master craftsman" in Swahili, and in it one of the students explains how she passed on her craft to them. The film includes scenes of tributes to Baker in the last years of her life. You can see Septima Clark, and Bob Moses, and wonderful praise from Wyatt T. Walker.

And at one event, an unnamed master of ceremonies tells the crowd: "Miss Baker to us is the mother of struggle." Then he introduces her to speak:

I want to bring to you now . . . this nurturer of those who needed nurturing, this scolder of those who needed scolding, this audacious champion of the right, this shining black beacon . . . Miss Ella Baker.

7

✛ ✛ ✛

ALICE PAUL WINS VOTES
FOR WOMEN

Acentury ago, American women did not vote. Today, of course, they do. How did it happen, exactly?

Most people know about the suffragettes, who marched in parades with banners flying. But who led them? Or were they simply one big movement without any leaders to speak of?

We know about Susan B. Anthony, who now graces the face of a dollar coin. During her lifetime, the press called her the "Napoleon" of woman suffrage. But Anthony helped start the movement back before the Civil War: She died in 1906, right when the marching began. Women won the vote fourteen years later, in 1920. Did anyone lead that final push, from 1906 to 1920, when decades of failure at last gave way to success?

There were several leaders, but one stands out above the others. Her name was Alice Paul. She worked behind the scenes, without fame or gain for herself. In those final years of struggle, Paul's *coup d'oeil* took the suffrage movement to victory. After Susan B. Anthony, Alice Paul was the single individual most responsible for winning American women the vote. Yet today, you don't hear much about her. The new generation of the women's movement hardly knows her name.

And so in our story of Alice Paul, we ask two questions: How did she do it? and Why do we know so little about her? Both answers give us precious insight about Napoleon's glance.

We catch a rare glimpse of Alice Paul in a book by one of her followers, Doris Stevens. The book is *Jailed for Freedom,* and the second chapter is titled "A Militant General—Alice Paul." Stevens writes:

Most people conjure up a menacing picture when a person is called not only a general, but a militant one. In appearance Alice Paul is anything but menacing. Quiet, almost mouselike, this frail young Quakeress sits in silence and baffles you with her contradictions. Large, soft gray eyes that strike you with a positive impact make you feel the indescribable force and power behind them. A mass of soft brown hair, caught easily at the neck, makes the contour of her head strong and graceful. Tiny, fragile hands that look more like an X-ray picture of hands, rest in her lap in Quakerish pose. Her whole atmosphere when she is not in action is one of strength and quiet determination. In action she is swift, alert, almost panther-like in her movements. Dressed always in simple frocks, preferably soft shades of purple, she conforms to an individual style and taste of her own rather than the prevailing vogue.

From her Quaker childhood in Moorestown, New Jersey, the "almost mouselike" Paul went on to Swarthmore College, and then spent a year studying social work at the New York School of Philanthropy, and then a year earning a master's degree in sociology at the University of Pennsylvania. In 1907, at the age of twenty-two, Alice Paul won a fellowship to study and practice social work in Britain. While taking courses at the University of Birmingham, she went to hear Christabel Pankhurst speak.

Five years older than Paul, voluptuous and beautiful, Pankhurst was anything but mouselike. She looked and spoke like a magnificent lion. Her subject was woman suffrage in Britain. The audience, mostly men, tried to shout her down. Pankhurst kept right on, through all the cries and catcalls.

Paul was hooked. She joined the Pankhursts.

There were three of them: the mother, Emmeline, and her two daughters, Christabel and Sylvia. Emmeline founded the Women's Political Suffrage Union in 1903, at the age of forty-five. Christabel was twenty-three and Sylvia twenty-one. The Women's Union was a break-away from the old-school suffrage association, the National Union of Women's Suffrage Societies. The older National Union elected their leaders from all the existing suffrage organizations in Britain. In the new Women's Union, Emmeline Pankhurst ran the show.

The breakaway Women's Union broke the law. Its constitution said so:

> *Object: To secure for women the Parliamentary vote as it is or may be granted to men . . . Methods: 1) Action entirely independent of political parties. 2) Opposition to whatever Government is in power until such time as the franchise is granted. 3) Vigorous agitation upon lines justified by the position of outlawry to which women are presently condemned.*

The old-school National Union shuddered at the very thought of "vigorous agitation" and "outlawry." They held conferences and wrote petitions to Parliament, and made sure not to criticize any politician or political party who expressed sympathy for other women's causes, like better food for women in poorhouses or better working conditions for women factory hands. The women of Britain made progress on these causes, thanks to their male allies in the various political parties, especially Labour and Liberal.

But the Pankhursts made no alliances with any politician or party. They opposed whatever party happened to be in power, to demand votes for women. The Pankhursts especially targeted Herbert Asquith, Liberal prime minister from 1908 to 1918. He supported other women's causes but opposed woman suffrage. So the National Union continued to court him while the Women's Union attacked him.

The attacks came in the form of parades, demonstrations, and disrupting government meetings with speeches and banners that proclaimed VOTES FOR WOMEN. The police ordered the women to stop. They refused, and went to jail. In jail, they went on hunger strikes. The jailkeepers fed them by force, a horrible ordeal much worse than hunger.

In Britain, Alice Paul lived all these methods firsthand, and noted how the Pankhursts played for spectacle. For example, their parades included riders on horseback. And a key follower, Flora Drummond, dressed in an army uniform and earned the nickname "General." The result was excellent coverage by the British press, who reported the Pankhursts' every move. Almost overnight, the question of votes for women moved from the margins to the very center of English politics. The country was in an uproar, and many politicians began declaring their support for woman suffrage, including two future prime ministers: David Lloyd-George and Winston Churchill.

There were two English methods that Alice Paul declined: breaking windows and arson. On some marches, Christabel and a few of her militants wrapped stones in pieces of paper with "Votes for Women" written on them, and hurled the stones through the windows of government buildings. And some tried to set fire to government buildings, without success. Perhaps Paul's Quaker background turned her away from violence of any kind. Or perhaps she saw that violence lost the Pankhursts more support than it gained. In any event, Paul practiced nonviolence throughout her life.

Paul first came to the attention of American suffragettes in November 1909. She was still in Britain, in jail at the time for disrupting the annual banquet of the lord mayor of London. Paul went on a hunger strike. Her jailers fed her by force, with a tube jammed down her throat. Paul weakened fast. Emmeline Pankhurst was on a speaking tour of the United States, and appealed to a New York meeting of suffragettes to press the American government to intervene on Alice Paul's behalf.

The leader of the New York group, Harriot Stanton Blatch, recalls the response: "I offered a resolution asking our government to intervene and this was adopted in spite of a few dissenters who cried out, 'Mrs. Pankhurst is not fighting for our vote or we for hers. Let the suffragettes take care of themselves.'"

The resolution did no good. Paul served out her thirty days in jail. Upon her release, she was far too ill to continue. So in January 1910, Alice Paul sailed back to America. Her first brush with suffrage had almost killed her. Paul went back to work on her doctorate in sociology at the University of Pennsylvania. But already, she had half her *coup d'oeil*. It would take two years for the other half to appear.

The first half had come in a London police station. Paul had been arrested with a group of suffragettes. The police ushered them into the station billiard room to keep them from the riffraff in the main station hall. Paul noticed a fellow suffragette who wore a pin of the American flag in her lapel. Paul struck up a conversation. It was their first meeting, but the two Americans connected like old friends. They sat on the billiard table and talked. Right away, they agreed that the American suffrage movement needed a dose of the British methods.

The other American was Lucy Burns. Six years older than Paul, Burns was a Vassar graduate, had taught high school in Brooklyn, and went to Germany to study German. Passing through England, she ran into the Pankhursts. In 1909, Burns switched her studies to Oxford but spent most of her time on suffrage.

For nearly a year after their first meeting, Paul and Burns demonstrated and went to jail together with the Pankhursts. But Burns was not there that time the jailers force-fed Paul. And Burns stayed behind in England when Paul returned to America.

That was the first half of Paul's *coup d'oeil*, on the billiard table with Burns. The second half came when Burns returned to America two years after Paul, who finished her doctorate at about the same time, in the summer of 1912. They visited each other at Moorestown and Brooklyn. The result was a concrete strategy to bring the British methods home to win a federal amendment for woman suffrage.

If Paul and Burns had the *coup d'oeil* together, perhaps we should credit them both. But as they put the strategy in motion, Paul became the senior partner and Burns her first follower. And Burns herself gave credit to Paul:

> *When Alice Paul spoke to me about the federal work, I knew that she had an extraordinary mind, extraordinary courage and remarkable executive ability . . . Her great assets, I should say, are her power, with a single leap of the imagination, to make plans on a national scale; and a supplementary power to see that done down to the last postage stamp.*

Burns refers to Paul's two assets: "leap of the imagination" and "power to see that done." These are the *coup d'oeil* and resolution of von Clausewitz—otherwise known as Napoleon's glance.

Another follower of Paul, Inez Irwin describes Burns:

> *Lucy Burns is as different a type from Alice Paul as one could imagine. She is tall—or at least she seems tall; rounded and muscular; a splendidly vigorous physical specimen . . . Lucy Burns' hair is a brilliant red; and even as she flashes, it flashes. It is full of sparkle . . . Mentally and emotionally, she is quick and warm. Her convictions are all vigorous and I do not think Lucy Burns would hesitate for a moment to suffer torture, to die, for them. She has intellectuality of a high order; but she overruns with a winning Irishness which supplements that intellectuality with grace and charm . . . Lucy Burns would*

*become angry because the President or the people did not do
this or that. Alice Paul never expected anything of them.*

Paul and Burns make a study in contrasts. We see Burns as
warm and strong, while Paul is cool and frail. They both might
"suffer torture" for the cause, but we imagine Burns bearing up and
Paul breaking down. And Paul "never expected anything"—a clear
indication of presence of mind, yet another key feature of
Napoleon's glance.

The federal strategy of Paul and Burns depended on two recent
developments back in America. First, women had already started
marching, thanks to the British example. One of the leading pio-
neers was the same Harriot Stanton Blatch who had offered the
resolution to free Paul from jail. She was the daughter of Elizabeth
Cady Stanton, the leading follower of Susan B. Anthony.

Second, it looked like the 1912 elections would give a solid
Democratic majority in the House and Senate and put a
Democrat—Woodrow Wilson—in the White House. With all
national offices controlled by one party, America would resemble
Britain. For in Britain, the party that won Parliament named the
prime minister. In America, it was a rare event for the same party
to win both houses of Congress and the presidency too. But in
1912, that rare event was nigh.

So first, Americans marching, and second, the 1912 elections,
brought the American suffrage movement closer to Britain's. Sure
enough, in October the elections delivered the Democratic victory
that everyone expected. The following month, November 1912,
was the annual convention of the National American Women's Suffrage Association—known as NAWSA. Paul and Burns presented
to Association leaders a plan to copy the British methods in the
United States: that is, demonstrations to force the Democratic
party to pass a federal suffrage amendment.

The NAWSA leaders listened carefully. Then they turned down the plan.

NAWSA was the leading suffrage organization in the United States. It was made up of state branches, much like the old-school National Union in Britain, and like its British cousin kept to meetings and petitions rather than demonstrations. But in America there was an extra twist: the states. NAWSA had given up on a federal amendment. Its local branches worked for suffrage state by state. So the November convention rejected the strategy of Paul and Burns not only for its militant character but also because the strategy aimed at a federal amendment, period. There was nothing in it about the states.

The federal-state debate went back a long way in the suffrage movement. After the Civil War, Susan B. Anthony and Elizabeth Cady Stanton noticed that each Confederate state would have to ratify the Fifteenth Amendment as a step to rejoining the Union. The Fifteenth Amendment gave voting rights to black men. So Anthony and Stanton opposed it. They wanted the amendment to include women, black and white. Otherwise, it would be fifty years before those same southern states would ever agree to votes for women. The one great chance for woman suffrage was to force the Confederate states to ratify votes for blacks and women together.

Most other suffrage leaders condemned Anthony and Stanton and supported the Fifteenth Amendment as a worthy step all its own. The amendment passed in 1870. But divisions endured: The suffrage movement split into two organizations, the National Women's Suffrage Association of Anthony and Stanton, and the American Woman Suffrage Association led by Lucy Stone and Lucretia Mott. Sure enough, just like Anthony and Stanton predicted, it was another fifty years before women won the vote.

The two organizations came back together in 1890 as NAWSA, with Anthony as president. But the organizer behind the scenes was

Carrie Chapman Catt. She was thirty-one years old, less than half Anthony's age. Catt made sure that each state had an Association branch. Each branch worked for a state amendment to give women the vote. In 1900, Anthony retired and Catt became president.

As of 1912, state suffrage had succeeded in nine states. If we date NAWSA from 1890, that makes one state every two and a half years. At that rate, all women would not vote until at least the year 2000. No wonder the younger generation of Paul and Burns pushed for a federal amendment instead.

But many southern women preferred state suffrage to a federal amendment. That way, their local Jim Crow laws could prevent black women from voting. A federal amendment meant that the federal government would have a hand in local voting rules, and so threaten the future of white supremacy. The compromise of 1890 committed NAWSA to work on both state and federal suffrage, but in reality the federal work died out.

By the time of the 1912 convention, the only vestige of federal suffrage in NAWSA was a standing Congressional Committee. Thanks to Anthony, the United States Congress had introduced the federal amendment in 1878. The Senate had voted it down in 1887, and the House never even took a vote. Once a year, NAWSA's Congressional Committee visited Congress to ask them to bring the federal amendment to debate again. Every year, the congressmen graciously listened and then did nothing. So for the past twenty-five years—from 1887 to 1912—there had been no progress at all on the federal amendment.

When the 1912 NAWSA convention rejected their "British" plan, Paul and Burns made an innocent request. They offered to organize a suffrage parade on the eve of Woodrow Wilson's inauguration in March. NAWSA agreed. There had been a few suffrage parades already in America, and many of the younger members wanted to march. What harm could there be in one more parade?

Paul and Burns swung into action. They took over the Congressional Committee, with Paul as chair and Burns as a member. That gave them access to NAWSA letterhead for stationery and lists of members and contributors. So they raised money and recruited marchers for what came to be America's first public demonstration for a federal suffrage amendment and the first step of a British-style campaign.

The mailing to Association members cited explicitly the chance for publicity:

WHY YOU MUST MARCH
Because this is the most conspicuous and important demonstration that has ever been attempted by suffragists in this country. Because this parade will be taken to indicate the importance of the suffrage movement by the press of the country and the thousands of spectators from all over the United States gathered in Washington for the Inauguration.

The parade took place on March 3, 1913. There were eight thousand marchers, twenty-six floats, ten marching bands, five contingents of cavalry, and six horse-drawn chariots. Black women joined the march, which outraged some of the southern Association members and only made them more certain of the evils of a federal amendment. And Paul had learned well the lesson of Christabel Pankhurt's beauty: Inez Milholland, a lawyer with the stunning looks of a fairy princess, led the parade with her long hair flowing, in flowing white robes, riding a big white horse.

Here are some newspaper headlines about the parade:

MOBS AT CAPITAL DEFY POLICE: BLOCK SUFFRAGE PARADE
                                                    —*Chicago Daily Tribune*

MOB HURTS 300 SUFFRAGISTS AT CAPITAL PARADE
—*New York Evening Journal*

CAPITAL MOBS MADE CONVERTS TO SUFFRAGE
—*New York Tribune*

The crowd numbered more than 250,000. At first the police ignored the parade and made no effort to control the mob that descended on the women. The *Chicago Daily Tribune* gave this report:

> *The most spectacular procession of women in equal suffrage history this afternoon buffeted its way westward along one of the widest streets in the country, through the greatest aggregation of spectators that ever turned out in Washington, while from beginning to end the police mismanagement was the worst in the known world . . .*

When the scene spun out of control, the secretary of war called out the cavalry from Fort Myer nearby. The *Tribune* reported some extra assistance: "Miss Inez Milholland, herald of the procession, distinguished herself by aiding in riding down a mob . . . "

The *Tribune* gave plenty of coverage to the suffrage beauty: "Miss Milholland, one grand ecstasy in white, with a golden crown on her head, and mounted astride a white horse, was down on the program as 'a mounted herald.' She wasn't any such thing. She was a peach. The crowd, jamming close, said so . . . "

Amid the melee, Paul and Burns showed their hand. Behind Milholland rode a rank of other women on horses. The *Tribune* reported what came next: "A wide, flat float, drawn slowly by two horses, followed the cavalry marshals, and bore in startling black letters on a white ground: 'We demand an amendment to the United States Constitution enfranchising women of the country.'"

The announcements for the parade had made no mention of the federal amendment. Now, there it was, at the front of the parade. After the amendment float, Paul and Burns put the NAWSA leaders. Again the *Tribune:* "Following on it marched the national officers ... Miss Anna Shaw, national president, stepping briskly and enwreathed in smiles ... "

Anna Shaw had succeeded Carrie Catt as president in 1904. The next parade contingent was "the worldwide movement for woman suffrage, headed by Mrs. Carrie Chapman Catt, president of the International Suffrage Alliance." The state contingents brought up the rear.

By all accounts, Anna Shaw was a kind, sweet intellectual who had no idea what Paul and Burns had just pulled off right under her nose: American and international leaders marched in support of a federal amendment. Perhaps even Catt, shrewder by far, did not pay close attention. Her eye was on the world stage. A month after the parade, Catt took off on another international speaking tour, to England, Germany, Czechoslovakia, and Austria. She ended up in Hungary, where she presided over the seventh annual meeting of the International Suffrage Alliance, which she had founded in 1904 when she gave up the presidency of NAWSA.

After the parade, Paul and Burns pressed on. They took advantage of the surge in public sympathy for suffrage. They lined up key Democratic and Republican allies, in the Senate and House, to introduce bipartisan motions to bring the federal amendment forward for debate. Six weeks after the parade, on the first day Congress opened, both motions passed.

And so with one bold stroke, Paul and Burns brought the federal amendment back to life, after a quarter-century of stalemate, since 1887. Perhaps as important, they gained thousands of followers and key allies among suffrage leaders. Two converts stand out: Harriot Stanton Blatch and Alva Vanderbilt Belmont.

We have already met Blatch, the daughter of Elizabeth Cady

Stanton and the first American suffrage leader to organize marches. Blatch continued her work in New York State, but also supported Paul and Burns on the federal amendment. In her memoirs, Blatch recalls that she had encouraged Paul and Burns in their original "British" plan before the Association leaders turned it down in November 1912. When the duo took over the Congressional Committee instead, Blatch applauded: "Now with young leaders of promise in Washington, trained in the Pankhurst school of direct dramatic action, it looked as if things were going to happen."

As for Alva Vanderbilt Belmont, she was one of the wealthiest women in the country. Her fortune came through divorce from one millionaire—Vanderbilt—and marriage to another—Belmont. She funded the New York State campaign until the Washington parade. After that, she put her money on Alice Paul.

Two weeks after the parade, Woodrow Wilson agreed to receive a delegation from the Congressional Committee. It was another first: No president before had ever received a suffrage delegation. Alice Paul and three others went. They made their case for a federal amendment. Wilson replied: No one had ever mentioned suffrage to him before, and so he would have to study the question. That was all. It was the only meeting ever between Wilson and Paul.

When Congress opened on April 7, there was a second parade: Paul and Burns had assembled delegates from all 435 congressional districts of the country to bring petitions in favor of the federal suffrage amendment. The delegates marched under their state banners to the Capitol and into the gallery to witness the House motion that brought the federal amendment forward. It was another coup: Paul and Burns had the states marching for a federal amendment.

On July 31, a third parade aimed at the Senate. In every state, women collected signatures and then traveled to Washington in festive train cars and automobiles, like a great parade converging from all quarters. They met in a final procession to the Capitol, where they handed the petitions to the Senate committee. At the same time, Inez Irwin reports that "processions, pilgrimages, petitions, deputations, and hearings, hundreds of public meetings organized by the Washington Headquarters" were held across the country.

And then came the annual convention of NAWSA itself, in December. Because it was in Washington, Paul and Burns organized it. Behind the podium they put a big sign with the same words as on the first float of the March parade: "We Demand an Amendment To The Constitution of the United States Enfranchising Women." And they put Burns among the opening speakers. She declared that the purpose of the NAWSA meeting was to ask the Democratic party and the government in power "to support the Woman Suffrage Amendment in Congress with its full strength."

Anna Shaw presided over the meeting, and hardly seemed to notice that Paul and Burns were committing not just the Congressional Committee but all of NAWSA to a federal amendment without any mention of state amendments. Then Alice Paul gave her official report from the committee, including a budget report: They had raised $25,343.88, of which the largest expense was $14,906.08 for the Washington parade.

The convention gave the Committee a standing ovation. But when the applause died down, Carrie Catt stepped to the podium.

She was back in the country from her international tour and did not like at all what she found. Later she wrote: "Many delegates to that suffrage convention in 1913 saw in the attitude of the chairman of the Congressional Committee a dark conspiracy to capture the entire 'National' for the militant enterprise." We do not know how many is "many," but we do know they included Carrie Catt.

Catt's first move was bureaucratic. After the standing ovation for the Committee, she could not attack Paul directly. So she invoked Association rules: It was not allowed for committees to control their own funds. The Congressional Committee would have to give their remaining funds, and all future funds they might raise, to the Association. Then the Association would decide on the budget for each of its various committees. It made no difference that NAWSA leaders had given special permission for the Committee to raise its own funds. Rules were rules.

As soon as Catt finished speaking, the NAWSA treasurer, Ruth McCormick, seconded the motion. Most of the delegates looked on in confusion, including Anna Shaw. But in the end they voted for Catt's proposal.

So Catt and McCormick succeeded in gaining control over the Congressional Committee in the name of NAWSA. They immediately forbade Paul and Burns to undertake any activity at all in any state without the permission of the state NAWSA branch.

Paul and Burns refused. They formed a new organization, the Congressional Union, separate from NAWSA. The Association appointed a new Congressional Committee, with McCormick as chair.

Catt made no secret of her opposition to Paul and Burns. Anna Shaw wrote to a fellow Association member: "Mrs. Catt said to me the other day that she had been looking for some time to a division among the suffragists of this country, and that the militants and militant sympathizers would gather into one group while those of us who really want suffrage and not advertising would gather in another."

Catt was one of the suffrage leaders that Paul had consulted early on, before she and Burns made their proposal to the 1912 Association convention. Catt told her then: "I feel that I have enlisted for life. This is something that cannot be done, we cannot get this federal amendment, and I did this deliberately knowing that I was enlisting for life."

Paul and Burns did not enlist for life. They wanted the vote right away. But Catt had built a successful career as a suffrage leader. She refused to let anyone rock her boat. She had many friends among Democratic politicians and wanted one more: Woodrow Wilson. Catt went out of her way to court him, while Paul and Burns attacked him.

Through 1914 and 1915, Carrie Catt went back and forth between her international activities and NAWSA. But during that time, more and more NAWSA members defected to the Congressional Union or called for NAWSA to fight for a federal amendment too. There was not enough money to hold NAWSA meetings in every state. And while NAWSA had thirty-six state chapters, by 1915 the Congressional Union had members and activities in all forty-eight states.

At the end of 1915, Carrie Catt returned to NAWSA full-time. In December, at the annual NAWSA convention in Washington, Anna Shaw stepped down. Catt became president again. The vote was unanimous. The first thing Catt did was meet with Paul.

The meeting took place at the Willard Hotel on December 17. Catt took along three other NAWSA officers, including Ruth McCormack, the treasurer who had helped Catt defeat Paul at the 1913 convention. Paul came with Burns and two other followers.

Catt began by inviting the Congressional Union back into NAWSA—on three conditions: drop the anti-Democrat campaign, stay out of political campaigns completely, and operate only in states where NAWSA did not have an active affiliate.

Paul, of course, declined. She offered instead that NAWSA and the Congressional Union coordinate their efforts as much as possible, as two separate organizations. In reply, Catt rose to go and spoke a last word to Paul: "All I wish to say is, I will fight you to the last ditch."

It was the last time Catt and Paul ever met. But now the battle was on.

Catt spent 1916 rebuilding NAWSA. She visited twenty-three

states herself and sent delegatives to the others. They visited hundreds of suffrage leaders and spoke at dozens of meetings. Catt found NAWSA members split between the federal and state amendments. So she came up with a grand solution: both. She called it the "Winning Plan."

In June 1916, the Republican and Democratic conventions both refused to endorse a federal amendment. That made Catt's Winning Plan even more urgent, before NAWSA lost even more members to Paul's federal campaign. Catt called the NAWSA convention early, in September instead of December, and held it in the resort of Atlantic City to entice more members to come. There she unveiled her Winning Plan: Some state chapters would work for the federal amendment and others would work for state suffrage. Catt gave each chapter detailed instructions on exactly how to proceed.

On the last night of the convention, the featured speaker was Woodrow Wilson. Catt arranged it, and introduced him to thunderous applause. In his speech, Wilson mentioned neither the federal nor state amendments to the women. Instead, he told them:

> *The whole art of practice of government consists not in moving individuals, but in moving masses. It is all very well to run ahead and beckon, but after all, you have to wait for them to follow. I have . . . come to congratulate you that there was a force behind you that will . . . be triumphant and for which you can afford a little while to wait.*

Wilson believed in moving masses, not individuals, and told the women to wait. Meanwhile, refusing to wait, Alice Paul turned her sights on a single individual as the key to federal suffrage: Wilson himself.

In June 1916, the Congressional Union changed its name to the National Woman's Party—NWP—with Paul still as president. The following month, Harriot Stanton Blatch, a member of the NWP executive committee, joined a delegation of Democratic women for an audience with Wilson. Blatch told him: "I am sixty years old, Mr. President. I have worked all my life for suffrage, and I am determined that I will never again stand up on the street corners of a great city appealing to every Tom, Dick, and Harry for the right of self-government."

Wilson explained why he opposed the federal amendment: the "Negro question."

Blatch replied: "But of course, you know the enfranchisement of women in the South would not decrease the proportion of white to black voters."

"Yes, I know it. But Congressmen don't." Wilson smiled. "In two states the blacks would still preponderate."

It was the same old story: If suffrage were left to the state amendments, Jim Crow laws in the South could prevent blacks from voting. The federal amendment risked actually giving blacks the vote.

Blatch gave up:

We left convinced that we could not change the President's mind, that he would do nothing for the Federal Amendment. The only alternative was to change Presidents.

In her New York campaign, Blatch had stationed "Silent Sentinels" at the State House in Albany. Now she turned to Washington: "How much more effective and stirring would be these Silent Sentinels at the White House!"

Silent Sentinels were pickets. No one had picketed the White House before. The NWP took up Blatch's idea in January 1917, following another delegation to Wilson. There were three hundred women in the delegation. They brought resolutions passed around the country at memorial services held Christmas Day, two weeks before. The services honored Inez Milholland, the suffrage beauty who rode the white horse.

In the three and a half years since she led the great Washington parade, Milholland had toured the country speaking for suffrage, sometimes astride a horse. She was anemic but kept going. In October 1916, she spoke in Los Angeles. Her speech concluded, "Mr. President, how long must women wait for liberty?" On the word "liberty," Milholland collapsed. A month later, she died.

Right away, she became a martyr to the cause. Drawings appeared of Milholland in white on her white horse, with the caption "Who Died for the Freedom of Women." The press called her an American Joan of Arc. And so to the delegation of January 1917, suffrage was a matter of life or death.

The delegation's spokeswoman, Sara Field, said to Wilson:

> *Mr. President, one of our most beautiful and beloved comrades, Inez Milholland, has paid the price of her life for a cause . . . In the light of Inez Milholland's death, as we look over the long backward trail through which we have sought our political liberty, we are asking, how long, how long, must this struggle go on?*

Wilson replied:

> *Ladies, I had not been apprised that you were coming here to make any representation that would issue an appeal to me. I had been told that you were coming to present memorial resolutions with regard to the very remarkable woman whom your cause has lost. I therefore am not prepared to say anything further than I have said on previous occasions of this sort.*

He then repeated his usual denial, that he was captive to the Democratic party: "As the leader of a Party, my commands come from that Party."

Another member of the delegation, Maud Younger, describes what happened next. "With a last defiant glance at us he abruptly left the room. Secret Service men, newspaper men, and secretaries followed him. Where the President of the United States had been was now a closed door." The women retreated. "Stunned, talking in low, indignant tones, we moved slowly out of the East Room and returned to our Headquarters. There we discussed the situation. We saw that the President would do nothing . . . We had had speeches, meetings, parades, campaigns, organization. What new method could we devise?"

The picketing began the next day, January 10, 1917. Four women carried lettered banners, and eight carried the purple, white, and gold banners of the Woman's Party. One banner read, MR. PRESIDENT WHAT WILL YOU DO FOR WOMAN SUFFRAGE? The other repeated Inez Milholland's last cry: HOW LONG MUST WOMEN WAIT FOR LIBERTY? The suffragettes split up, to stand at the east and west gates of the White House.

At first, they suffered only wind and rain and sometimes jeering and jostling crowds. The police just looked on, for picketing was legal. Every day, except for Sunday, legions of women took their turn at the White House gates. Then on April 7, 1917, America entered World War I by declaring war on Germany. Now some of the press and the crowd called the picketers "traitors" for opposing the government in wartime.

Then on June 20, a Russian delegation visited Wilson to discuss their common fight against Germany. An elected Russian government had just replaced the czar and given women the vote—it was still four months before the Bolsheviks took power there. As the Russians passed through the White House gates, the suffragettes unfurled a new banner:

PRESIDENT WILSON AND ENVOY ROOT ARE DECEIVING RUSSIA.

THEY SAY "WE ARE A DEMOCRACY. HELP US TO WIN THE WAR SO THAT DEMOCRACIES MAY SURVIVE." WE WOMEN OF AMERICA TELL YOU THAT AMERICA IS NOT A DEMOCRACY. TWENTY MILLION WOMEN ARE DENIED THE RIGHT TO VOTE. PRESIDENT WILSON IS THE CHIEF OPPONENT OF THEIR NATIONAL ENFRANCHISEMENT. HELP US MAKE THIS NATION REALLY FREE. TELL OUR GOVERN-MENT THAT IT MUST LIBERATE ITS PEOPLE BEFORE IT CAN CLAIM FREE RUSSIA AS AN ALLY.

The crowd around the suffragettes swiftly tore down the banner. But the incident drew more press coverage than any suf-frage event since the great Washington parade.

Washington's chief of police called Alice Paul on the phone: "You will be arrested if you attempt to picket again."

She reminded him that picketing was legal.

The arrests started on June 22: Lucy Burns and Katherine Morey. They were released without trial. More arrests followed, and sometimes the suffragettes spent a few days in prison. Then, on July 14, the judge sentenced a group of sixteen to sixty days in prison, on the charge of "obstructing traffic." That same day, Alice Paul entered a hospital in Philadelphia, ill from overwork. It took her a month to recover.

The prison was the Occoquan Workhouse outside Washington. Some of the husbands visited their wives, including J. A. Hopkins, a member of the 1916 Democratic National Campaign Com-mittee. He was so upset by the prison's conditions that he went straight to the White House. Wilson was "shocked"—he claimed to know nothing about the prison. After three days, he ordered the women released.

The picketing resumed without arrests. But the crowd grew more violent, especially as soldiers in uniform joined them, but the police just looked on. Then on August 14, the picketers unfurled a new banner:

KAISER WILSON, HAVE YOU FORGOTTEN YOUR SYMPATHY WITH THE POOR GERMANS BECAUSE THEY WERE NOT SELF-GOVERNING? TWENTY MILLION AMERICAN WOMEN ARE NOT SELF-GOVERNING. TAKE THE BEAM OUT OF YOUR OWN EYE.

Wilson brought America into World War I on the side of democracy—that is, Britain and France. Now here the women painted him as an enemy of democracy, like the German kaiser.

The banner lasted a half hour before the crowd tore it down. The women retreated to headquarters, but the crowd followed. Inez Irwin reports:

> *By this time the mob . . . had become a solid mass of people, choking the street . . . The crowd began to throw eggs, tomatoes, and apples . . . Suddenly a shot rang out from the crowd. A bullet went through a window of the second story, directly over the heads of two women who stood there . . . Three yeomen climbed up onto the balcony . . . Lucy Burns . . . held her banner until the last moment. It seemed as though she were going to be dragged over the railing of the balcony, but two of the yeomen managed to tear it from her hands before this occurred.*

The next day, the picketing resumed. Again, the crowd attacked. The next day, August 16, the police attacked. They arrested six picketers. The judge gave the women thirty days in the Occoquan Workhouse. Over the next few weeks, through September and into October, the arrests continued. The longest sentence was two months, until Alice Paul went to jail too.

In Britain, Emmeline Pankhurst had gone to jail many times. At some point, Paul had to join her followers in prison. So on October 20, 1917, Alice Paul went out to picket and went to jail with three other suffragettes. It was her first arrest in America, eight years after the month she spent in a London prison that broke her health.

When the judge asked how the suffragettes pleaded, Alice Paul rose and spoke calmly: "We do not with to make any plea before this court. We do not consider ourselves subject to this court, since as an unenfranchised class we have nothing to do with the making of the laws which have put us in this position."

It was the same speech the Pankhursts made whenever they were arrested.

The judge sentenced Paul's three accomplices to six months in Occuquan. He sentenced Paul to seven.

Seven months! Eight years ago, one month in prison had almost killed her.

Right away, Paul and her fellow prisoners began a hunger strike, just like in London. And just like in London, the Occoquan wardens force-fed her.

Meanwhile, the prison denied Paul contact with the outside world: no lawyer, no family or friends. Lucy Burns went to jail on November 14 with another group of picketers, but once inside Occoquan, she was not able to see Paul. Burns and her group began a hunger strike too. Again, the wardens force-fed them. The guards roughed up the women as they took them in and out of their cells. Lucy Burns resisted so fiercely that they punished her by taking away her clothes. She slept in only a blanket. Once, they tied her arms to the wall above her head and left her that way all night.

Outside, the NWP put on tour the suffragettes who had already served time in prison. They spoke at meetings and traveled the country in a train, the "Prison Special," dressed in prison outfits. They described the harsh conditions, the rough treatment, and the force-feeding. Democrats started to worry, and called on Wilson to do something. For example, the Democratic chairman in Illinois wrote to him: "Chances for Democratic success in the Congressional elections are being severely hurt by the unhuman treatment of ... women ... in Occuquan ... Cannot you use your influence to have these women released and the situation cleared up by passage of the federal amendment?"

A close friend of Wilson, Dudley Malone, resigned his presidentially appointed post as collector of the Port of New York in protest. Malone then offered himself as lawyer to the suffrage prisoners. But he could not find Alice Paul.

Where was she?

In solitary confinement. Ruth Winslow, in solitary, too, smuggled out this note:

We have been in solitary for five weeks now ... I have felt quite feeble the last few days—faint, so that I could hardly get my hair combed, my arms ached so ... Alice Paul and I talk back and forth though we are at opposite ends of the building ... Yesterday was a bad day for me in feeding. I was vomiting continually during the process. The tube has developed an irritation somewhere that is painful ... Don't let them tell you we take this well. Miss Paul vomits much. I do too ... The feeding always gives me a severe headache. My throat aches afterward, and I always weep and sob, to my great disgust, quite against my will. I try to be less feeble-minded.

Paul and Winslow grew so weak that the wardens transferred them to the prison hospital. Then they moved Paul to the psychiatric ward. In addition to breaking her body, now they tried to break her mind. They replaced the wooden door of her cell with metal bars and let other inmates of the ward come over to shriek at her. Once an hour, all through the night, a nurse came in to wake Paul and shine a light in her face.

At this point, none of her allies knew where she was, not even Ruth Winslow.

In these crisis months of the suffrage movement, let's pause for a picture of our three key suffrage leaders. We see Carrie Catt at her gala convention in the resort of Atlantic City, welcoming Woodrow Wilson onstage. We see Lucy Burns wrestling two sailors on a Washington balcony, or naked in bed in a filthy prison, hands tied above her head, with her wild red hair and booming voice singing away through the night.

And there lies Alice Paul, fading fast, alone, victim of a stubborn president and her own resolution to follow her great *coup d'oeil*. Nothing remained before her to do but die to see it through.

Then Dudley Malone found her.

He quickly obtained a court order to transfer Paul out of the psychiatric ward, back to the regular hospital. There, a few days later, David Lawrence appeared.

He was a journalist. Dozens of journalists had tried to get into the prison—how did Lawrence succeed? He was a close friend of Woodrow Wilson's. Unlike Malone, Lawrence stayed on Wilson's side. He came to Paul because Wilson, of course, could not.

Lawrence told her that Wilson would try for the federal amendment to pass the House in 1918 and the Senate in 1919. Would that stop the picketing now?

In other words, he was offering Paul a deal.

She turned it down. Her reply to Lawrence: "Nothing short of the passage of the amendment through Congress will end our agitation." Once the House and Senate both passed the amendment, then the picketing would stop. If that was in 1919, then so be it. Nothing else would make the women stop.

So Lawrence left without a deal. But he did reveal Wilson's intention: to declare at last for a federal amendment and encourage the House to pass it. So a few days after Lawrence's visit, the prison released all the suffrage prisoners, including Alice Paul.

Suddenly, the House declared it would vote on the federal

amendment in just a few weeks, on January 10, 1918. On January 9, Wilson convoked twelve key House members and advised them to vote in favor. The next day, the amendment passed the House.

So ends our story of Alice Paul in victory won at the edge of defeat.

As Wilson promised, the Senate passed the amendment in 1919, and as Paul promised, the picketing continued right to the end. But the arrests stopped. The states ratified the amendment in 1920.

As for Wilson, he went down in history as a man of peace, the founder of the League of Nations, instead of the killer of Alice Paul.

On the day the suffrage amendment passed the last state, Wilson received a victory delegation from Carrie Catt. She went down in history as the victorious leader of NAWSA, which became the League of Women Voters after 1920. In the decades that followed, the League of Women Voters made a great contribution to American politics by stationing women at voting places to prevent cheating.

In 1923, Catt published a comprehensive history, *Woman Suffrage and Politics: The Inner Story of the Suffrage Movement*. It became the primary source for suffrage historians. In over five hundred pages, the book mentions the name Alice Paul exactly once.

Alice Paul was also busy in 1923. That was the year she wrote the Equal Rights Amendment, or ERA, and succeeded in having Congress introduce it, like Susan B. Anthony with the suffrage amendment in 1878. So history knows Paul for the ERA, not for her suffrage campaign. But her presence of mind made her ready to see the Pankhurst achievements, her *coup d'oeil* showed her the path to bring those past achievements to America, and her resolution kept her going—until Alice Paul won votes for women, thanks to Napoleon's glance.

8

✠ ✠ ✠

STRATEGY REBORN:
PATTON VS. THE PLANNERS

I n World War II, three hundred and ninety-five Americans held the rank of general. Today, more than fifty years later, George S. Patton remains the most famous of them all. He is the only one whom Hollywood made a movie about. It was a good movie too. *Patton* shows up on most lists of the best films of all time.

Another general of World War II, Dwight D. Eisenhower, also gained lasting fame, but as president, not as a soldier. As it turns out, Patton and Eisenhower knew each other well. They met right after World War I at Camp Meade, Maryland. Both were West Point graduates and avid tank officers. Once the two of them took apart a whole tank and put it back together. They rode horses, hunted wild game, made bathtub gin, and practiced pistol shooting. Their wives, Beatrice and Mamie, were best friends too.

But in other ways, Patton and Eisenhower were completely different. Patton was a rich city boy from Los Angeles, handsome, loud, a show-off with a raw temper and a foul mouth. Eisenhower was a poor country boy from Kansas, homely, soft-spoken, and charming to everyone. By the time the United States entered World War II, Eisenhower outranked Patton by several grades, even though Patton was five years older. When Eisenhower became head of all Allied forces in Europe, he had a chance to name Patton head of the American contingent. Instead, he picked Omar Bradley, a poor country boy from Missouri, who spoke, behaved, thought, and even looked like Eisenhower himself.

There was another difference between Patton on one hand and Eisenhower and Bradley on the other. Patton fought by *coup d'oeil.*

Eisenhower and Bradley were classic Jomini planners. While his two superiors plodded along, Patton rode a roller coaster of bitter frustration, spectacular triumph, sudden tragedy, and timeless glory. Again and again, Eisenhower and Bradley tried to rein him in. Again and again, Patton broke out.

We can hunt for clues to Patton's *coup d'oeil* in his letters, his diaries, a rough draft of a short memoir, and notes in the margins of the books he bequeathed to West Point. He was dyslexic, so he had a hard time writing things down. Martin Blumenson brought these various sources together in two volumes of *The Patton Papers* and Carlo D'Este combed these various sources for a massive, masterful biography, *Patton: A Genius for War*, taking the title from von Clausewitz's chapter on *coup d'oeil*, "The Genius for War." And some of Patton's men published their own accounts. Last but not least, Bradley spoke often of Patton in his own memoir, which served as the basis for the movie *Patton*.

In all these accounts, Patton's *coup d'oeil* remains elusive. But if we look hard enough, we can find it. The first place to look is in Patton's oddest quirk of all: his belief in reincarnation.

Patton's family and fellow soldiers reported many occasions when he would show them an old battlefield, in the United States or later in Europe, and point out what happened in each exact spot. When they asked him how he knew, Patton always gave the same answer: "I was there." When the British general Sir Harold Alexander remarked, "You know, George, you would have made a great marshal for Napoleon if you had lived in the nineteenth century," Patton replied, "But I did."

He wrote about reincarnation only once, in a peculiar poem in 1922, at the age of thirty-seven:

Through the travail of the ages, midst the pomp and toil of war
Have I fought and strove and perished, countless times upon this star

Still more clearly as a Roman, can I see the legion close
As our third rank moved in forward, and the short sword
found our foes
I have fought with gun and cutlass, on the red and slippery deck
With all Hell aflame within me, and a rope around my neck
And still later as a general, have I galloped with Murat
When we laughed at death and numbers, trusting in the
Emperor's star
So but now with tanks a clatter, have I waddled on the foe
Belching death at twenty paces, by the starshell's ghastly glow
So as through a glass and darkly, the age-long strife I see
Where I fought in many guises, many names—but always me
So forever in the future, shall I battle as of yore
Dying to be born a fighter, but to die again once more

In this poem, Patton not only fought before: He fought and died. Throughout his career, Patton threw himself into battle, like Napoleon at the Lodi bridge, exposing himself to enemy fire while other generals led from the safety of headquarters behind the lines. A belief in reincarnation gave Patton courage to face death—he would come back a soldier to fight again.

But how much was this a belief in reincarnation, or a very strong ability to "see" historic battles, like Napoleon before him? In *coup d'oeil*, you draw on successful tactics from history: You return to the past, and the past lives again through you.

We know that Patton was a student of war from the earliest age. He was named for his grandfather, George Smith Patton, who fought for the South in the Civil War and died at the Third Battle of Winchester in the Shenandoah Valley. The Union general who won that battle was Philip Sheridan. It was September 1864, after Grant had become Union commander, and freed Sheridan and Sherman from Jomini, planning to fight instead by *coup d'oeil*.

That was how the Civil War finally ended, when Grant discovered Napoleon's glance.

Patton's grandfather and his father, also named George Smith Patton, and many other Pattons attended the Virginia Military Institute. The family moved to Los Angeles before the third George Smith Patton was born in 1885. Young George grew up steeped in stories of battle. His father told them or read them to the boy from books. When he learned to read, George studied the stories himself. He dressed in soldier suits, wore toy swords and guns, and inherited the Civil War saddle that his grandfather was riding when he died. On the pommel was a stain that young George believed was his grandfather's blood.

Patton's childhood pranks re-created the battles he read about. One time he led his cousins to turn a farm wagon into a make-believe armored vehicle, like John the Blind, a Czech general of the fifteenth century, who put cannons on horse carts and fired them in motion. It was John the Blind who invented tank warfare—and Patton who mastered it, five hundred years later.

Patton's school essays were all about war. For example, at the age of sixteen he wrote about the battle of Marathon:

Most of the credit belongs to Miltadeos who was the first to use Greek troops in open field in so thin a formation, and his use of the second line saved the Greeks from destruction and won the battle for them.

Not bad for a kid in high school. But Patton's dyslexia made schoolwork difficult. His grades were not good enough for West Point, so he went to the Virginia Military Institute instead. After two years, in 1904, he was able to transfer to West Point. He was the first Patton to go there—a sign that the Civil War was now past.

We know about Patton's West Point years from the notebooks

he kept. They are full of references to past battles, great generals, and the lessons of history. In one telling remark, he summarized a key principle of von Clausewitz's: that a general must study history to become:

> ... so thoroughly conversant with all sorts of military possibilities that whenever an occasion arises he has at hand without effort on his part a parallel. To attain this end I think it is necessary for a man to begin to read military history in its earliest and hence crudest form and to follow it down in natural sequence permitting his mind to grow with his subject until he can grasp without effort the most abstruse question of the science of war.

Here is more evidence that Patton's belief in reincarnation came from studying past battles "so thoroughly" that he saw himself in them. He had "at hand" so many "parallels" that his mind "grew with his subject" until the past blended with the present in one great theater of war.

But what about von Clausewitz himself, or, rather, his formidable opus, *On War*? And what about Jomini? By the time Patton arrived at West Point, both von Clausewitz and Jomini were required reading. But while Jomini remained the classic text of strategy, von Clausewitz never found much favor. In fact, many experts considered him out of date.

In 1908, a year before Patton graduated from West Point, a new translation of *On War* came out. It featured an introduction by the editor, Colonel F. N. Maude of the British army. For Maude, military strategy had changed beyond recognition:

> The difference between "now and then" lies in this, that, thanks to the enormous increase in range (the essential feature in modern armaments), it is possible to concentrate by surprise,

on any chosen spot, a man-killing power fully twentyfold greater than was conceivable in the days of Waterloo; and whereas in Napoleon's time this concentration of man-killing power ... depended almost entirely on the shape and condition of the ground, which might or might not be favorable, nowadays such concentration of fire-power is almost independent of the country altogether.

Maude's disregard for the "condition of the ground" contrasts strongly with the first description of *coup d'oeil* by Frederick the Great, who applied the term to a general's ability to "read" the terrain at a glance. Von Clausewitz later broadened the term to include all aspects of strategy. In contrast, Maude's view is pure Jomini, updated with modern artillery:

Thus, at Waterloo, Napoleon was compelled to wait till the ground became firm enough for his guns to gallop over; nowadays every gun at his disposal, and five times that number had he possessed them, might have opened on any point in the British position he had selected, as soon as it became light enough to see . . . . Nowadays there would be no difficulty in turning on the fire of two thousand guns on any point of the position, and switching this fire up and down the line like water from a fire-engine hose, if the occasion demanded such concentration.

For Colonel Maude, modern artillery made mobile war and the commander's *coup d'oeil* obsolete. Instead, long-range guns would kill from a distance, with "no difficulty." It was a chilling thought, but Maude was not alone in his assessment. His description above fits how both sides of World War I would fight just a few years later. The result was tragedy on a monumental scale.

The war broke out in 1914, while Patton was a cavalry

instructor at Fort Riley, Kansas. An extra year to graduate from West Point, in 1909, plus his two years at Virginia Military Institute, made him three years older than his classmates. He ranked forty-sixth out of one hundred three graduates. All in all, his dyslexia made him an average-to-poor student. But after graduation, he thrived as a cavalry officer. Patton was a member of the American pentathlon team at the 1912 Stockholm Olympics: The contestants were mostly other cavalry officers, as the five sports were riding, fencing, swimming, running, and shooting. The event followed a military story: Carrying orders to his general, an officer rides as fast as he can, encounters the enemy, who shoots his horse, so he fires at the enemy until he is out of ammunition, fights them off with his sword, swims a river to escape, and then runs to deliver the message.

Patton finished fifth. That allowed him to claim that he was one of the greatest cavalrymen in the world. He then spent the summer of 1913 studying fencing at the French Cavalry School in Saumur and touring the historic battlefields of Europe. On his return, he designed a new cavalry saber for the U.S. army, following a French design from the days of Napoleon. The army adopted it as its official sword. Tall, slim, blond, and handsome, Patton fancied himself a dashing cavalry officer in the old European tradition.

When the World War broke out the following year, Patton wrote to his superiors:

> I have always wanted to have the experience of actual combat, not as an observer but as a participant . . . I know officers and several French regiments who would take me as an extra man . . . Therefore if I can get leave I can manage the rest.

The army said no. For the moment, the United States intended to keep as far away from the war as possible.

Instead, Patton saw some brief action chasing Pancho Villa,

after the sometime-revolutionary and sometime-bandit killed eighteen Americans in the border town of Columbus, New Mexico. Patton led a convoy of three automobiles into Mexico. In a skirmish at a ranch near the village of Rubio, they killed three of Villa's men with a hail of gunfire. It was Patton's first taste of warfare. He used an ivory-handled 1873 Colt .45 revolver, and wore it years later throughout World War II.

Patton's chance for real combat came when the United States finally entered World War I. In the summer of 1917, he arrived in France as part of the headquarters staff for the American army. It took months of training and logistics to ready the troops for battle. Confined to desk work, Patton chafed in frustration. But in September, he wrote to his wife:

> *There is a lot of talk about "Tanks" here now and I am interested as I can see no future in my present job.*

It was the British who invented the tank. While most of their army shared Colonel Maude's blind faith in long-range artillery, a few skeptics started working on building a tank right after the war broke out in 1914. They judged that bombing could only weaken the enemy: The army still had to storm the enemy lines, which tanks could do better than infantry. The biggest supporter of tanks was Winston Churchill, who sponsored the early models even though he was naval secretary at the time. The first tanks entered combat in 1916 at the Battle of the Somme.

The Somme was a classic Jomini battle, modernized as Meade foresaw with a wallop of long-range artillery. The generals who planned it stayed miles behind the front, in beautiful chateaus in the French countryside. They sent their orders by messenger, telegram, or telephone to commanding officers at the front. Those commanders sent further orders to junior officers along the trenches, who passed them on to attacking officers, who led the troops out of the trenches toward the enemy lines. The "chateau generals" of World War I were the exact opposite of Napoleon at the Lodi bridge, leading from the front.

The Battle of the Somme began on July 1. After a week and a half of intensive shelling, just like Maude prescribed, thousands of British soldiers walked out of their trenches toward the German lines. Some carried walking sticks, as if out for a morning stroll. They expected to find nothing but stacks of dead soldiers in the German trenches. Instead, they met German artillery and machine-gun fire. As it turned out, the Germans had just burrowed deeper into their trenches, safe from the British shells.

Following orders, the British infantry kept advancing. They fell like harvested wheat. There were sixty thousand casualties in one day.

But that was only the beginning. The next day the British tried again. And the next. And the next.

Then the French joined in.

From July to November, the British and French lost 600,000 men at the Battle of the Somme. The Germans lost 450,000. It was the greatest disaster in military history. The result was that the Germans pulled back a few miles, only to dig new trenches and resume the stalemate.

The British tanks came in halfway through the Battle of the Somme, in September. Forty-nine of them spread out along the front and advanced with the infantry. Most of the tanks broke down, but a few made it far enough to smash through the German lines. That was just how Patton's boyhood hero, the Czech general John the Blind, used his tanks—as battering rams on wheels, with guns. The tanks were too few to make much difference, but the Germans took note and rushed to start making their own.

A year after the Battle of the Somme, when the Americans arrived and Patton heard talk of the tanks, he wrote to his superiors again, volunteering for the new tank corps:

I speak and read French better than 95% of American officers so could get information from the French direct. I have also been to school in France and have always gotten on well with Frenchmen. I believe I have quick judgment and that I am willing to take chances. Also I have always believed in getting close to the enemy and have taught this for two years at the Mounted Service School where I had success in arousing the aggressive spirit in the students.

Accepted.

On November 10, 1917, one day before his thirty-second birthday, Patton became America's first tank officer.

But wait—Patton did not see tank warfare the same way his superiors did. We get a hint of this in his request above. He talks of "quick judgment"—*coup d'oeil*—and taking chances, getting close to the enemy, aggressive spirit. This does not fit the image of chateau generals picking targets from afar, massive infantry attacks on those targets, and tanks falling in line as battering rams to help the infantry smash through the enemy defenses.

Here's an excerpt from "Light Tanks," a report that Patton wrote in December 1917:

If resistance is broken and the line pierced, the tank must and will assume the role of pursuit cavalry and "ride the enemy to death."

"Ride the enemy to death" was a favorite saying of Frederick the Great's. Napoleon liked to use the same quote. We can see that Patton's view of the tank was a throwback to Napoleon's cavalry. But you never knew where you might pierce the line for the cavalry to ride through and win the day. That meant you needed flexibility, mobility, *coup d'oeil*—to swing your tanks one way or the other depending on how the battle unfolded. Patton even recommended forgoing the sacred artillery barrage before the advance, because "it tears up the ground" and slowed the tanks, as well as announcing exactly where the attack was about to take place.

All in all, his view was the exact opposite of how World War I had been fought so far. What would happen when the two views clashed, when the chateau generals sent Patton into battle?

After months of testing and training, Patton's tanks at last entered combat. In September 1918 they joined the Battle of Saint-Mihiel, which was the first major engagement of American troops in the war. Saint-Mihiel was a French village along the Meuse River. There were hills with forest behind it, then another river. The rivers were in wide valleys where the Germans faced the British and French in trenches half a mile apart. In rain, the valleys turned to mud.

Right away, Patton did something odd. Instead of relying on the usual reports, he surveyed the terrain himself. He went along on a French night patrol, where they came close enough to the enemy trenches to whistle and hear the Germans whistle back. It was worth it: Patton decided that the reports made too much of the mud—his tanks would do fine even in the rain. From then on, Patton insisted on the "absolute necessity for a tank officer to personally see the ground" before a battle. Again, just like Napoleon, and completely out of the ordinary in World War I. The worst case of ignoring the condition of the terrain was the four-month Battle of Passchendaele in 1917, when the British actually discontinued terrain reports. Only after losing 250,000 men did the British commander find out that the battlefield had been a sea of mud throughout the battle.

After inspecting the ground at Saint-Mihiel, Patton tried to eliminate the artillery barrage before the attack. He lost the argument. Next he requested smoke canisters mixed in with the shells, to give his tanks cover. The artillery officer refused, because it meant changing the plans. Once again, von Clausewitz-style mobility conflicted with Jomini-style planning.

Patton complained to his commander, Colonel Rockenbach, who intervened in Patton's favor. But Rockenbach ordered Patton to keep out of the actual combat. The night before the battle, Rockenbach told him explicitly: "Keep control of your reserve and supply, you have no business in a tank and I give you the order not to go into this fight in a tank." Like the infantry officers, Patton had to stay in a particular spot with a telephone so that Rockenbach could call him in case he had further orders. Patton was then supposed to send messengers to the tank commanders to pass on Rockenbach's orders. That was how the chain of command worked in World War I—and made flexible, mobile war impossible.

The shelling began at one o'clock in the morning. It lasted four hours. The weather changed from a light summer rain to a cold, heavy downpour. Nevertheless, at the first break of dawn at five o'clock, right on schedule, the ground attack began. Patton's tanks moved out.

Patton stayed behind at his post with six of his men, just like Rockenbach ordered. They inched forward as much as possible, until the telephone wire stretched straight and could go no farther. Patton stood on a hill to peer out over the battlefield. He saw ground burnt bare and black by constant bombardment, huge craters filled with rain, rows of barbed wire raised onto Xes of twisted wood, mud and debris splashing up as German artillery met the attackers, the bodies of dead soldiers contorted in every possible position. There was a deafening din of whining shells, the rattle of machine guns, crackling rifles, and exploding bombs.

Shivering with cold, Patton kept his eyes on his tanks. Some took direct hits by German shells. Others had to change course as they reached the German trenches. As Patton predicted, the ground was firm enough to hold the tanks despite the rain, but some of the trenches were too wide and deep for the tanks to cross. The Germans pulled back from the trenches, but the tanks could not pursue them. The tanks changed course to find a way over, only to encounter more trenches. They lurched back, around, and looked for another route. Even when they found a way across, the tank officers had trouble locating their new position on the map. So they wandered around, shooting at retreating Germans and wondering where to go. The infantry came up behind and started wandering too.

Despite the rain, Patton was able to see well enough to know what to do. The tanks needed a commander to lead from the front, to show the way again and again as the battle unfolded, like Napoleon at the Lodi bridge. But Patton had orders to stay out of the fighting. His frustration mounted. Then, at seven o'clock, two hours after the start of the battle, Patton broke. He disobeyed his superior and left his post. He ordered one of his men to stay behind at the telephone. The other five he took along. They just walked down the hill into the thick of battle.

As a lieutenant colonel, Patton outranked both his own men and most of the infantry he met. So he was able to gather contingents of foot soldiers and tanks wherever he found them and point them the right way. On one occasion there were five tanks poised to enter the village of Pannes, but they feared a German ambush in the narrow streets ahead. Patton jumped on the lead tank and took them through.

In his first combat, Patton showed extreme bravery in the face of death. Shells burst close around him, sending others diving for cover, while Patton just stood there calmly. He wrote later:

I admit that I wanted to duck and probably did at first but soon saw the futility of dodging fate . . . It was much easier than you think and the feeling, foolish probably, of being admired by the men lying down is a great stimulus.

One time he went first across a bridge that everyone thought was mined. Word of his courage spread quickly through the ranks—in a war where commanding officers stayed safe behind the lines, ordinary soldiers were quick to praise the exception.

By nightfall, the Germans had fallen back a few miles, so the battle was a success. Many American soldiers received medals for bravery. Patton came close to a demotion. Rockenbach was furious that he had left his post. It was a clear case of insubordination, and of the very worst kind—during combat. Both sides in World War I punished insubordination severely—sometimes with a firing squad. It kept the troops obedient. How else could you get them out of their trenches to attack the enemy? But in the end Rockenbach let the incident pass. After all, Patton did not refuse to go into battle. He refused to stay out of it.

There was one bad omen in Patton's first combat. As he walked onto the battlefield, the first American soldier he saw was just sitting in a foxhole while the fighting moved far beyond him. Patton went at the soldier in a fury, ready to "cuss him out" for cowardice. As Patton came close, he saw the soldier was dead. Many years later, Patton would lose a key promotion thanks to a similar incident.

The Battle of Saint-Mihiel was the first of many that the American army would fight on European soil. Patton had only a minor role in it. He tried to fight the battle his way, with mobility and *coup d'oeil* in the style of Napoleon. But the rest of the army had other ideas—the chessboard strategy of Jomini.

World War I ended in stalemate, where it began. The Americans fought for a few months alongside the British and French. They made progress, but not much. Then the German government collapsed, the kaiser fled the country, and the new German leaders signed an armistice on November 11, 1918. It was Patton's thirty-third birthday. He had been a tank officer exactly one year, and fought in battle exactly five days.

After the war, both sides dismantled their armies. The American army abolished the Tank Corps and gave the tanks to the infantry. Patton despaired. He had missed his chance to "fight and strive and perish," to "laugh at death and numbers," to "battle as of yore," like the eternal soldier he later celebrated in his poem on reincarnation.

As he waited to return to the United States, Patton met Sir Edmund Allenby, the commanding officer of Lawrence of Arabia. It was Lawrence, not Patton, who won fame in World War I for daring mobile warfare. Lawrence had even used a form of cavalry—camels—and described *coup d'oeil* in writing: "Nine-tenths of tactics are certain, and taught in books. But the irrational tenth is like the kingfisher across the pool, and that is the test for generals."

Allenby told Patton that for every great hero of history, such as Napoleon and Alexander the Great,

> . . . *there were several born. Only the lucky ones made it to the summit. In every age and time, men were born ready to serve their country and their god, but sometimes were not needed. You had to be at the right place at the right time—you had to be lucky.*

Patton swallowed his disappointment and returned to the life of a nineteenth-century cavalry officer, at Fort Myer, Virginia. He joined the army polo team, went fox hunting, and entered fencing competitions and horse shows around the country. His family wealth let him entertain lavishly despite his meager army pay. Horses were a rich man's sport, so Patton fit right in.

He played jolly, but his unhappiness kept breaking through. As the years went by, he angered more and more quickly and cursed more often. A photograph from 1929 shows him sitting in a living room, surrounded by his wife, Beatrice, their two teenage daughters, Ruth Ellen and Beatrice, and their young son, George IV: Patton wears a splendid dress uniform with gold braid, shiny buttons, a chestful of medals, and a look on his face of infinite sadness.

The rest of the family looks sad too. Patton came to take a fiendish delight in giving offense in public, like the time at a Boston social event he tried to show a group of women a "war wound" and asked them to help him take off his pants.

But Patton's real war wound was the fear that he would never get a chance to fight. It was during this time that he wrote to a fellow officer, "War is the only place where a man really lives." His poem on reincarnation dates from the same period—maybe he would have more luck in a later life. But he also dove deeper into military history, just in case.

The library at West Point inherited his collection of books, and there you can see the volume of *On War* that Patton had rebound after too much use. In Volume 1, Patton underlined almost every word of the key chapter, "The Genius for War," including von Clausewitz's discussion of *coup d'oeil*. Patton read everything he could find about Napoleon, and made many notations from Napoleon's own sayings, especially his key advice: "The only right way of learning the science of war is to read and reread the campaigns of the great captains." And in *The Generalship of Ulysses S. Grant* by J.F.C. Fuller, Patton penciled in "the true art" next to Fuller's discussion of how Grant held the enemy's front while moving swiftly to strike his rear.

This "true art" later became Patton's signature method of tank warfare. He explained it in a rousing speech to his troops on the eve of the D-day invasion in World War II, like Napoleon before his first Italian campaign:

> *I don't want to get any messages saying that we are holding our position. We're not holding anything. Let the Hun do that. We are advancing constantly and we're not interested in holding on to anything except the enemy. We're going to hold on to him by the nose and kick him in the ass. We're going to kick the hell out of him all the time and we're going to go through him like crap through a goose.*

This speech shows Patton's rough humor and his emphasis on mobility. Most important, "hold on to him by the nose and kick him in the ass" expresses Grant's "true art." We can find the same art in Napoleon: Many of his victories came from this "pin and flank" method, including the great battles of Jena and Friedland. It is the purest form of mobile war: Set out without a clear destination, and when you run into the enemy, pin him down with part of your force and send the rest the long way around to attack from another direction.

But Patton had to wait twenty long years for his chance to practice the "true art." He kicked around from post to post across the United States—Maryland, Virginia, Kansas, Washington D.C., Hawaii, Texas—until December 1938, when the army gave him command of Fort Myer. At the age of fifty-three he was still only a colonel, while many of his classmates at West Point had long been generals. And Fort Myer was a ceremonial post, close to the national capital. Its commander spent most of his time entertaining visiting dignitaries with colorful cavalry parades and lavish parties. The previous commander had no outside income, so his parties were meager affairs. The army appointed Patton because his wife was rich. The Pattons gave excellent parties.

It was the end of the line. Patton's moods grew worse. He gave up polo and hunting. He frightened his family with his anger and stark silences. When his daughter Ruth Ellen wanted to marry, Patton objected violently to her choice. She persisted. The tension rose up to the wedding, but the ceremony went off without a hitch. As the bride and groom drove off, Patton leapt onto the roof of the car, screamed to the sky, and emptied two pistols into the air.

Then everything changed.

War.

In May 1940, Patton went as an umpire to maneuvers in Louisiana. A division of horse cavalry faced an experimental tank division. Five days into the exercise, everyone paused to hear the news: The German army had launched a blitzkreig against France. A "panzer" force of tanks and armored cars sped through and around the French, British, and Belgian armies. Paris fell. The remnants of the British army barely escaped at Dunkirk. The Germans—including Hitler himself—had studied von Clausewitz and converted wholesale to mobile war.

In the Louisiana war games, the tank division trounced the cavalry. At the end of the exercise, a group of officers met in the basement of a nearby high school. Patton was one of them. They wrote a joint recommendation to the head of the army, declaring that the time had come for the United States to form a panzer force like the ones that just won the Louisiana games and conquered France in a week.

In normal times, this unauthorized group action would have risked a court-martial. Instead, the chief of the army agreed. In July 1940 he created two armored divisions. Patton became the commander of one of them. With the assignment came promotion, at last, to general.

It was the end of Patton's days as a washed-up cavalry officer and the start of his second life as a tank officer in battle. He identified the German victory in Europe as a replay of the battle of Cannae in 216 B.C., where Hannibal defeated a larger Roman force by "double envelopment." Patton called it "the oldest plan in the world . . . invented by the cavemen when they surrounded the mammoth to destroy him." He further noted that the German infantry broke through the enemy defenses first. The tanks followed, "exactly as Murat used his cavalry corps in the days of Napoleon." That is, they "rode the enemy to death."

For the next two years, the American army rushed to produce tanks and try them out. In war games across the country, Patton made his name right away as the army's best tank commander. He turned the games into a lesson in mobile warfare and leading from the front. At one briefing before the exercise began, Patton put a wet noodle on a plate and held it up for all to see. First he tried to push the noodle from behind. Of course it just folded, without moving forward. Then he pulled it from the front, and it moved across the plate. "Gentlemen," he concluded, "you don't push a noodle, you pull it. In other words, you lead."

In July 1941, Patton appeared on the cover of *Life* magazine as America's leading tank commander. He rode his men hard and held to strict discipline on uniforms, saluting, and respect for officers. He started with raw recruits who knew nothing about tank warfare and quickly whipped them into shape. Most were young enough to be his sons. Before every exercise, Patton gave a version of his usual speech to crush the enemy, to spill the "blood and guts" of the "Hun." And so his men, and then the press, gave him the name "Old Blood and Guts."

In the games of September 1941, back in Louisiana, Patton had a *coup d'oeil.*

Instead of advancing directly on the "enemy," he saw a way to drive far but swiftly around them, to attack from behind. His route took him off the map of the official zone for maneuvers. Patton led his tanks completely out of Louisiana and into Texas, using ordinary road maps. He refueled at gas stations with cash instead of hauling his own army-issue gas, which would only slow him down. His side won the battle so fast that the army called off the games five days early.

The other side complained that Patton had broken the rules. He grinned and replied, "I didn't know war had any rules."

Meanwhile, Eisenhower rose through the ranks. In 1942, he became head of all Allied forces in Europe and the Mediterranean and picked Bradley as his second-in-command. But from the first, everyone knew that they needed Patton to lead the actual fighting. Eisenhower's superior in Washington, General George Marshall, sent Patton to join the new Allied headquarters in England. Eisenhower wrote to Marshall, "I am delighted you fixed upon him as your choice for leading the American venture."

But once in England, Patton only made trouble for Eisenhower. Their first task was to land American troops in North Africa, where the British were already fighting the Germans and Italians. Patton wanted to skip the whole enterprise and invade Europe right away. The British insisted on winning in North Africa first, and Eisenhower aimed above all to keep the Allies together. So Patton gave in and joined the North Africa planning. He wrote in his diary on August 9:

> *Had supper with Ike and talked until 1:00 AM. We both feel that the operation is bad and mostly political. However, we are told to do it and intend to succeed or die in the attempt.*

Patton continued to talk openly against the British. So when it came time to enter the fighting in North Africa, Eisenhower sent other generals into action first. Eisenhower recognized Patton's talent but warned him that he lacked diplomacy—that he spoke before he thought. Patton wrote Eisenhower a letter that he never mailed, where he said:

> *For years I have been accused of indulging in snap judgments. Honestly, this is not the case because, like yourself, I am a profound military student and the thoughts I express, perhaps too flippantly, are the result of years of thought and study . . . It may be that I am not over-awed in the presence of high personages and therefore speak too freely.*

This letter shows that Patton saw his "snap judgment"—*coup d'oeil*—as the cause of his lack of diplomacy. Eisenhower seemed to agree. He told Marshall, "Patton is a problem child, but he is a great fighting leader in pursuit and exploitation."

In February 1943, the American army arrived in North Africa to fight alongside the British. Patton stayed behind. At the Kasserine Pass in Tunisia, Eisenhower sent his troops into their first battle of World War II without his best combat commander. They met a force of German panzer tanks. It was a total defeat for the Americans.

In the United States, the news came as a great shock. Everyone was hoping that the American army would end the war quickly. In one blow, Kasserine destroyed that hope. The British argued that the Americans were incompetent and that Eisenhower should step down as supreme Allied commander.

So Eisenhower sent in Patton—but along went Bradley as Eisenhower's eyes and ears. Patton's first reaction to Bradley was "I'm not going to have any goddamn spies running around my headquarters." But Bradley was a good diplomat even with Patton, so in the end they got along.

When Patton arrived at the front, he found the headquarters of the American commander, Lloyd Fredendall, sixty-five miles behind the lines, in a huge underground bunker—just like in World War I. Patton destroyed the bunker and quickly whipped the defeated troops back into shape. He ordered all officers down to the rank of lieutenant to lead their troops into battle.

In a series of short battles, Patton succeeded in regaining Kasserine and pushing the Germans back. But he quickly realized that the plans he had to follow kept the Americans in a sideshow, while giving the main event to Field Marshall "Monty" Montgomery, the British commander. Patton wrote in his diary:

> It is noteworthy that these instructions definitely prohibit American advance to the sea. In other words, we continue to threaten the enemy's right flank, but we do not participate in cutting him off. In brief, this is to pinch us out so as to insure a British triumph . . . I am fed up with being treated like a moron by the British. There is no national honor left to us. Ike must go.

Throughout the war, Patton complained about Montgomery

receiving equal treatment with himself, but he never blamed Montgomery. He blamed Eisenhower. In private, he complained, "Ike is more British than the British and is putty in their hands." But still, Patton followed orders.

In May, the Allies pushed the Germans all the way out of North Africa. Next came a landing on the island of Sicily. Again, the Americans' job was to protect the flank of the British army advancing north to the key city of Messina.

The Allies landed on the island. After six days, the fighting bogged down.

Then Patton had a *coup d'oeil*.

He saw that by taking the ancient town of Agrigento, he could break out in the opposite direction, circle the long way around the island, and take Messina from the west. Agrigento first drew his attention because of an invasion there in 470 B.C., when the Greeks ruled Sicily.

Patton did not disobey orders, but, rather, asked his British superior, General Alexander, for permission to take Agrigento through "reconnaissance in force." That is, it was just a minor sortie to check the strength of the German fortifications. Alexander agreed. Patton took Agrigento and then kept on going. Now if Alexander objected, it would seem like the British were jealous of American success. In a month of mobile fighting, Patton swept along the coast of Sicily and entered Messina first.

Patton had turned the battle into a classic pin-and-flank maneuver. The British held on to the enemy "by the nose" while Patton swept around to "kick him in the ass."

During the campaign, Patton was everywhere along the moving front. At the village of Naso, he urged on the lead commander with anger—"Are you afraid to fight?"—and encouragement—"Remember Frederick the Great: *L'audace, l'audace, toujours l'audace!* I know you will win."

After the capture of Messina, Patton was the most famous

Allied general of the war. Reporters swarmed around him. They delighted in his every coarse word, his ivory pistol, the time he shot two mules on a bridge when they blocked his tanks from crossing.

But the reporters came too close. They saw his ugly side too. They found out that on two occasions, just before reaching Messina, Patton had come upon two soldiers in hospital tents without any visible wounds. Patton called them cowards and slapped them. The hospital staff told the press. Word reached Eisenhower just as the story broke.

Eisenhower sent Patton a written rebuke, the only one of its kind to an American officer in all of World War II. The incident would have ended the career of anyone else. But back in Washington, the assistant secretary of war observed: "Lincoln's remark when they got after Grant comes to mind when I think of Patton— 'I can't spare this man—he fights.'" At a press conference, President Roosevelt said he recalled what Lincoln said when told that Grant drank too much: "It must be a good brand of liquor."

Napoleon, Grant, Patton—flawed humans, but great strategists.

The controversy died down, except for one more decision by Eisenhower. Until the slapping incident, Patton was the obvious choice to lead the American army on D-Day, which was only a few months off. Instead, Eisenhower gave the job to Bradley.

Patton was stunned. Once again, he figured his career was over. Worse, the fate of the Allied invasion of Normandy was in the hands of Bradley. In Sicily, Patton had given Bradley command over troops, but then regretted it. He complained to Eisenhower that Bradley was "not aggressive enough." Bradley returned the complaint: "To George, tactics was simply a process of bulling ahead. He never seemed to think out a campaign. Seldom made a careful estimate of the situation. I thought him a shallow commander."

Bradley versus Patton, Jomini versus von Clausewitz: pure and simple.

Patton brooded in a castle in Sicily while the rest of the army prepared for D-Day. The Germans knew an invasion was coming. But where? Eisenhower's staff came up with a clever trick—they leaked false information that Patton would lead the invasion at Calais, two hundred miles from Normandy. The Germans paid close attention to Patton. He was the only Allied commander they feared.

As for the real invasion, Eisenhower and Bradley left Patton out. They judged him too headstrong to get along with the British and French to invade Normandy together, so they planned to bring him in afterward.

In his memoirs, Bradley includes a photograph that shows the Allied planning team for the Normandy invasion. Seven senior officers sit around two rough wooden tables pushed together, with two detailed maps on the wall behind. Eisenhower holds the center. On his flanks are two British generals: Sir Monty Montgomery, the head of British forces on the ground, and Sir Arthur Tedder, Eisenhower's second-in-command. Next to them are two more British generals: Sir Trafford Leigh-Mallory, head of the combined Allied air forces, and Sir Bertram Ramsay, head of the combined Allied naval forces. On the wings are two American generals: Bradley, head of American forces on the ground, and Walter Smith, Eisenhower's chief of staff. The seven sit stiffly, each with a single sheet of paper on the table before them. In truth, it is hard to imagine Patton among them. On every decision it would be seven against one, until Patton insulted them all and stormed out.

So Patton had no role in the D-Day invasion. Sure enough, it ended up a classic Jomini battle, carefully planned rather than mobile and flexible. On four of the five beaches—Utah, Sword, Gold, and Juno—the landing went well. On the fifth—Omaha—the plans broke down. The result was slaughter.

But four out of five was good enough. D-Day succeeded in putting the Allied army ashore in France. And the Patton trick worked—the Germans kept most of their troops guarding Calais instead of Normandy.

In his memoirs, Bradley explains what he planned to do next after D-Day: "We had long ago concluded that the best point for breakout lay somewhere along the 16-mile line between St.-Lo and Coutances." For a month, the Allies made little progress, just like in World War I. Instead of mud, they faced a patchwork of forest—*bocage* in French—that hid the enemy well. Then a month after D-Day, Bradley picked his spot for breakout and concentrated his forces there.

He explained: "How then were we to turn this battle of the *bocage* into a war of movement? First, we must pick a soft point in the enemy's line; next, concentrate our forces against it. Then, after smashing through with a blow that would crush his front-line defenses, we would spill our mechanized columns through that gap before the enemy could recover his senses."

The attack began on July 3.

The breakout failed. Bradley wrote: "By July 10, we faced a real danger of a World War I–type stalemate."

Bradley's mistake would have been obvious to von Clausewitz: You can't plan a breakout. The spot for a breakout appears as the battle unfolds. The commander sees it in a *coup d'oeil*, like Patton saw Agrigento in Sicily.

About the same time, early July, Patton arrived in Normandy. Only now did the Germans give up their belief in a Calais invasion. They rushed troops west to meet the invading force—and Patton.

Patton's first impression was dire. For advice, Bradley turned to General Courtney Hodges, commander of the First Army, not to Patton, commander of the Third Army. Patton wrote in his diary:

Brad and Hodges are such nothings. Their one virtue is that they get along by doing nothing. I could break through in three days if I commanded.

Then it happened: Patton sent out scouts to probe the front, and on July 31 they entered the village of Avranches. They found two bridges intact over the River See.

Patton had a *coup d'oeil*: This was the breakout.

In a snap, he sent his whole army—200,000 troops and 40,000 tanks and trucks—down a narrow country road to Avranches. It was forty miles from St.-Lo, very far indeed from where Bradley had planned a breakout.

As Patton swept through Avranches and then across France, Bradley wisely transferred half of Hodges's First Army to Patton's Third. For commanders on the ground, it came as quite a shock. Major General Manton Eddy told his staff: "What the hell kind of war is this? I've been fighting for two months and have advanced five miles. Now in one day you want me to go fifty miles?"

But after a reassuring phone call to Patton, Eddy went ahead and succeeded in taking the village of Sens. He called Patton again: "General, I had a lovely drive. I'm in Sens. What's next?" Patton replied, "Hang up and keep going."

Despite Patton's success where Hodges had failed, Bradley still preferred Hodges as a commander: "Whereas Patton could seldom be bothered with details, Hodges studied his problems with infinite care and was thus better qualified to execute the more intricate operations. A steady, undramatic and dependable man with great tenacity and persistence."

Bradley might have been describing himself.

Yet he also appreciated Patton's achievement at Avranches:

Every manual on road movement was ground into the dust. He and his staff did what the whole world knew couldn't be done: It was flat impossible to put a whole army out on a narrow two-lane road and move it at high speed. Everything was going to come to a screeching halt. He even intermingled units. Yet out of the other end of the straw came divisions,

*intact and ready to fight. If anybody else could have done it, no
one ever got that man's name.*

How can we reconcile these two statements? On the one hand,
Bradley thought Hodges was better qualified to execute intricate
operations because he studied problems with infinite care. On
the other hand, Patton executed an intricate—no, impossible—
operation at Avranches, and no one else could have done it. Was
Bradley contradicting himself?

No. He meant that Patton could not be bothered with details
before making a decision. *After* Patton made a decision, he worked
out everything in great detail, in true von Clausewitz style. Hodges
and Bradley, like true Jomini planners, worked out all the details
beforehand—they thought that was how you made decisions in
the first place.

And where was Patton during the breakout? Everywhere up and
down the line. Once he found a traffic jam in the middle of
Avranches itself, so he jumped out of his jeep and directed traffic
for an hour and a half, cursing the whole time.

After Avranches, Patton kept going. He needed more troops
and tanks, which Bradley gave him right away from Hodges's inert
First Army. Patton needed air support, gasoline, and ammunition
too, not according to Bradley's original plan but in the moment,
day by day as the sweep unfolded. In the air force Patton found a
ready ally in General Otto Weyland, who dropped everything else
to give him what he wanted. But when Patton's gasoline ran out, he
had to ask Bradley for more.

Bradley asked Eisenhower.

Eisenhower asked Montgomery.

Montgomery said no.

The gas ran out on August 29. Patton wrote in his diary:

It was evident at that time there was no real threat against us as long as we did not stop ourselves or allow ourselves to be stopped by imaginary enemies. Everything seemed rosy when suddenly it was reported to me that the 140,000 gallons of gasoline which we were supposed to get for that day did not arrive. I presented my case for a rapid advance to the east for the purpose of cutting the Siegfried Line before it could be manned. It is my opinion that this was the momentous error of the war.

Thanks to Patton, less than three months after D-Day the Allies approached the German border, a full eight months ahead of Bradley's original plan. But in September, Patton had to send his men out to pilfer gas from other American troops. They could never get enough, of course. They slowed to a halt. Eisenhower and Bradley even withdrew some of the troops and tanks they had shifted to Patton.

There was nothing Patton could do. After the slapping incidents, he dared not complain too much. But he wrote later:

In every case, practically throughout the campaign, I was under wraps from the Higher Command. This may have been a good thing, as perhaps I am too impetuous. However, I do not believe I was, and feel that had I been permitted to go all out, the war would have ended sooner and more lives would have been saved. Particularly I think this statement applies to the time when, in the early days of September, we were halted, owing to the desire, or necessity, on the part of General Eisenhower in backing Montgomery's move to the north. At that time there was no question of doubt but that we could have gone through and on across the Rhine within ten days.

Montogomery not only refused to give up gas to Patton—he proposed a breakout of his own. Like Bradley at St.-Lo, Montgomery tried to plan his breakout on maps in advance rather than find it as the battle unfolds, like Patton at Avranches. Montgomery's plan, code name Market-Garden, diverted troops, tanks, and supplies to a swing north around the main German lines, through Belgium. It was a classic Jomini battle, planned out in advance rather than as the situation unfolded. Eisenhower gave the green light.

Montgomery attacked on September 17. He aimed to take a bridge at Arnhem as the key to the breakout—unlike the Avranches bridge, which Patton saw as the key to breakout only *after* his men took it. Eight days later, on September 25, Montgomery signaled retreat. Market-Garden had failed completely. The Arnhem bridge remained in German hands.

The Western Front fell into stalemate again.

Bradley and Eisenhower dusted off their original plan to advance along a broad front that gave each general, American and British, an equal role. It was classic Jomini again. The Allies advanced, but slowly, at the pace of World War I. Bradley and Hodges planned another breakout in early December, again in the north, again on maps beforehand, at Huertgen. Again, it failed.

Then Patton had another *coup d'oeil*.

His troops held the southernmost end of the front. On November 25, he noted that Hodges was making a big mistake in the Ardennes, a hundred miles to the north. This was where the German blitzkreig had broken through at the start of the war: The Allies had left it lightly defended, thinking the terrain too rough for the Germans to pass through. Now, nearly five years later, it was right in the middle of the Western Front. Patton thought Hodges needed to attack more forcefully, before the enemy did: "It is highly probable that the Germans are building up east of them."

Patton's head intelligence officer, Major Oscar Koch, noted the German buildup from mid-November through early December. On December 9, Koch gave a briefing at Patton's temporary headquarters in Nancy, France. He judged that the recent movements gave the Germans a two-to-one advantage over the Allies in the Ardennes. It was a strong sign of a possible counterattack.

Patton asked about American troops in the area. Koch listed four divisions in the field, plus one division undergoing "rest and refitting" just to the south. They were all under other generals.

Patton concluded the briefing with a long silence. Then he rose and said, "We'll be in a position to meet whatever happens."

Koch's report went on to Bradley's headquarters, along with all the others from the Western Front that day. Bradley's intelligence officers ignored it. Koch's sector was a hundred miles to the south. To them, what happened in the north was none of Koch's business.

But Patton swung into action. On December 12 he drove forty miles northeast—toward the Ardennes—to visit the armored division in rest and refitting. In the village of Dommon-les-Dieuze, he dropped in on the 8th Tank Battalion. The battalion commander, Major Albin Irzyk, remembered the visit well. Years later, in an article in *World War II* magazine, he wrote:

> *On the fourth day the troops were excited and energized by the visit of the Third Army commander, General Patton, who swooped in for a quick stop. He arrived at high speed in his jeep, with a wide, crooked grin and all his stars blazing. He was jolly, animated and interested in how we were doing. After jumping out of his jeep, he worked his way along the entire length of the small town. He stopped at every vehicle, talked with every cluster of soldiers and had something to say to each—a question, a word of encouragement or appreciation, a compliment, a wisecrack, a good-natured dig. He was a master at this kind of rapprochement. His visits were brief, and he kept moving. But in thirty minutes or so, he had worked his magic—he had "touched" virtually every man in that battalion.*

What was Patton up to?

In that quick visit, he both assessed the quality of Irzyk's battalion and made it loyal to him.

Why?

As he told Koch at the Nancy briefing, to be "in a position to meet whatever happens." Irzyk's unit was the only one that Patton visited. In his diary that day he started to work out assignments in case the Germans made their move. He would take over some of Hodges's units that were closer to the action than his own troops. First on the list was Irzyk's battalion. So we can date Patton's *coup d'oeil* as starting December 9 with the Nancy briefing and concluding on December 12, when he visited Irzyk's men.

Meanwhile, in his daily reports Koch continued to cite evidence of a German counteroffensive at Ardennes, including a high-ranking German prisoner who said explicitly that such a move was coming. On the night of December 15, six days after the Nancy briefing, the counterattack began.

At first, the American troops in the Ardennes could not know the scale of the attack. But as it continued, the Germans pushed deep into the Western Front, making a big bulge in the line. The Allies called it the Battle of the Bulge. It was the Germans who threatened a breakout now. If they succeeded, it would prolong the war by months, even years. The Allies thought they were on their way into Germany, but instead the Germans were on their way back into France.

Bradley was far behind the lines at the time, conferring with Eisenhower at Versailles, outside Paris. He had ignored all warnings from Koch. Instead, he agreed with Montgomery's rosy report of December 16, just before the news of the attack reached the British: "The enemy is at present fighting a defensive campaign on all fronts; his situation is such that he cannot stage major offensive operations."

But Eisenhower insisted that the German attack was serious. He ordered Bradley to meet it. Bradley met with Patton on December

17. Patton laid out his plans to meet the attack, and Bradley approved them. In other words, Patton already knew what to do. Bradley at last was ready to let him do it.

So the tide shifted again. Now that Bradley knew the trouble was serious, he gave Patton all the troops he wanted.

Patton's first move was to set Irzyk's column in motion. At first, all Irzyk knew was that his previous orders were canceled and he had to move his men quickly, "in a totally different direction—north!"

Irzyk's battalion moved out at 12:50 A.M. on December 19. And so began the largest, swiftest movement of an entire army in the history of warfare. Over the next four days, Patton shifted a quarter of a million men from an eastward thrust into Germany to a northward thrust to the Ardennes. And at the head of the column was the one battalion he visited on December 12, when it was under another general's command.

Irzyk had no information about the situation ahead of him. His 8th Tank Battalion "led the odyssey north into the cold, black, night . . . At the head of the 8th was my tank, making it the lead element of the Third Army in its advance to the north." They had only one map, and had to stop often and read the road signs to find their way. Thankfully, after twenty-two hours the convoy made it to their destination, the village of Vaux-les-Rosières, without running into the enemy. Just ahead was the town of Bastogne, where Patton saw a major battle unfolding in just a few days. Until then he was simply moving his troops into place.

On December 19, the same day that Irzyk led his column north, the most important meeting of the Battle of the Bulge took place in the small French city of Verdun. Eisenhower and Bradley drove all night from Paris, while Patton drove up from Nancy. Other generals and staff came too. They met in the Citadel, which was a fortress in the center of the town. Bradley had quickly set up a second headquarters there, in case he had to abandon his main base in Luxembourg because of the German advance.

Verdun was twenty miles from Saint-Mihiel, where Patton had fought in World War I. Verdun first entered history in 843, when the empire of Charlemagne broke up. The Treaty of Verdun divided the empire among three of his grandsons. The western piece was most of France, the eastern piece was most of Germany, and the middle piece ran as a wedge between them, from the North Sea to the Mediterranean. Many of the great battles of European history took place in this middle wedge, including most of World War I, Napoleon's Italian campaign, and Waterloo.

The Citadel of Verdun was built in the seventeenth century, after the French king took control of the region. After the Germans won the war of 1870 against France, the French dug tunnels under the Citadel to turn it into a modern fortress. There were barracks, ammunition dumps, a hospital, and a workshop. During World War I, the Germans spent ten months trying to take the Citadel. Half a million soldiers died. It was the second-worst battle of the war, after the Somme. After the war, in 1920, the French government selected an unmarked coffin from the Citadel and reburied it under the Arc de Triomphe in Paris as the Tomb of the Unknown Soldier. This was the first such tomb in the world: Other countries quickly followed.

Verdun was a fitting site for the meeting of December 19. It was a tragic shrine to the static, chessboard strategy of Jomini. Now the top brass of World War II met there to hand over leadership to the one master of mobile war among them. In their hour of crisis, the Jomini generals turned to Patton.

The meeting took place in one of the Citadel's cold, damp, gloomy rooms. It was never warm there, even in summer, but in winter the chill came off the stone walls and through your flesh like a fever. The officers sat down around a potbellied stove. Their mood matched the room—glum and fearful—except for Patton. He was cheerful and confident, with a plan in his pocket and Irzyk already in motion.

There were seven senior officers present, just like in the photograph in Bradley's memoirs for the planning of D day. Four of those seven from the photo were also there at Verdun: Eisenhower; Bradley; Walter Smith, who was Eisenhower's chief of staff; and Sir Arthur Tedder, Eisenhower's second-in-command. The three newcomers were Patton, General Jake Devers, and Major General Francis de Guingand. Devers was head of the Sixth Army, which was to take over from Patton in the south while the Third Army sped north to the Bulge. De Guingand was Montgomery's chief of staff. Montgomery himself refused to come, and had already informed Eisenhower that he, not Patton, deserved to take over. As for Hodges, he wanted to be at the Verdun meeting, but he was busy retreating from his headquarters in the face of the German advance.

Eisenhower started the meeting by declaring all previous plans null and void, and making Patton temporary commander of all Allied troops facing the Bulge, "under Brad's supervision, of course." Eisenhower asked Patton how soon he could start. Patton replied, "As soon as you're through with me." Eisenhower tried a more specific question: "When can you attack?" Patton said, "The morning of December 21."

That was only forty-eight hours away—Eisenhower had expected an answer of at least a week. "Don't be fatuous, George," he said.

Patton went on to explain how he would do it. His staff had prepared three possible plans, sending different combinations of armored divisions on three different routes to three different placements around the Bulge. Eisenhower listened, and then chose one of the three options. Everyone else was quiet, including Bradley. At the end of the two-hour meeting, Bradley reported that Patton turned to him:

George was itching to start the counter-attack. He lighted a fresh cigar and pointed to the Bulge where it pierced the thin blue lines on our war map. "Brad," he exclaimed, "this time the Kraut's stuck his head in a meatgrinder." With a turn of the fist, he added, "And this time I've got hold of the handle."

As at Avranches, Bradley acknowledged Patton's achievement in the Battle of the Bulge:

Within two days George had made good on the start of his attack ... Patton's brilliant shift of Third Army from its bridgehead in the Saar to the snow-covered Ardennes front became one of the most astonishing feats of generalship of our campaign in the West ... More than 133,000 tanks and trucks joined that round-the-clock trek over the icy roads. From the windows of my office overlooking the gorge where the medieval dungeons and battlements of Luxembourg had been cut into the rock, I could count the double-banked columns as they crossed the arched stone bridge. In heavy greatcoats still caked with the mud of the Saar, troops huddled against the wintry cold that knifed through their canvas-topped trucks ... Day and night those columns rattled over the cobblestoned pavements until on December 21 a new carpet of snow muffled their passage and they glided through like ghosts.

Once again, Patton stayed at the front. He rode in an open jeep to show his men that he faced the same cold that they did. So many of the troops were new to him, but like Irzyk's battalion, Patton made them his.

In taking over the Bulge sector, Patton got more than extra troops. A movie star fell into his arms.

Marlene Dietrich was there at the front, entertaining the American soldiers. She gave a performance the night of December 15 right in the path of the German advance the next day. She awoke in the morning and ran for her life. Dietrich was born in Germany and began her career there, so if the Nazis caught her, they would execute her as a traitor.

Books on Patton do not mention Dietrich, but other books on the Battle of the Bulge claim that she ended up in Patton's entourage and in his bed. The only trace of her in any of the published Patton sources is a diary entry from a month before, November 5. Patton wrote:

Had Marlene Dietrich and her troupe for lunch. Later they gave us a show. Very low comedy, almost an insult to human intelligence.

In a biography of Dietrich, *The Blue Angel* by Donald Spoto, the Hollywood director Billy Wilder asks her if she had really slept with Eisenhower instead of Patton. Dietrich replies, "But darling, how could it have been Eisenhower? He wasn't even at the front!"

By early January, Patton's troops had erased the Bulge. They beat back the German counteroffensive, but there was plenty of fighting left. They were not in Germany yet. Patton wrote in his diary on January 4: "We can still lose this war. The Germans are colder and hungrier than we are, but they fight better."

Montgomery stayed out of the Battle of the Bulge rather than serve under Patton, even temporarily. Then in January, after the danger had passed, Eisenhower dusted off the old Jomini plan again. The Allies pushed ahead on a broad front, with all generals playing an equal role. Once again, Eisenhower transferred away some of the troops he had given to Patton during the emergency. Patton complied, but complained to his staff:

It would be a foolish and ignoble way for the Americans to end the war by sitting on their asses . . . It may be of interest to

*future generals to realize that one makes plans to fit circum-
stances and does not create circumstances to fit plans. That
way danger lies.*

Which comes first, circumstances or plans, is the essence of the
difference between Jomini and von Clausewitz.

In mid-March, Patton broke out again. But this time it was not
a single *coup d'oeil*. From March 13 to March 22, his troops swept
through the Palatinate, a triangle of German land between the
Rhine and Moselle rivers and the French border. They went all
which ways, even crossing each other in violation of Jomini doc-
trine but perfectly fine under Patton. The various commanders
carried through on their own *coups d'oeil*.

In September 1940, as Patton started training his tank corps, he
had recalled translating a Latin quotation:

*In the winter time, Caesar so trained his legions in all that
became soldiers and so habituated them in the proper performance of their duties, that when in the spring he committed
them to battle against the Gauls, it was not necessary to give
them orders, for they knew what to do and how to do it." This
quotation expresses very exactly the goal we are seeking in this
division. I know that we shall attain it and when we do, may
God have mercy on our enemies: They will need it.*

The winter Battle of the Bulge prepared Patton's legions for the
Palatinate spring. Now they fought like him, by the "true art" of
Grant. In notes for the memoir he never finished, Patton explained:

*Any operation, reduced to its primary characteristics, consists in
moving down the road until you bump into the enemy. It may
be one road or it may be several roads. When you have bumped,
hold him at the point of contact with fire with about a third of*

*your command. Move the rest in a wide envelopment so that
you can attack him from his rear flank. The enveloping attack
should start first. The initial nose attack starts to move forward
only when the enemy has properly reacted to the enveloping
attack. Then the direct attack can go in easily and fast.*

It sounds easy, but to know you have hit on a battle worth
fighting and above all, one you can win—this takes *coup d'oeil.*
And to pick which way to go to envelop requires another. By the
Palatinate campaign, Patton's troops had learned the "true art"
well enough to take charge themselves. It was the exact opposite
of chessboard planning, and they faced not the sparse defenses of
France but a thick concentration of German forces fighting on
German soil.

On March 23, Patton's troops crossed the Rhine and kept on
going. They swept across Germany, liberating concentration camps
and prisoners-of-war, and capturing more German soldiers than
the rest of the Allies combined. Since again, Eisenhower gave
Patton all the troops and gas he needed. The Third Army grew to
540,000 men, twice the number that Patton commanded before the
Battle of the Bulge. In early May, they went out the other side of
Germany, into Czechoslovakia.

So ended the war on the Western Front. Germany lost on the
Eastern Front too, as the massive Russian army closed in. On May
8, the Germans surrendered.

And so ends the story of Patton at war.

In early December, Eisenhower and Bradley returned to the
United States. Eisenhower went on to become president, and
Bradley became the obvious choice for the first head of the Joint
Chiefs of Staff. Eisenhower wanted to avoid the kind of rivalry
among different commanders that happened on the Western
Front, so he put the army, navy, marines, and air force all under one
commander. The job required a great diplomat, and that was

Bradley. So after the war, Eisenhower and Bradley continued to prove their political skills.

As for Patton, all he knew was war. He spent a few months as part of the army of occupation. Eisenhower made him military governor of Bavaria. It was the same post that Jomini had held in Vilnius more than a century before. Patton hated the job. Instead of ridding Germany of Nazis, he wanted to start the next war right away, with the Russians. But they were still on the side of the Allies. Patton didn't care. He wanted to fight them.

In public and private, Patton said exactly what he thought. For example, to the press he railed:

You cannot lay down with a diseased jackal. Neither can we ever do business with the Russians. Even the stupidest man thousands of miles away, back home, should have realized that.

And to Walter Smith, Eisenhower's chief of staff, Patton said of the Russians:

We are going to have to fight them sooner or later . . . Why not do it now while our Army is intact and we can have their hind end kicked back into Russia in three months? We can do it easily with the help of the German troops we have, if we just arm them and take them with us. They hate the bastards.

In late September, Eisenhower relieved Patton of his command.

Patton hung on in Europe for two more months, and then decided to head back to the United States, to find whatever job he might in the regular postwar army. On December 9, the day before his departure, he set out one last time to go hunting for pheasant and visit some Roman ruins outside the German town of Mannheim. He went in a Cadillac with a fellow general, Hap Gay, and a new driver, Private Horace Woodring. Patton's usual driver,

Sergeant John Mims, had already gone home to America. Woodring was nervous but proud to serve the great General Patton.

It was exactly one year since the briefing at Nancy that started Patton's *coup d'oeil* to save the Battle of the Bulge.

They left around nine in the morning. At 11:45, Patton was studying the terrain, as usual, as if he were in his jeep in battle. "Look at all the derelict vehicles!" he said. "How awful war is. Look at the waste."

Mims would have ignored him, but Woodring took it as an order. He looked.

At the same moment, an army truck cut across in front of them. Woodring swung his eyes back to the road, but it was too late. He braced for the impact. So did Gay. Patton's eyes were still on the countryside, not on the road ahead.

The truck was going only ten miles per hour. The Cadillac was going thirty. It was a minor accident, except that Patton flew around inside the big car like a stone in a bottle. He gashed his head and snapped his spine. No one else was hurt.

More than a year before, in the full flush of the Avranches breakout and before Eisenhower cut off his gas, Patton wrote in his diary:

Civil life will be mighty dull—no cheering crowds, no flowers, no private airplanes. I am convinced that the best end for an officer is the last bullet of the war.

He came close to getting his wish. He held on for five days after the accident. Generals came to visit, and his wife made it over from the United States in time. Among his last words were "What chance have I to ride a horse again?"

Patton died on December 14, 1945, at the age of sixty. The army buried him on Christmas Eve in a military cemetery in the Ardennes. German prisoners captured by Patton dug his grave.

Some military historians think that Patton saved thousands of lives in the camps he liberated by arriving before the Germans let the inmates die. Others agree with Patton's own assessment that the war would have ended many months earlier—thereby saving thousands of casualties—if Eisenhower had given Patton a free hand. But one thing no one disputes: Patton was the best Allied general of the war.

His loyal intelligence officer, Oscar Koch, explains why:

Many times the question has been asked whether Patton possessed an intuition—a sixth sense or whatever—which contributed to the exploits of his commands and to his ability to catch his enemy unaware. If one can call anticipation of enemy reactions based on a lifetime of professional training and on thinking and application "intuition," he had it . . . He was a professional soldier, a student of history . . . A firm believer in the cavalry motto Mobilitate Vigemus—"In mobility lies our strength"—Patton was a master of the old horse cavalry tactic of the breakthrough, its exploitation, and pursuit.

A strategist reborn—from an earlier era of war, from disappointment in World War I to triumph in World War II—and a master of Napoleon's glance.

9

✛   ✛   ✛

THE BAREFOOT BANK
OF BANGLADESH

On August 1, 1971, former Beatle George Harrison put together a concert of rock stars in Madison Square Garden, in New York City, to raise money for the country of Bangladesh. Harrison wrote a song for the occasion. Here is the chorus:

Bangladesh, Bangladesh
Where so many people are dying fast
And it sure looks like a mess
I've never seen such distress
Now, won't you lend your hand and understand
Relieve the people of Bangladesh

The concert recording became a best-selling album that raised even more money. It was the first rock concert for a worthy cause. These days, there is at least one every year: to save the rain forest, for AIDS research and treatment, African famine relief, the victims of 9/11. But it all began with Bangladesh.

At the time of the concert, Bangladesh was still officially East Pakistan, on the east side of India. West of India, the main part of Pakistan ran the whole country for years. Then a political party from the East won a national election: The main Pakistan party refused to accept the victory. So East Pakistan declared independence as Bangladesh. Pakistan sent in the army. So began Bangladesh's war for independence. More than a million of its citizens died. But four months after the concert, in December 1971, Bangladesh won the war.

George Harrison knew about Bangladesh from his sitar

teacher, Ravi Shankar, who also played at the concert. Shankar, from India, had relatives across the border in Bangladesh. The country was poor to begin with, but the ravages of the Pakistan army turned much of the population into refugees. The concert raised money for the United Nations to distribute food and medicine throughout Bangladesh.

After the war ended, the new country had a fresh start to climb its way out of poverty.

But how?

As it turned out, there were two paths ahead: one followed Jomini, and the other followed von Clausewitz. Once again, it was planning versus *coup d'oeil*.

The Jomini planners work in government departments and dozens of development agencies. They got their money from rich countries, who spent more than sixty billion dollars in Bangladesh over thirty years, from 1972 to 2002. Over the same period, the same agencies spent more than a trillion dollars in development aid to all poor nations together. Yet most of the target countries, including Bangladesh, remain desperately poor. The aid did not work. So many citizens of the rich countries want to put a stop to the aid. However worthy the cause, it makes no sense to throw good money after bad.

But there is another path.

Over the same thirty years, the world's most successful development project for poor countries arose in Bangladesh. It reaches 12 million poor people—ten percent of the country's total population—in half of the country's 80,000 villages. And it costs a tiny fraction of other development projects: It pays for itself, through loans. It's a bank for poor people. Most of the borrowers are women, who in poor countries are poorest of all.

The name is the Grameen Bank. The word *grameen* means "of the village." Instead of paying huge interest rates to village moneylenders, the borrowers pay a small rate to Grameen. So they save money and work their way up to a better life. The bank is an astounding success by any measure: No other project in poor countries reaches so many poor people at such low cost with such good results.

Yet the Jomini planners continue on their usual path. They admire Grameen, and some of them try to copy it, but the vast majority just keep on doing what they always did even if it doesn't work.

But why?

Because Grameen follows von Clausewitz. Napoleon's glance, not Jomini planning, brought Grameen to life.

To follow the Grameen path, the planners would have to redo their entire procedures, their rules and guidelines, their whole operation from stem to stern. Like the Prussian army facing Napoleon: You would like to do what he does, but you can't, at least not in time to win the battle. It took the Prussians more than fifty years to make all the changes to fight like Napoleon. In 1870, thanks to von Clausewitz and his students, the Prussians routed the French army under Napoleon's nephew, Napoleon III.

Maybe it's the same for the world's development agencies: Their Jomini planners need fifty years to learn the lesson of the Grameen Bank. Let's hope it goes faster than that. When people are starving, fifty years is a very long time.

The lesson of Grameen's success is to study not what they did but how they did it. The details will be different for every country: The size of the loans will vary, as will what they're used for, the interest rate, and how you organize the bank. And poor countries need many things other than loans. But always: Keep your presence of mind; wait for a battle you can win by building on past achievement; it comes to you in a *coup d'oeil*; then resolution carries you on.

Such is the lesson of Napoleon's glance, and the lesson of the Grameen Bank.

The founder of Grameen is Mohammed Yunus. He grew up in Chittagong, the main port city of Bangladesh. For a few years after college, he ran a family business that made paper cartons. In 1965, he won a scholarship to the United States. A Ph.D. in economics from Vanderbilt University in Nashville, Tennessee, led to a job teaching at Middle Tennessee State University.

When the Bangladesh war broke out, Yunus joined with other Bangladeshis in the United States to raise money and lobby the American government to take the side of Bangladesh. And like many other Bangladeshis, victory brought him home to join the great cause to raise their country from poverty.

Yunus arrived back in Bangladesh in 1972, right after the war. He was thirty-two years old. In the capital, Dhaka, he became the deputy chief of the General Economics Division of the government's National Planning Commission. With "nothing to do all day but read newspapers," Yunus resigned.

Yunus applied to teach at Dhaka University but was turned down. Instead, he became the head of the economics department at Chittagong University. It was a step down from Dhaka but right in his hometown.

How could Yunus have "nothing to do" at the planning commission? The country was struggling to pull itself out of poverty. Foreign aid was flowing in. Wasn't it up to the planning commission to plan how to use the money?

Not quite. The international development agencies controlled the foreign aid. They're the ones who planned how to use it. They involved some Bangladeshis, but there were far too many graduates like Yunus to give them all something to do.

At Chittagong University, Yunus found himself out of the struggle. The professors taught, and the students learned. They fought about grades, not the fate of the country. Meanwhile, the battle of poverty raged all around. Yunus could not ignore it. He reports in his memoirs:

At that time I lived with my parents in town. My father

*allowed me to use his car to commute to the campus every day.
Along the way, I drove through the village of Jobra . . . I noticed
barren fields next to the village, and asked a colleague, Professor H. I. Latifee, why they were not being cultivated for a
winter crop. As he did not know, I proposed that we go talk to
the villagers and find out the reason. It turned out that there
was no water for irrigation.*

Bangladesh is a very wet country: high rainfall, and regular
floods from the great rivers that run through it from the Himalaya
Mountains. But that's in summer. To get a second crop in winter,
you need to irrigate the fields. The answer is a tube well: You drill
deep in the ground and attach a pipe with a pump. And then you
buy special seeds that give a higher yield.

It was the time of the Green Revolution, when development
agencies helped poor countries adopt pump irrigation and special
seeds to grow more food. The Green Revolution worked, except
that the pump and the seeds cost a lot of money. So the poorest
farmers could not afford it. And worse, sometimes they lost their
land as the richer farmers expanded. There was nothing wrong
with that as long as the poor had something else to do.

But what? The Green Revolution had no answer.

Like so many other students from poor countries, Yunus wrote
his doctoral dissertation on the Green Revolution. The title was
"Optimal Allocation of Multi-Purpose Reservoir Water: A
Dynamic Programming Model." So Yunus, the Green Revolution
economist, set out to bring water to the barren fields of Jobra.

The government owned the tube wells, so Yunus went from
agency to agency to put one in Jobra. It took him nearly a year, but
in the end he succeeded.

And then: The tube well stayed empty. No one used it. The
farmers argued over how to collect fees to pay for gas and oil. And

Jobra was not alone: Yunus reports at the time "almost half the deep tube wells in Bangladesh had fallen out of use." When there was a big farmer to profit from the well, he paid for its upkeep. But in Jobra and many other villages, the small farmers had to all chip in to keep their tube well running.

So Yunus organized a cooperative, Three Share Farm. The landowners gave land, sharecroppers gave labor, and Yunus lent the money for seed, fuel, and insecticide. These three parties would divide the harvest in three. Yunus used his students: As part of their classwork, they found out who had claims to the land, explained the idea, calculated how much fuel and seeds and other supplies they needed, and then how much money. Yunus paid the students a small stipend out of a research grant from a foreign agency, the Ford Foundation. Many professors had similar grants, but they used them for research. Yunus used his grant for action.

To cover Three Share's other costs, Yunus took out a personal loan of $1,250 from the Janata Bank. The campus branch of Janata only took deposits—the bank made all its loans in the cities. But the branch manager made an exception for Yunus, who got the loan and passed it on to the farmers. They reaped a good harvest. The farmers were happy but Yunus "lost 13,000 takas because some farmers gave me less than the one-third they had promised."

A Bangladeshi taka was about four cents, so Yunus lost more than $400. Since the total was $1,250, that means the farmers cheated by a third. Yet the government considered the project a success and copied it in other villages. It solved the problem of half their tube wells that went unused. Yunus received the President's Award.

So the government program took over support for the Three Share Farm in Jobra. But without Yunus. He had nothing more to do with it.

Why?

Besides losing money, and the cheating, Yunus did not consider the Three Share Farm a success: "It was clear to me that the wealthier the farmer, the more he earned." Even if all the farmers paid their share, not enough benefit went to the poor. The farmers were men, and the poor were women.

He noticed the poor women for the first time at the Three Share harvest. They were a problem "I had not focused on before:"

Once the rice was harvested, labor was needed to separate the rice from the dry straw. This mindless, boring work was offered to the cheapest day laborers: destitute women who would otherwise be reduced to begging. For hours on end these poor women would separate the rice with their feet. What a terrible life—to earn forty cents investing the weight of your body and the tiresome motion of your bare feet for ten hours a day! These women, many of them widowed, were too poor even to be sharecroppers. They were landless and assetless and without any hope.

Forty cents a day, for twenty days of harvest, made eight dollars total. With the tube well, there were now two harvests a year. That made sixteen dollars a year for two months of work. The women could not possibly survive on just that. What did they do the rest of the year?

The poor of Jobra were very poor indeed. They earned much less than the Bangladesh average, which was low enough to begin with, about a dollar a day. In the United States, the figure is fifty dollars. So fifty Bangladeshi earn the same as one American.

And the poor in Bangladesh are many. The total population is 130 million, a little less than half the United States. New York and New Jersey combined are about the same land area, but total about 30 million people. The extra 100 million people in Bangladesh live in thousands of villages cramped so close together they touch: The farmland of one meets the farmland of the other, on and on across the country. The land is fertile—it's the floodplain of the Ganges and Brahmaputra, two great rivers that flow down from the Himalayas. When the rivers flood, they enrich the soil. But also, they wash away the villages.

As a city dweller, Yunus did not know much about village life. He knew even less about the poor, who hardly ever dealt with the government or other outsiders. When he set up the Three Share Farm, Yunus talked to the wealthier farmers, not with the poor who worked the fields. But now:

> In 1976, I began visiting the poorest households in Jobra to see if I could help them directly in any way. There were three parts to the village: a Muslim, a Hindu, and a Buddhist section. When I visited the Buddhist section, I would often take one of my students, Dipal Chandra Barua, a native of the Buddhist section, along with me. Otherwise, a colleague, Professor H. I. Latifee, would usually accompany me. He knew most of the families and had a natural talent for making villagers feel at ease.

Latifee again: He was the one who first introduced Yunus to Jobra. Some people have a flair for village life, they can feel at home anywhere in the world even without speaking a word of the language. From the various accounts of the start of Grameen, we get a hint that Latifee was like that. Yunus was not. He began as an outsider—studying, watching, listening, searching. Latifee had the heart of a villager, while Yunus had the eye of a strategist.

> One day as Latifee and I were making our rounds in Jobra, we stopped at a run-down house with crumbling mud walls and a low thatched roof pocked with holes ... A woman squatted on the dirt floor of the verandah, a half-finished bamboo stool gripped between her knees. Her fingers moved quickly, plaiting the stubborn strands of cane ... On hearing Latifee's call of

greeting, she dropped her bamboo, sprang to her feet, and scurried into the house.

They were in the Muslim section. The women were in purdah, which meant they stayed in seclusion and did not talk to men, except for close relatives. But Latifee coaxed some of the women outside. Yunus tried to help:

Complimenting a mother on her baby was a natural way to put her at ease. I now picked up one of the naked children beside me, but he started to cry and rushed over to his mother.

Latifee had better luck. He engaged the child's mother in small talk, and then Yunus started asking questions.

She was in her early twenties, thin, with dark skin and black eyes. She wore a red sari and had the tired eyes of a woman who labored every day from morning to night.

Her name was Sufiya Begum. She bought bamboo from a trader on five takas credit—about twenty-two cents. She made the bamboo into a stool and sold it back to the trader for five and a half takas. That gave her a profit of half a taka, or about two cents.

She made a stool a day, so her daily income was one fiftieth the national average of a dollar a day. So an average American earned fifty times more than an average Bangladeshi, and an average Bangladeshi earned fifty times more than Sufiya Begum.

Two cents a day: Yunus had found real poverty.

He asked more questions, to really understand it.

Sufiya could buy the bamboo directly rather than from the trader on credit for much less than five takas. And she could sell her stool in the market instead of to the trader for much more than five and a half takas. That would give her much more profit. But for that she needed cash. There were moneylenders in the village, so why not borrow from them?

Sufiya replied:

Yes, but the moneylender would demand a lot. People who deal with them only get poorer ... Sometimes he charges ten percent per week. But I have one neighbor who is paying ten percent per day.

Enough questions: "Sufiya did not want to waste any more time talking. I watched as she set to work again, her small brown hands plaiting the strands of bamboo as they had every day for months and years on end ... She squatted barefoot on the hard mud. Her fingers were callused, her nails black with grime."

Note how Yunus recalls the "calluses," the "grime." If you spend a lot of time in the poor villages of the world, you get used to these signs of poverty. To Yunus they were new, and more: He did not want to get used to them. He wanted to change them.

Sufiya Begum earned two cents a day. It was this knowledge that shocked me. In my university courses, I theorized about sums in the millions of dollars, but here before my eyes the problems of life and death were posed in terms of pennies ... I had never heard of anyone suffering for the lack of twenty-two cents. It seemed impossible to me, preposterous. Should I reach into my pocket and hand Sufiya the pittance she needed for capital?

That was it.
Coup d'oeil.

Or at least the start of one. Yunus did not actually give Sufiya the money, at least not yet. But he saw himself do it in his mind's eye.

He saw what she needed most was a loan from someone like him, on fairer terms than the trader or moneylender. Yet:

That would be so simple, so easy. I resisted the urge to give Sufiya the money she needed. She was not asking for charity. And giving one person twenty-two cents was not addressing the problem on any permanent basis.

So Yunus sent a student to find out how many Sufiyas there were in the village. It took a week to come up with the list. There were forty-two, who borrowed a total of twenty-seven dollars at a time.

"My God, my God. All this misery in all these families all for the lack of twenty-seven dollars!" I exclaimed.

But:

My mind would not let this problem lie . . . I wanted to help these forty-two able-bodied, hard-working people. I kept going around and around the problem, like a dog worrying a bone . . . No formal financial structure was available to cater to the credit needs of the poor. This credit market, by default, had been taken over by the local moneylenders. It was an efficient vehicle; it created a heavy rush of one-way traffic on the road to poverty.

In this passage, we see the start of the Grameen Bank: a "formal financial structure," like the Janata Bank that lent him money for the Three Share Farm—plus the "efficient vehicle" of the village moneylender. Grameen put the two together. And Yunus knew the details of Sufiya's finances, so he had a clear picture of his model customer.

He gave twenty-seven dollars to his student, Maimouna:

"Here, lend this money to the forty-two villagers on our list. They can repay the traders what they owe them and sell their products at a good price."

"When should they repay you?" she asked.

"Whenever they can . . . They don't have to pay any interest. I am not in the money business."

He was not in the money business—yet.
Maimouna gave out the money.
The women paid it back.
Yunus went to the Janata Bank to get more.
He was in the money business—now.

The campus manager of Janata turned Yunus down, but the regional manager, R. A. Howladar, approved a loan fund of $300. Six months later, the money came through. The Jobra Landless Association began, but in name only. There was no association in place yet, or even on paper. Years later, David Bornstein interviewed Yunus about those early days:

"I didn't know what I was doing," Yunus recalled. "I certainly had no intention of starting a bank."

In other words, Yunus had no plan. He just saw a problem he could solve, a battle he could win: to give forty-two poor women of Jobra the credit they need to make a living. From Bornstein's account, we know that the women started paying back the first loans "at a local tea stall" before Yunus went to the bank. But:

"This was not a solution," he said. "Every time they needed money they couldn't come to me . . . "

Yunus decided to pay another visit to the manager of the Janata Bank . . . He had an idea.

"Ten taka loans?" the manager exclaimed. "That's not even worth the paperwork they have to fill out . . . we can't give loans to poor people . . . They don't have any collateral . . . "
  Yunus explained that the villagers were repaying his loans. Why wouldn't they repay the bank's loans?

When Yunus gave out the first loans to the forty-two women, he did not really want the money back. But put yourself in Sufiya Begum's shoes. Along comes the same rich man who got the men money for their Three Share Farm. He asks you some questions about traders and moneylenders. Then his assistant arrives with a five-taka loan at no interest. What do you do?

You take the loan. Then you pay it back in hopes of getting another loan, and another and another. Just like a loan from a moneylender, but without the high interest.

This was the moment that Grameen started, when the women repaid the first loans. That success completed the *coup d'oeil*. Yunus saw that lending small amounts of money to poor women worked: They paid it back. So he went on to do it again and again, for hundreds then thousands, then millions of borrowers.

Yunus showed great presence of mind in turning away from Three Share Farm to the unknown world of the Jobra poor. He entered that world with a blank mind. He had no preconceptions, no expectations of what he would find or what he should do. What he did find, and what he should do, were completely outside his expertise and experience. He started out as a Green Revolution economist. Now he became a moneylender.

I never intended to become a moneylender. All I really wanted was to solve an immediate problem. Out of sheer frustration, I had questioned the most basic banking premise of collateral. I did not know if I was right. I had no idea what I was getting myself into. I was walking blind and learning as I went along.

Yunus questioned the "basic banking premise of collateral" because he saw a no-collateral system already working: the moneylenders. Their borrowers paid them back not from fear of the moneylender seizing their property—they had no property worth seizing. The borrowers repaid the moneylenders in order to get the next loan, and the next. So Yunus did the same thing. He became a moneylender, but at much lower interest.

An economist might ask: How could Yunus afford a lower rate? If the moneylenders ran an "efficient" system, as Yunus himself admitted, that meant they charged a market rate. If Yunus tried to charge less, didn't that mean he would lose money?

There are four answers.

First, the poor women of Jobra were a "captive market." If they shopped around to other villages to look for a better interest rate, they would spend the day walking instead of working. So they had to accept what the local moneylenders charged. When Yunus brought in outside money at a better rate, the women took it right away. Like Americans turning to Japanese cars in the 1970s instead of American models. The American car market was "efficient." The Japanese just offered a better product, and American customers bought it.

Second, Yunus kept his costs low at first by using his students. As part of their classwork, they had helped him start the Three Share Farm. Now he did the same thing for the loans. The Ford Foundation renewed its research grant, so he was able to continue a small stipend for the students. And he drew no salary himself, again like Three Share.

Third, Yunus achieved "economies of scale." That is, he reached far more borrowers than any moneylender could even dream. So he spread out his costs over many more loans.

As Yunus added borrowers, he started hiring staff, but slowly. His first employee was Priti Rani Barua, a Buddhist widow, who would work with the Muslim women in purdah. She did not have a husband to answer to, and was not in purdah herself, so that made her free to work for Yunus. Priti had a ninth-grade education, and her pay was fifty takas a month—about two dollars. This was the fourth way Yunus kept costs down: In Bangladesh, wages for all kinds of workers were very low.

When the Janata fund came through in January 1977, the Jobra Landless Association gave out its first loans, to seven women. The first was Sufiya Begum. Instead of buying bamboo to make stools, she stocked up on bangles and candy. Sufiya became a peddler, house to house in the village.

Right away, in this first loan, we see a key reason for Grameen's success. It was up to Sufiya to decide how best to use her money. Contrast this with the loan programs of development agencies. There, the Jomini planners decide what the country needs to invest in: for example, tube wells. So they set up a program to offer loans for tube wells. Or the planners decide that the country needs to plant more coffee, so they set up loans for that. Or bamboo stools. But if Sufiya Begum takes that loan, she cannot switch to something else that she judges might earn more money, like peddling.

Over the past thirty years, studies have shown that Sufiya is typical: The poor shift from job to job, crop to crop, craft to craft, as they see a chance to earn a bit more. Grameen helps them do just that—just like a moneylender. The development agencies, on the other hand, set up more special loan programs: one for tube wells, one for coffee, one for bamboo stools, one for cotton, one for fishing nets, and so on. Why? Because they can't just let Sufiya decide for herself. She might invest in something that's not in their plan.

Like peddling. Most development agencies think that peddling is "nonproductive." Which means they don't approve of it. But even if they do approve, they assign it "low priority." What is "high priority"? Whatever is in their plan.

So in many villages today, in poor countries around the world, you might find someone with a coffee loan, one with a fishing loan, and so forth. The loan locks the borrower into a specific activity. In the village, there is usually a credit cooperative to handle the individual loans. Or a bank branch, like Janata, makes loans from the nearest town. To change activity, you change to a different loan program with a different cooperative. So you stop paying one loan and go get another from a different cooperative. So each program has unpaid loans as people leave it for another program. And each program has just a few borrowers, which means costs per borrower are high, so the loans have to be bigger to make each one worthwhile. Or sometimes you simply take one big loan with no intention of ever repaying or asking for another loan.

Yet development aid for Bangladesh kept flowing to the cooperatives and Janata. Why? It was in the plan. The Jomini planners decided that the country needed what the loans were for—tube wells, fishing nets, improved rice seeds—so they kept giving money to pay for them. To stop the funding would throw into question their entire system of planning.

Through 1977, Yunus went back to Janata for a larger loan fund. So loans went out to fifty-eight more villagers. During that year, Yunus started working out exactly how to organize the loans in the village. First he asked the villagers. With cooperatives in mind, they suggested a milk-cow group, a chili-trading group, a bamboo-stool group, and so on. Yunus tried that, but it did not work. The groups were not really groups; they were lists of names on a sheet of paper under different headings. Just like the cooperatives. Just like Three Share Farm.

So instead, the Jobra groups formed themselves from people who knew each other. As Yunus explains it:

A prospective borrower first has to take the initiative and explain how the bank works to a second person . . . She often has a difficult time convincing her friends—who are likely to be terrified, skeptical, or forbidden by their husbands to deal with money—but eventually a second person, impressed by what Grameen has done for another household, will take the leap of joining the group. Then the two will go out and seek out a third, then a fourth, then a fifth.

A bank worker does a home visit to verify that each of the five is poor: that is, has less than half an acre of farmland or its equivalent in other property. The five get at least seven days of training on Grameen policies. After, each one has to pass an oral exam, alone:

The night before her test, a borrower often gets so nervous that she lights a candle in a saint's shrine and prays to Allah for help. She knows that if she fails she will let down not only herself but also the others in her group.

If she fails, "The Bank worker will send the group away, telling all the members to study some more, and the others in the group will chastise her."

Bornstein reports how Yunus arrived at the size of the group: "After trial and error, Yunus settled on the number five. Part of this was intuitive: A working hand has five fingers, there are five pillars of faith in Islam, and each day has five calls to prayer." The number could have been four or six or seven. In the end, Yunus picked a number and stuck to it, so everyone knew the rules.

Each member gets her own loan at the same time as the rest of the group. You repay the loan in equal weekly installments over the year, with the interest at the end. If any member of the group fails to repay, no one in the group can get a new loan. There is no charge for late payments. Pay what you owe, and then the group can get a new loan.

In 1977, Yunus charged an annual interest rate of 13 percent. Over the years, it rose to 20 percent. The moneylenders charged 120 percent. No wonder the women flocked to Grameen.

But not right away. At first, Yunus had trouble pulling in enough women borrowers beyond his original forty-two. For the first six years, more than half the borrowers were men.

Yunus explains:

> The first and most formidable opposition came from the husbands, who generally wanted the loans for themselves. The religious leaders were very suspicious of us. And the moneylenders saw us as a direct threat to their authority in the village. These objections I had expected, but what surprised me was to hear educated civil servants and professionals arguing against us. They contended that it made no sense to lend money to women while so many men were jobless and without income.

A woman feared that taking a loan might turn the men of the village against her, starting with her husband. Yunus and his staff spent long hours drumming up business, house to house through the village. It helped greatly when the staff were women too. But women workers were hard to find, as Yunus explains:

> The nature of a bank worker's job requires that he or she walk alone in rural areas, sometimes for distances as long as five miles in each direction. The parents of many prospective female bank workers found this demeaning—even scandalous. Though they might have allowed their daughter to sit behind an office desk, they did not accept her spending her day working in the villages for Grameen.

Yunus tells of Nurjahan, a Muslim female staff member with a master's degree: She did not tell her family what kind of bank Grameen really was. Yunus recounts:

> Nurjahan had a special gift for dealing with the poor. I was

*very pleased to have her on my team of workers. Then one day
Nurjahan's sister-in-law's brother came to give Nurjahan some
family news. When he arrived at our office, he saw that it was
only a tin-roofed shack with no telephone, toilet, or running
water. He was shocked. This was not at all the image he had of
a commercial bank.*

Worse, the office manager gave the visitor directions to find
Nurjahan in the village:

*The man went and found Nurjahan seated on the grass under
a tree talking to some village women.*

It was a family scandal, but with a happy ending. After much
torment, her mother let her stay. Yunus even sent Nurjahan to rep-
resent Grameen at official gatherings, "to break the myth that a
woman could not travel alone . . . As she had never traveled alone
before, she prayed to Allah to give her strength and courage, and
away she went."

Yunus says of Nurjahan today:

*She is one of the three general managers of the Grameen Bank
and heads our training division, where she helps hundreds of
our future young bank workers to become self-reliant.*

Yunus's *coup d'oeil* of 1976 showed him how to make loans to
poor women and get the money back. It took several years to fill
in the details, like figuring out the group structure, the interest
rate and repayment schedule, and attracting enough women borrowers and staff.

Another key detail was where he got the money. In 1977, it came
from the campus branch of the Janata Bank. But Yunus wore out
his welcome there. Janata never expected so many borrowers. They

all repaid, but the paperwork was a nightmare. Every little loan needed Yunus's signature and went to the head office in Dhaka, the capital, for approval. At first it took days, then weeks, then months. Janata was just not set up to become a village bank.

At the end of 1977, Yunus had to go to New York for three months of meetings at the United Nations. So he would not be around to sign the Janata paperwork. At this point, Yunus was still an active university professor: Grameen was not yet big enough to take up all his time. Before he left, a chance meeting threw him together with the head of the Kishi Bank in Dhaka. The meeting solved his Janata problem, and made Yunus a full-time banker.

Kishi means "agriculture": It was the national agricultural bank. The Kishi head, A. N. Annisuzzaman, saw that Yunus was from the university, so he launched into a lecture on ivory-tower professors who did nothing to help the country. Yunus thought quickly: Here was a bank with a rural slant. So he explained his credit program and made a request: "I would like the agriculture bank to set up a branch in Jobra and leave it at my disposal."

Annisuzzaman said yes.

So early in 1978, after Yunus returned from New York, he set up the Jobra Experimental Grameen Branch of the Kishi Bank. Kishi made loans for farming, while most of Grameen's borrowers had no land to farm. And as the population increased, the number of landless grew every year. When Grameen started, more than half of Jobra was landless.

At first, Yunus kept his university job. "I devoted much of my day to managing our Jobra branch of the agriculture bank, which was staffed by my ex-students." They eliminated the steps that made the Janata Bank so slow. Business boomed.

Bornstein gives this report:

By September, the bank had spread to three villages and disbursed more than half a million takas—about $15,000—to *four hundred villagers, one quarter of whom were women. The default rate was less than one percent.*

Yunus reported his progress at a national credit seminar. Bankers filled the audience. They did not know what to make of Grameen. Then one of them replied:

Professor Yunus, your Jobra experiment is nothing, only a fly speck compared to the big national banks we manage. Our hair has not turned gray for nothing. We have a lot of experience. If you want to prove your point, show us success over a whole district.

This was not rejection. It was a challenge.

In the audience was A. K. Gangopadhaya, deputy governor of the Bangladesh Central Bank. Yunus recalls:

After the meeting, he called me into his office and asked me if I was serious about wanting to extend my experiment. I told him I was. A month later he invited me to a meeting of all the managing directors of the state-owned banks to discuss my proposal. They agreed to sponsor Grameen in a whole district.

For the third time, Yunus found a key ally right when he was ready to move to the next step. After the first forty-two borrowers repaid, the manager of the campus branch of the Janata Bank gave Yunus a loan fund. When Yunus outgrew Janata, the head of the Kishi Bank stepped forward. Now he was ready to take on a district with the help of the Bangladesh Central Bank. Each time, Yunus had no plan: After each success, he kept his eyes open for the next battle he saw a way to win.

The University of Chittagong granted me a two-year leave of absence. On June 6, 1979, before I knew what had happened, I had officially joined the Grameen Bank Project in the District of Tangail.

Tangail is two hundred miles from Chittagong, on the other side of Bangladesh. The bankers who sponsored the Grameen expansion picked it for that reason. Chittagong is Yunus's hometown—perhaps the villagers of nearby Jobra followed him as a "big man" of the region. In Tangail, Yunus was unknown. Also, it was close enought to Dhaka for the bankers to visit and see for themselves.

At this point, Grameen was three years old. Over those three years, Yunus and his students, then his staff, had worked out all the basic elements, with great success: repayment of more than ninety-eight percent. Now his sponsor banks offered their local branches to work from: nineteen in Tangail, plus another six in Chittagong. With Jobra, that made twenty-five branches in all.

But all eyes were on Tangail. There, the biggest problem was staff. Could Yunus find the right people and train them fast enough? At first, he brought only three staff with him from Jobra—all men. Then, when it was safe, he brought two women, including Nurjahan. The rest he hired in Tangail.

Safety in Tangail was not just a question for the women. Men, too, feared the Gonobahini—the "People's Army." Yunus recalls:

These guerrillas killed with little compunction. They simply pointed a gun and fired. In every village we came across dead bodies lying in the middle of the road, hanging from trees, or shot by a wall.

Yet it was the Gonobahini's last days. The Bangladesh army defeated them. Grameen reaped an odd bounty:

The ex-Gonobanini turned out to be excellent workers . . . They had wanted to liberate the country with guns and revolution, and now they were walking around those same villages

*extending micro-loans to the destitute. They just needed a
cause to fight for. We channeled their energies into something
more constructive than terrorism.*

And, of course, the former fighters came cheap. So once again,
Yunus found a way to keep his costs down.

Bornstein reports: "Each office was staffed with a manager and
guard and five bank workers who carried out the same work that
Yunus' students had been doing in Jobra: organizing and training
villagers, disbursing and collecting loans, and troubleshooting."
That made twenty-five managers, twenty-five guards, and a hundred twenty-five workers. Yunus himself worked out of a main
office in Tangail town, the capital of Tangail district. Two students
supervised the managers, while Nurjahan took the special assignment of finding and training female staff and borrowers.

Within a year, Grameen had 12,000 borrowers—a third of them
women, thanks to Nurjahan. There were problems galore: Rich villagers took over new groups, the regular bank staff hated the extra
work that Grameen brought in, new staff in their own villages caved
in to pressure to cheat. But repayment remained over ninety percent.
A six-month training program for new staff, and careful matching of
which staff to which village, solved most of the problems.

So Grameen passed the Tangail test with flying colors.

What next?

Bornstein reports:

*In 1980, the International Fund for Agricultural Development
(IFAD), a Rome-based aid organization created by the United
Nations, sent a Project Identification Mission to Bangladesh
... After identifying all the worthy projects they could find, the
IFAD mission had a few million dollars left over and they were
finding it difficult to justify returning to Rome with money
unspent, particularly from Bangladesh.*

A few million dollars—"left over"! Such was the world of the international development aid.

Bornstein continues:

> *When an official of the Bangladesh Bank mentioned that they had an experimental credit program working with landless villagers in Tangail, the IFAD mission declined: the project had nothing to do with agriculture and didn't really sound like banking. A few days later, still unsuccessful in their search, they called back. They would take a closer look at the Grameen Bank Project.*

Note that the Bangladesh Central Bank claimed ownership of Grameen. That was fine with Yunus: It meant he had their full support. And here they were pointing IFAD in Grameen's direction. IFAD's first reaction was typical of a Jomini planner: They were looking for credit programs that fit what they decided that Bangladesh needed.

When IFAD took their closer look, they judged Grameen too "risky"—even though it had a far better repayment rate than anything else they funded. Instead of protesting, Yunus looked for a guarantee—the way he himself guaranteed the first Jobra loans from Janata Bank.

He still had an active research grant from the Ford Foundation, so he tried there. Their representative in Dhaka, Adrienne Germaine, was the first woman to head a Ford office anywhere in the world. She was not a banker, but she became one overnight: Thanks to Germaine, Ford came through with a guarantee of $800,000. Yunus recalls:

> *I assured them we would never need to dip into it. "The fact that it's there," I said, "will do the magic."*

So once again, Yunus found a key ally when the time came to

expand. IFAD lent Grameen $3.4 million at 3 percent interest, and obliged the Bangladesh Central Bank to match it, at 6 percent. That made $6.8 million in all, at an average of 4.5 percent interest. It took a year to put the whole deal together. So in 1982, Grameen spread to a hundred branches in five of the country's fourteen districts.

And now Yunus declared independence.

In Tangail, he worked out of the branches of the various sponsor banks that the Bangladesh Central Bank brought together after the credit conference of 1978. Using the other banks kept costs down, but a hundred branches gave Yunus the scale to cover all his costs himself. And he made money on his money: Grameen charged borrowers 20 percent interest, but the $6.8 million loan cost only 4.5 percent. Yunus made a profit of 15.5 percent on the loan. That amounted to more than a million dollars, enough to run his own branches.

So Yunus took Grameen from a project of the Bangladesh Central Bank to a separate bank all its own. He had high-level help. Kamal Hussain, drafter of the country's first constitution, now drafted the Grameen charter. And the finance minister, A. M. A. Muhith, took the charter through official channels. Final approval came in September 1983, seven years after Sufiya Begum repaid her first loan.

On its public Web site, Grameen publishes its balance sheet from 1983 to 2000, and its loan figures all the way back to the beginning. We see the number of borrowers grow: 10 in 1976; 70 in 1977; 290 in 1978; 2,200 in 1979; 15,000 in 1980; 58,000 in 1983; 234,000 in 1986; 1.0 million in 1991; 2.0 million in 1994; and 2.4 million in 2000. As each borrower has five or six family members, the loans reach about 13 million people.

Also from 1983 to 2000, Grameen's ownership changed. At the start, the government appointed sixty percent of the board of directors. The borrowers elected the other forty percent. Over time, Yunus won a larger share for the borrowers. Today they have ninety percent of the seats. So Grameen calls them not borrowers but "members"—who legally own the bank.

We also see the repayment rate: 100 percent in 1976; 100 percent in 1979; 100 percent in 1982; 98 percent in 1987; 99 percent in 1993; 93 percent in 1997; 89 percent in 2000. And women members grew to 95 percent, an astounding achievement in its own right. The volume of loans grew from $498 in 1976 to $270 million in 2000. The total for all the years put together was $3.2 billion.

Over the years, other international agencies joined IFAD and Ford in providing loan funds: from Norway, Sweden, Belgium, Japan, Holland, Germany, and Canada.

But not the World Bank. Yunus explains:

Even before I started the Grameen Bank, I had been a critic of international aid agencies in Bangladesh. By far the most influential agency, and the one I have most criticized, is the World Bank.

In 1986, Yunus had a "public confrontation" with the World Bank president, Barber Conable. They were panelists on a World Food Day teleconference, broadcast to thirty countries around the world. Yunus "had not expected to go into battle against the World Bank president," but Conable "provoked" him by saying the Bank funded Grameen. Yunus corrected him. Conable said it again. Yunus corrected him again. "Conable ignored my protest and repeated that the World Bank provided financial support to the Grameen Bank."

We don't have Conable's account, so we can't know what he was thinking. The World Bank typically works in every sector of a country: Perhaps he could not imagine something of Grameen's scale beyond the World Bank's reach. In any event, Yunus went on to tell the audience why he refused to take the Bank's money:

Their experts and consultants often take over the projects they *finance. They do not rest until they have molded things their way . . . Indeed . . . we had actually rejected a $200-million low-interest loan from the World Bank. I also told Conable, who was bragging about employing the best minds in the world, that hiding smart economists does not necessarily translate into policies and programs that benefit the poor.*

The World Bank was a bastion of Jomini planning. They hired the "best minds" to analyze a country, decide what it needs, design a massive loan for that purpose, and then make a plan to carry out the design. They "take over" a project to make sure it follows their plan. But Yunus did not design Grameen: He saw it in a *coup d'oeil*. The plans came after, and they changed each time he saw a way to expand Grameen again.

A few years later, Yunus did accept World Bank support, but not for Bangladesh. Starting with Malaysia in 1987, other countries started imitating Grameen. One or two people would visit, go home, and start things up, and then Yunus or some of his senior staff would go there to offer advice. At a conference in Chicago in 1994, Yunus proposed a special fund to support the replications. In the audience was Adele Simmons, head of the MacArthur Foundation. Right away she agreed to kick off the fund. From there, many other funders joined in with grants and loans, including the World Bank.

In 1998, Yunus reported "sixty-five Grameen replication projects in twenty-seven countries," with "more than $88 million in loans to some 280,000 poor people." A separate arm of Grameen, the Grameen Trust, supports the replications. The head of the trust is none other than H. I. Latifee, who first led Yunus into Jobra so many years before.

Throughout Grameen's history, key people gave up their previous ideas to support it—starting with Yunus himself. It might seem like luck that R. A. Howladar was regional manager of Janata,

Annisuzzaman was head of Kishi, Gangopadhaya was deputy director of the Central Bank, Germaine was head of Ford in Bangladesh, and Simmons was head of MacArthur. And Yunus seems doubly lucky to run into each one at just the right time.

But was it luck—or *coup d'oeil?* Yunus talked about Grameen to everyone he met. Hundreds of people through the years criticized him, ignored him, or praised him. A precious few had their own *coups d'oeil* about how they might help him succeed. Those few include Grameen's employees: They grew in number from Priti the Buddhist widow in 1976 to 43 in 1979, 420 in 1982, 4600 in 1987, and over 12,000 from 1994 on.

Sometimes it was not clear right away what role an ally might play. For example, Khalid Shams was on the staff of the government's Management Training Center. His students first told him about Grameen, so Shams went to see for himself. When IFAD came around, Yunus suggested Shams join their mission from the government side. We recall that the IFAD mission first turned Grameen down: Shams helped bring them around.

A few years later, Shams joined Grameen as Yunus's second-in-command. When Bornstein interviewed him, Shams made this comment about the Grameen staff:

Yunus has shown the way. Pardon the comparison: Columbus discovered America, but once he established the track, other ships could follow.

So as Grameen borrowers are "members," the staff and various allies are "followers." They follow the trail that Yunus blazed. They give up the trail they were on before and switch to Grameen, because it succeeds in helping the poor, at scale and low cost, in one of the poorest countries of the world.

Some international agencies now "follow" Grameen, but still most do not. Support of Grameen and its replications account for a tiny fraction of total aid to poor countries. As Yunus notes, "There have always been a few individuals in the World Bank who understand." Same with some individuals at other agencies. But overall the agencies have not changed. They still refuse to follow.

To follow, you have to give up your own ideas, your own plans, your own designs. This is very hard to do, especially for development experts. They think they know the answer. But you don't "know" an answer, you see it in a *coup d'oeil*. And then you follow it with resolution.

For the World Bank and other agencies to truly follow Grameen, they would have to stop designing massive multi-year projects from scratch. Instead, you would go on a treasure hunt, to look for something that already shows some elements of success, where someone like Yunus spent years already working out the "track." When you find it, *coup d'oeil* will tell you what to do next, and resolution will carry you through to do it.

And as you hunt, you need presence of mind. It would be a great coincidence—no, a miracle—for what you find to match what you expect to find. So you have to expect the unexpected, like Yunus when he first explored the unknown world of Jobra's poor.

Thanks to his Grameen achievement, Yunus imagines "a world without poverty":

> *We have created a slavery-free world, a smallpox-free world, an apartheid-free world. Creating a poverty-free world would be greater than all these accomplishments while at the same time reinforcing them. This would be a world that we could all be proud to live in.*

As with other great achievements of history, Napoleon's glance shows the way.

10

✝ ✝ ✝

SAMURAI STRATEGY:

THE MEIJI REVOLUTION OF JAPAN

Three times in its history, Japan as a nation had a great *coup d'oeil.*

The first time came in the seventh century A.D., by way of Korea. Japan was still very new, a tiny kingdom on the southern end of its biggest island, Honshu. On a map the country looks like a dragon: The head is Hokkaido island, Honshu is the body, and the islands of Shikoku and Kyushu make two feet. From southern Honshu, the tail, Korea is just over a hundred miles away by sea.

At the time, Korea was a small kingdom too, very much like Japan. The two countries traded back and forth. Then the Koreans made a discovery: a wonder of the world, a marvel of marvels, heaven on earth. It was Ch'ang-an, the capital city of China, a thousand miles to the west.

The Koreans spread the news to Japan. In A.D. 600, the Japanese royal court sent a delegation to see for themselves.

Over the next century, the Japanese went back again and again. For the first few years the Sui dynasty ruled in China, but in 618 began the Tang. At the time, Tang was the largest empire on earth and Ch'ang-an the greatest city. The Silk Road brought prosperity through trade with India and all the way to the Mediterranean. It was China's golden age. The Tang let religion and philosophy boom: Tao and Confucius from China itself, Buddhism from India, Zoroastrianism from Persia, and even a Christian church. Traders from all nations mixed freely in Ch'ang-an. It was during the Tang that block printing spread through China: You carve

223

characters in blocks and press paper over them. Thanks to block printing, millions of Chinese learned to read and write.

Coup d'oeil.

The Japanese brought it all back to Japan.

They built a new capital modeled on Ch'ang-an. Prince Shotoko wrote a constitution modeled on China's government: It became the longest-lasting written constitution in the history of the world, from 604 to 1946. The Japanese had no written language, so they borrowed Chinese characters and block printing. Chinese music, dance, architecture, fashion, pottery, cavalry, martial arts, and courtly manners—Japan took them all.

The third *coup d'oeil* of Japan as a nation came in 1946, after the Second World War.

A gang of military officers had led their people to the brink of total destruction: Japan lay in ruins from American bombing. The American army occupied the country, at first in fear. They expected fanatic resistance like the kamikaze pilots who plowed into American ships, or the Japanese soldiers and civilians of the small island of Okinawa who fought to the death or jumped from cliffs instead of giving up.

Once in Japan, the Americans found the opposite. The Japanese greeted them with open arms. It helped that the emperor told them to do it. But even so, the Americans marveled at how the Japanese "picked things up."

Coup d'oeil.

The Japanese studied what the Americans did, to do the same themselves. After all, America was many times greater an industrial power than Japan even before the war. It worked: Over the next twenty years, Japan bounced back to become the second greatest industrial power in the world, with the fastest rate of growth in history.

Both the first and third *coups d'oeil*—in the seventh century and 1946—brought fortune to the country while keeping it Japan. Despite massive imitation, Japanese culture remains distinct and strong. So, too, with the second *coup d'oeil*, in the 1860s—but this one was greatest of all.

In the seventh century, China and Japan were both peasant kingdoms. The Japanese saw a way to make their peasant kingdom better. In 1946, America and Japan were both industrial countries. The Japanese saw a way to make their industry better. In contrast, the *coup d'oeil* of the 1860s vaulted Japan from peasant nation to industrial power. It was a great transformation that touched every corner of Japanese life, every hill and valley of the country, every Japanese.

There were many heroes of the tale. Here we follow only one, Yukichi Fukuzawa. He helped the country take up more achievements from other nations than anyone else in Japan.

Fukuzawa was a samurai. That made him a follower of Zen Buddhism, which came to Japan from China. Zen is "Chan" in Chinese, from "dhyan" in Sanskrit, the original language of sacred Buddhist texts. The word means "meditation." Zen is more philosophy than religion: We recognize "Zen mind" as "presence of mind" in von Clausewitz. Samurai enter battle thinking of nothing, predicting nothing, ready to spring into action with whatever combination of actions the situation demands. They expect the unexpected.

Samurai thrived in peasant Japan. In the 1860s, they were suddenly obsolete. But Yukichi Fukuzawa used his samurai mind for a new battle, to bring Japan into the modern world.

I will begin by telling something about my family. My father, Fukuzawa Hyakusuke, was a samurai in the service of Oku-daira, the lord of Nakatsu in the province of Buzen on the island of Kyushu. My mother, called O-Jun as her given name, was the eldest daughter of Hashimoto Hamaemon, another samurai of the same clan.

So begins *The Autobiography of Fukuzawa Yukichi*. From the first, we see how much Fukuzawa's samurai heritage meant to him. Old Japan had four classes: samurai, farmers, artisans, and merchants.

The samurai were the highest class. They were nobles. Like knights in Europe, the samurai fought for their king and received land in return. The peasants on that land paid tax in rice to the samurai, who in turn paid a tax to the lord.

As king fought king, samurai fought samurai. One king defeated the others, and he became the emperor. In 1600, a samurai knight rose to conquer Japan, and he became the shogun. For the next two hundred and fifty years, the shoguns ruled, while the emperors kept to their palace. Peace reigned in the country.

And then:

My exact age was nineteen years and three months when in February of the first year of Ansei (1854) I set out to Nagasaki. At that time there was not a single one in our town who could understand the "strange letters written sideways"... But it was a few months after the coming of Commodore Perry. And the news of the appearance of the American fleet in Tokyo had already made its impression on every remote town of Japan... Now all those who wanted to study gunnery had to do so under the Dutch who were the only Europeans, after the seventeenth century, permitted to have intercourse with Japan.

The first year of "Ansei" is the reign of a new emperor. In 1860, the Emperor died and his heir began a new reign, so that was the first year of "Mannen." As for the "strange letters" written sideways"—that was Dutch. Japanese and Chinese writing went up and down. In the 1600s, the shogun barred all foreigners from setting foot in Japan, except for the Dutch in the port of Nagasaki. They allowed the Dutch one ship per year. This was the Chinese model, where the emperor of China closed the country to foreign trade except for Hong Kong and a few other ports.

But on July 8, 1853, an American fleet sailed into Tokyo Bay. Commodore Matthew Perry brought four ships, two steam frigates and two sailing sloops. The steam frigates had sails plus a paddlewheel on the side, turned by great steam engines. The engine chimneys spewed black smoke. At the time, as Fukuzawa tells us, "A steam engine could not be seen anywhere in the whole of Japan." The country feared invasion: For defense, many Japanese turned to study "gunnery" from the Dutch in Nagasaki.

The Chinese model had proved a dead end for Japan. In 1842, Britain defeated China in the First Opium War. As a result, foreign traders overran the country, buying and selling at will. The chief product they sold to China was opium from India. In just a few years, China fell into ruin. Perry arrived in Tokyo Bay to open Japan up next. Other foreign nations followed. In 1858, Japan signed a Treaty of Five Nations—with America, Holland, Russia, England, and France—to open the country up like China.

The Japanese had no choice. If they tried to resist, foreign armies would destroy the country. But they still had time: The country was much smaller than China, so fewer foreign traders arrived. And China had long, flat rivers that reached deep into the country, which made it easy for traders to travel. Japan was a nation of hills, which made travel harder. So Japan had a few years' grace before foreigners took over the country.

Most educated Japanese looked down on foreigners, but a few rebels started to study them. Fukuzawa was one of the first. We saw in 1854, right after Perry's visit, Fukuzawa went to study Dutch in Nagasaki. After the 1858 Treaty, he visited Tokyo Bay to practice his Dutch on the foreign traders arriving:

> *To my chagrin, when I tried to speak with them, no one seemed to understand me at all. Nor was I able to understand anything spoken by any one of all the foreigners I met. Neither could I read anything of the signboards over the shops, nor the labels on the bottles which they had for sale.*

The new traders spoke English, not Dutch.

I realized that a man would have to be able to read and con-
verse in English to be recognized as a scholar in foreign sub-
jects in the coming time. In my disappointment my spirit was
low, but I knew that it was not the time to be sitting still. On
the very next day . . . I took up a new aim in my life and deter-
mined to begin the study of English.

So Fukuzawa started over, this time with English. But how did
a samurai decide in the first place to become "a scholar in foreign
subjects"? Wasn't a samurai supposed to fight?

By Fukuzawa's day, thanks to centuries of peace, the samurai did
very little fighting. The highest ranks of the samurai class lived as
lords on their bountiful rice tax. The lowest ranks has a lowly share
of the rice tax, so many of them became farmers, merchants, or artisans. The middle ranks worked for the upper, as officials of the lordly
courts. Fukuzawa came from a middle rank: His father handled the
extra rice from his lord's estates and sold it to merchants for cash.

Japan's samurai class was far larger than the noble class of
Europe. That meant the ranks within the samurai mattered very
much. So the upper samurai looked down on everyone else,
including Fukuzawa. The highest of all were the "shogun's men,"
who wore on their robes the *aoi* crest, in the shape of a hollyhock.
Fukuzawa had a low opinion of them: "They did not really have
brains to think with or even physical initiative." Yet:

We might leave our inn on a cold winter morning to take a
ferry. After waiting for an hour on the windy river bank . . . just
as we were about to step in, should some men wearing the aoi
crest come, we would have to wait another hour for the next
ferry. Again at some wayside station . . . we would look every-
where for vacant litters. Once we had found some ready, and
were about to stow ourselves in, up would stalk a wearer of the
aoi crest, and we would have to stand aside . . . I decided that
here was the worst government in the world.

In Europe, the French Revolution and then Napoleon over-turned such noble privilege. Could Japan now do the same?

At first, it seemed impossible. Anti-noble meant pro-West. Officially, the government made peace with the West through the Treaty of Five Nations. But:

> *If one were to examine the individual official, one would have found each one an ardent hater of anything new and Western. All those who had any influence or commanded respect were wearing long swords. Many of the fencing masters of the city had been honored with commissions by the government, and they suddenly became the idols of the people. It was no time for the students of foreign culture to hold up their heads above others.*

The "long swords" were the symbol of samurai rank for men. You wore them through the cloth belt of your robes. Even as a poor student, Fukuzawa always wore his swords whenever he went out in public:

> *... the majority of the students ... had pawned their swords so that there were perhaps only two or three pairs in the whole dormitory . . . Yet we had no difficulty, for the few pairs of swords were our common property, and anyone wore them who wished to appear in formal dress. On ordinary days they went around with only one sword so as not to lose entirely the dignity of belonging to samurai.*

Fukuzawa never used his sword, but he did know how:

> *As a young man I had learned iai-nike, the art of drawing the long sword in an emergency, and I had frequently practiced it at home and at school in Osaka.*

But now Japan could never defend itself with swords. The

230 · NAPOLEON'S GLANCE

black-smoke steamships of Perry's first visit made that very clear. Yet Fukuzawa's samurai training served him well in other ways.

The greatest classic of samurai training is *Book of Five Rings* by Miyamoto Musashi, written in the 1640s. Musashi was known as the "Sword Saint"—the greatest samurai of his era. Here are some excerpts from his *Book:*

> *It is said the warrior's is the twofold Way of pen and sword, and he should have a taste for both Ways. Even if a man has no natural ability he can be a warrior by sticking assiduously to both divisions of the Way . . .*

> *In China and Japan practitioners of the Way have been known as "masters of strategy." Warriors must learn this Way . . .*

> *If you merely read this book you will not reach the Way of strategy. Absorb the things written in this book. Do not just read, memorize or imitate, but so that you realize the principle from within your own heart study hard to absorb these things into your body.*

For Musashi, strategy applies to "pen and sword." He himself, a great fighter, wrote a book, and he urges his students to study it. So Fukuzawa can follow the samurai "Way" even as a scholar. The *Book* continues:

> *In strategy your spiritual bearing must not be any different from normal. Both in fighting and in everyday life you should be determined though calm. Meet the situation without tenseness yet not recklessly, your spirit settled yet unbiased . . .*

> *It is necessary in strategy to be able to look to both sides without moving the eyeballs. You cannot master this ability*

quickly. Learn what is written here: use this gaze in everyday life and do not vary it whatever happens.

These passages apply the principles of Zen to both "fighting" and "everyday life." Musashi describes presence of mind, and the "gaze" that leads to a *coup d'oeil.*

And more:

The strategist makes small things into big things, like building a great Buddha from a one-foot model . . .

The Way of strategy is the Way of nature. When you appreciate the power of nature, knowing the rhythm of any situation, you will be able to hit the enemy naturally and strike naturally . . .

When you attain the Way of strategy there will not be one thing you cannot see.

You must study hard . . .

Masters of the long sword are called strategists . . . To master the virtue of the long sword is to govern the world and oneself, thus the long sword is the basis of strategy.

From a "one-foot model" to a "great Buddha" sounds like building on past achievement. To strike "naturally," with the "rhythm of any situation," sounds like Napoleon, who never tried to control circumstances but, rather, followed them. Again Musashi applies samurai strategy to "the world and oneself," not just fighting. And again he praises study.

At the end of the first chapter, the Book offers this summary:

This is the Way for men who want to learn my strategy:

- *Do not think dishonestly*
- *The Way is in training*
- *Become acquainted with every art*
- *Know the Ways of all professions*
- *Distinguish between gain and loss in worldly matters*
- *Develop intuitive judgment and understanding for everything*
- *Perceive those things which cannot be seen*
- *Pay attention even to trifles*
- *Do nothing which is of no use . . .*

If there is a Way involving the spirit of not being defeated, to help oneself and gain honor, it is the Way of strategy.

This summary makes no mention of fighting. It is Zen for life. Fukuzawa gave up the sword and applied Musashi's samurai strategy to a life of the "pen" instead. He helped Japan avoid "defeat" and "gain honor," in the true samurai Way.

The year after I settled in Tokyo—the sixth year of Ansei (1859)—the government of the Shogun made a great decision to send a ship-of-war to the United States, an enterprise never before attempted since the foundation of the empire. On this ship I was to have the good fortune of visiting America.

At the time, Fukuzawa was twenty-four years old. He had graduated from poor student to poor teacher: His clan had sent him to Tokyo to open a school on the clan's estate there. First he taught Dutch, then English. He received from his clan enough rice to live on, but that was all. When Fukuzawa heard about the ship to America, he begged the captain to take him along as a personal servant. The captain said yes right away.

There were no other candidates. No one else wanted to go.

The ship was a little corvette, with twelve cannons, sails, and a small steam engine for moving in and out of harbor. It was built in Holland in 1856 and sold to Japan the next year.

Since the second year of Ansei (1855), after the opening of the ports, officers had been studying navigation and the science of steamships under the Dutch residents of Nagasaki. By now their skill and practice had made them able to venture; so the council of the Shogun had decided that Japanese officers and crew should take a ship across the Pacific to San Francisco at the occasion of our first envoy's departure to Washington.

The envoy himself and his grand entourage sailed on a big American warship. The little Japanese ship went along as an escort. It was a test of skill for the crew. Many thought they would never make it—including some "elder officials of the government." But the corvette left in January 1860 and landed safely in San Francisco after thirty-seven days at sea.

I am willing to admit my pride in this accomplishment for Japan. The facts are these: It was not until the sixth year of Kaei (1853) that a steamship was seen for the first time; it was only in the second year of Ansei (1855) that we began to study navigation from the Dutch in Nagasaki; by 1860, the science was sufficiently understood to enable us to sail a ship across the Pacific.

This was the start of Fukuzawa's great *coup d'oeil.* He witnessed his countrymen learn and apply correctly Western knowledge for the benefit of Japan. And still they remained Japanese. A photograph taken in San Francisco shows Fukuzawa and five other members of the crew: They wear flowing robes and two swords each.

From then on, Fukuzawa set out to help his countrymen acquire other Western skills for the benefit of Japan, while still remaining Japanese. He followed *Book of Five Rings:* "the Way is in training," "Become acquainted with every art," "Know the Ways of all professions." Art after art, profession upon profession, Fukuzawa saw its essence—its Way—and showed it to Japan.

In San Francisco, the crew saw modern industry, dancing, and other "strange customs of American society." Fukuzawa and the Japanese interpreter each brought back a Webster's dictionary, the first in Japan. Back in Tokyo, he wrote a short English-Japanese dictionary. It was his first publication.

And then:

> A little later I was taken by the government to become a translator of messages from foreign legations . . . My chief advantage in holding the position under the Shogunate government was that I had the opportunity to practice English.

This position led to a second voyage overseas. In 1862, the government sent envoys to Europe too. Fukuzawa went along as an official translator. The whole trip took a year:

> On this tour I was at last somewhat able to use English . . . I was given opportunities to visit the headquarters and buildings of the naval and military posts, factories, both governmental and private, banks, offices, religious edifices, educational institutions, club houses, hospitals—including even the actual performances of surgical operations.

Fukuzawa also studied "the most commonplace details of foreign culture:"

> Europeans would not describe them in books as being too obvious. Yet to us those common matters were the most difficult to comprehend. So whenever I met a person whom I thought to be of some consequence, I would ask him questions and would put down all he said in a notebook.

He did not bother with Western science, "which could more readily be obtained in text books." Instead, as *Book of Five Rings* told him, Fukuzawa "perceived those things which cannot be seen." He sought out Western "strategy:"

For instance, when I saw a hospital, I wanted to know how it was run—who paid the running expenses; when I visited a bank, I wished to learn how the money was deposited and paid out. By similar first-hand queries, I learned something of the postal system and the military conscription then in force in France.

Fukuzawa returned to Japan with a full picture of how the country might use Western strategy to its own advantage. His *coup d'oeil* was complete. His samurai training had served him well.

But then:

Back in Japan once more, I found the country at the height of the anti-foreign movement.

While Fukuzawa was in Europe, China lost the Second Opium War. The European powers divided up the country and declared themselves completely free of Chinese law. Instead of a warning, many samurai saw China's loss as a call to combat.

I had never thought of having a public enemy, or felt any fear of assassination. But now, since our return from Europe, the situation had changed. The ronin were appearing in the most unexpected places; even some of the merchants engaged in foreign trade suddenly closed up their shops for fear of these lawless warriors.

A "ronin" was a samurai warrior without a lord. They had always existed, as bandits or as swords-for-hire. In the 1860s, anti-Western samurai now took up the name as a badge of honor.

The reason the ronin included us in their attack was that they

thought we scholars who read foreign books and taught for-
eign culture were liars trying to mislead the people and make
way for Westerners to exploit Japan.

During Fukuzawa's voyage home, an Englishman had ridden
his horse across the path of a local lord. The lord's samurai killed
him at once. In return, a British warship destroyed the local port,
Kagoshima. It was the first shots fired against Japan since Perry's
ships arrived. Everyone expected many more.

Right away, a ronin revolt broke out against the shogun. Forty
ronin, including some from Fukuzawa's home island of Kyushu,
took over the emperor's estate at Yamato. They beheaded the
shogun's local governor and issued a call to arms:

In recent years, since the coming of the Western barbarians . . .
our country has fallen more and more into the barbarians'
toils, has become a slave of the barbarian worms; and . . . it is
the Emperor's wish . . . to put himself at the head of an army of
chastisement.

They did this without consulting the emperor. They wanted
troops from the rest of the country to join them at Yamato: to
mount an army, overthrow the shogun, and fight the foreigners. Instead, the shogun sent ten thousand troops, who
crushed the revolt.

But the Yamato rebels were very popular. Other revolts broke
out. Ronin murdered more shogun officials. Yet over time, the rebels
switched their slogan from "Honor the Emperor, Expel the For-
eigner" to "Enrich the Country, Strengthen the Army." Now they
permitted Western knowledge if it fortified Japan.

So Fukuzawa started publishing. *The Rifle Instruction Book,* in
three volumes, and *Western Ways,* also in three volumes, both came
out in 1866. The next year Fukuzawa went to America again, as interpreter on a mission for the shogun government to buy American

warships. He brought back dozens of books in English. In 1867 and 1869, he published seven more volumes of *Western Ways*.

Meanwhile, in 1868, the rebels won. They removed the shogun and replaced him with the emperor Meiji. So began the Meiji Revolution. The race was on, to make Japan an industrial power before it collapsed like China.

Like the art of *iai-nike* he practiced in his youth, Fukuzawa drew his sword at just the right moment. Here is a description of *Western Ways* by Eiichi Kiyooka, who translated Fukuzawa's *Autobiography* into English:

> *This was an invaluable guide to everyone who wanted to study the European civilization. It proved a great help to the Meiji government. Also it opened the eyes of men in business and students of general sciences to many new possibilities. About one hundred and fifty thousand copies of the authorized version were sold. When the forged edition that was printed in Osaka was added, the total number amounted to no less than two hundred thousand. Its table of contents includes such subjects as political systems of European nations, methods of taxation, national debts, joint-stock company, schools, newspaper, library, hospital, poorhouse, schools for the blind and the deaf and dumb, asylum for the insane, museum, steam engine, steamship, railway, telegraph, gas light, the European ideas on society and social economy, the meaning of liberty and self-government; also outline histories and government and military organizations of all the principal countries of Europe and America.*

All together, the ten volumes of *Western Ways* make a single *coup d'oeil*. From his trips to America and Europe and from the books he brought back, Fukuzawa's samurai eye picked out the Western achievements of use to Japan. He put them together as a single Way for Japanese to follow.

And so they did. But not all at once, and not right away.

Anti-foreign feeling stayed strong. Ronin still roamed. Assassinations continued. Fukuzawa reports:

The period ... to the sixth or seventh year of Meiji ... was for me the most dangerous. I never ventured out of my house in the evenings during that period. When obliged to travel, I went under an assumed name, not daring to put my real name even on my baggage ... The final purpose in all my work was to create in Japan a civilized nation, as well equipped in both the arts of war and peace as those of the Western world ... It was natural then that I should be disliked by the older type of Japanese, and suspected of working for the benefit of foreigners.

Fukuzawa's closest call came on a visit to his hometown:

Back in Nakatsu was a second cousin of mine, Masuda Sotaro, ... a pronounced advocate of "Honor the Emperor and Expel the Foreigners" ... Sotaro came and hid himself in our yard ... I happened to be entertaining a guest that evening. It was my senior friend, Hattori Gorobei, and a very hearty sort of man he is. He and I were sitting together in the living room, drinking and talking ... All the while, outside in the dark, Sotaro was watching our every move. At midnight we were still talking and drinking ... Finally Sotaro was worn out and gave up his cherished plan. This seems to be an instance where the merit, or perhaps the coincidence, of my habit of drinking really saved my life.

The Meiji government "was yet busy organizing itself ... And so ours was the only center in the country where Western learning was being taught." Fukuzawa's school expanded to three hundred students, many from "the battlefields:"

Among them was a certain young warrior from the Tosa clan who wore a pair of swords in red lacquered sheaths . . . he was a typical soldier with all the fiery spirit of the old military, ready to draw at the least provocation.

Fukuzawa's school was the first one that charged tuition and taught in English. Until then, schools depended on gifts from the students, following "the Chinese custom." Fukuzawa himself took no salary from the school: He depended on income from books. When the Meiji government asked him to take over all government schools, Fukuzawa declined. If he did that, he would have no time for writing.

Even after his monumental *Western Ways,* he continued to publish every year on other subjects. For example: *Summary of the Western Art of War,* five volumes, in 1869; *Bookkeeping* in 1873; *An Elementary Book of Penmanship and Reading,* two volumes, in 1871; *Popular Economics* in 1877; *On Currency* in 1878; *The People's Rights* in 1878; and *On Business* in 1893.

Sometimes he wrote special pieces. In 1871, in exchange for more space for his school, Fukuzawa helped out the city of Tokyo:

The city of Tokyo was still using a system of military patrol, and soldiers of various clans appeared in the streets, carrying guns on their shoulders as they marched along. The practice . . . made Tokyo seem to be continually in a battle area. The government was planning to adopt a Western police system, but being unable to secure exact information on its organization, one of the officials called on me one day to ask me privately to make a study . . . I collected several English books on civic government and translated the portions dealing with police systems, making a book out of it which I presented to the prefectural office. Soon the Tokyo authorities set about creating their new police organization,

basing it on my translation though with due changes for the
existing conditions of the Japanese city.

There was one last anti-modern revolt. In 1873, the Meiji government abolished the privileges of the samurai class. It was the Napoleonic Code for Japan, based on writings by Fukuzawa and other students of Western ways. In reaction, samurai from Fukuzawa's home island of Kyushu mounted a rebel army. At the battle of Shiromaya in September 1877, forty thousand samurai with swords met sixty thousand government troops with rifles. The soldiers knew how to use their weapons thanks to Fukuzawa's first published manual, *The Rifle Instruction Book.*

The samurai never had a chance. Sword against rifle: The battle was a massacre. Among the samurai dead was Masuda Sotaro, the cousin of Fukuzawa who had crouched in the dark, waiting to kill him, seven years before.

Fukuzawa kept writing and teaching until his death in 1901 at the age of sixty-six, three years after he finished his *Autobiography.* By then Japan was a great industrial power. Annual steel production had grown from zero in 1868 to over five thousand metric tons. Rail lines went from zero to nearly four thousand miles. And so on throughout the economy. Even rice production doubled.

Fukuzawa's great *coup d'oeil* of *Western Ways* played its part. Hundreds of Japanese visited America and Europe in the 1850s and 1860s, and many of them played important roles in the Meiji Revolution. But Fukuzawa saw more "Ways" than anyone else by far. And thanks to him, millions of Japanese saw their way through turbulent, fearful times.

I am not sure whether most of the scholars of the age were
unskilled in writing, or whether they were so absorbed in the
prospect of gaining high posts in the government . . . I
seemed to be alone in the field of writing for popular causes,

and it became the sole basis of my livelihood and later of my reputation.

In later decades, some Japanese criticized Fukuzawa on two counts. First, for too much support to the army, which forty years later led the country into World War II. In Fukuzawa's defense, his last years were the great era of colonial conquest: He feared Japan becoming an English, French, German, or American colony. On the second count, in more than a dozen publications he pioneered women's rights—but not beyond Western women at that time. His school admitted only men, like the colleges of the West. And women did not vote in any Western country, so Fukuzawa did not argue for woman suffrage. Japanese women only won the vote in 1946.

As Fukuzawa drew from Western achievements, we might ask as well: did anyone draw from him? Especially—any women?

Let's go back to Perry's warships.

As they steamed into Tokyo Bay, among the samurai watching from shore was Tsuda Sen. He was eighteen years old—two years younger than Fukuzawa. Right away he set to studying Dutch. Like Fukuzawa, he soon switched to English. Tsuda was one of the other interpreters on Fukuzawa's second American visit in 1867. In 1871, Tsuda's daughter, Umeko, was the youngest of five girls on the first female delegation from Japan to America. She was seven years old at the time.

Little Tsuda Umeko grew up to become the Fukuzawa of women's education. She spent eleven years in American schools and came back to teach in Japan. But all she could teach was domestic arts: cooking, sewing, decorating, hygiene, and entertaining. There was no academic schooling for girls. So in 1889, she used her American contacts to return for college, at Bryn Mawr, outside Philadelphia.

Coup d'oeil.

Fukuzawa plus Bryn Mawr.

Tsuda graduated in 1892. Back in Japan, she helped other Japanese women find American scholarships to American colleges. In 1900, she opened her own college in Tokyo: the Women's Institute for English Studies. She modeled it on Fukuzawa's school and taught the same academic courses as Bryn Mawr, in English. In contrast, the government opened Tokyo Women's College also in 1900, as a training school for teachers of domestic arts. The schools of Fukuzawa and Tsuda became Japan's leading private universities, and remain so to this day.

Fukuzawa Yukichi and Umeko Tsuda were notable examples of Napoleon's glance in Meiji Japan. Many others made it into history books, like Umeko Tsuda's father. And then there were millions of ordinary Japanese who had their own *coups d'oeil*, about how to combine "Western ways" with elements of old Japan in their life and work. They were all followers of Miyamoto Musashi, students of the *Book of Five Rings:*

> *The strategist makes small things into big things, like building a great Buddha from a one-foot model . . .*

Their one-foot model was each combination of Japanese and Western elements, and their great Buddha was the thriving nation of Japan. Scholars call Meiji a "revolution from above," because one group of upper samurai replaced another to take control of the country. But thanks to Fukuzawa and many others, there was a "revolution below" as well, where ordinary Japanese played their part. Many failed to find their way—like the thousands of samurai dead on the field at Shiromaya. But the rest, as a nation, once again proved themselves masters of Napoleon's glance.

11

✛ ✛ ✛

JOAN OF ARC SAVES FRANCE

In my town they called me Jeannette, and since I came to France I have been called Jeanne ... I was born in the town of Domremy ... My father was called Jacques d'Arc and my mother Isabelle.

So begins the testimony of Jeanne d'Arc, or "Joan of Arc" in English, at her trial for witchcraft in 1431. The court found her guilty and burned her at the stake. Twenty-five years later, in 1456, another court cleared her name. Centuries later, in 1920, she became an official saint of the Catholic church. Joan of Arc is the patron saint of France and of soldiers, and one of the most famous heroes of all time.

Yet a mystery remains: How did Joan succeed? She was a peasant girl of only eighteen, but in less than a year she saved France from certain conquest by England. She turned the tide of the Hundred Years' War, the longest in Europe's long history of fighting among its various nations. That fighting lasted to 1945, the end of World War II. Six centuries later, after dozens of wars, Joan of Arc still stands out among hundreds of military leaders.

How did Joan do it? At the time, both sides thought it was magic. The English, her enemy, called it bad magic: witchcraft. Her own side, the French, called it good magic: a holy miracle. It was an English court that condemned her, and a French court that cleared her name. Joan herself claimed that voices sent by God told her what to do. So Joan believed it was magic too.

And it was: the magic of Napoleon's glance. Looking back, you can find all the elements: past examples, presence of mind, *coup d'oeil*, and resolution. When it happens, no one really knows how to explain it. Some call it luck or chance or fortune. In the Middle Ages, they called it divine intervention. For the French in the throes of the Hundred Years' War, that divine intervention was Joan.

Here is Joan's account of her voices:

> *When I was thirteen years old, I had a voice from God to help me govern my conduct. And the first time I was very fearful . . . When I came to France, often I heard this voice . . . The voice was sent to me by God and, after I had thrice heard this voice, I knew that it was the voice of an angel. This voice has always guarded me well and I have always understood it clearly . . . Saint Michael, when he came to me, told me that Saint Catherine and Saint Margaret would come to me and that I should act by their advice.*

Throughout her testimony, Joan refers to four voices: one sent "by God," plus three saints. Why these three: Michael, Catherine, and Margaret?

In the Middle Ages, paintings and drawings showed St. Michael in armor, at battle against Satan. In 1425, the year Joan first heard voices, the French won a rare victory in the Hundred Years' War by repelling an English attack on the fortress of Saint-Michel. As for Catherine and Margaret, they numbered among the statues in Joan's local church. Margaret of Antioch tended sheep, like Joan, while Catherine of Alexandria came from a noble family. They both refused to submit to pagan Romans, who had them put to death.

So Joan's saints were a great soldier plus two virgins who died at the hands of foreign rulers. And St. Michael in 1425 saved his namesake town. In the Middle Ages, stories of saints gave you inspiration: You picked out saints to imitate, prayed to them, and their spirits came inside you. Different saints gave different inspiration. Joan set out to become a soldier, like Michael. For that she had to remain pure, like Margaret and Catherine. Otherwise her fellow soldiers would take her for sex instead of obey her commands. Even so, she knew the risk: death at the hands of a foreign ruler, also like Margaret and Catherine.

In 1428, when Joan was sixteen, the English attacked Orléans. The city guarded the key bridge over the Loire River. If Orléans fell, France was doomed:

> *The voice told me that I should go to France and . . . raise the siege of Orléans . . . And . . . to come to the aid of the King of France . . . The voice told me also that I should make my way to Robert de Baudricourt in the fortress of Vaucouleurs, the Captain of that place, that he would give me people to go with me . . . Robert twice refused and repulsed me, and the third time he received me and gave me men.*

Vaucouleurs was the nearest main town to Joan's little village of Domremy. Captain Baudricourt of the Vaucouleur fortress ignored her at first. But then:

> *For fear of the Burgundians, I left my father's house and went to the town of Neufchateau in Lorraine . . . where I stayed for about fifteen days.*

The "Burgundians" sacked Domremy and other villages around Vaucouleurs. Baudricourt changed his mind because the enemy arrived at his doorstep. On the verge of defeat, with nothing to lose, Baudricourt did what Joan asked: He sent her on to the king of France.

The Burgundians were French allies of the English. Note how Joan says she left her home and went "to France"—that means she started from somewhere else. At that time, her village was stuck in no-man's-land between the Duchy of Burgundy, the English, and the Duchy of Lorraine. Lorraine stretched into Germany and stayed out of the Hundred Years' War. When Joan wrote her name, she used a German spelling: "Jehanne," like Johanna in German. Neufchateau, where she escaped the Burgundians, was safely in Lorraine.

Vaucouleur and Domremy were in a last pocket of northeast France loyal to the French king. When Joan's voices told her to go "to France," they meant the Ile-de-France, the core of the French kingdom, around Paris and Orléans. At the time, Paris was in English hands, and Orléans was under siege, so the French king held court at Chinon, just south of English control. So Baudricourt sent Joan to Chinon.

But first, the Duke of Lorraine asked to see her. She went to his castle in nearby Nancy:

> I told him that I wanted to go to France, and the Duke questioned me about the restoration of his health and I told him that of that I knew nothing . . . I said to the Duke that he give me . . . some men to take me into France and that I would pray to God for his health.

Already we see Joan's reputation for magic: The duke thought Joan could heal him. Note her answer: "Send me to France and I'll pray to God." On the one hand, it was perfectly normal to pray for someone's health. On the other hand, was Joan hinting her prayers had special force?

Baudricourt sent Joan to Chinon with four knights and two servants. She wore men's clothes for the journey, to prevent her escorts from getting ideas. They traveled eleven days through enemy territory. Joan dictated letters that reached the king first—she did not know how to read and write but only sign her name. Once in Chinon, Joan waited two days for the king's advisers to let her see him.

Who were the king's advisers? Let's single out two. Georges de la Trémoille led the anti-Joan faction. The Duke of Alençon led the pros.

Both Trémoille and Alençon had been taken prisoner by the English and released on payment of ransom. Trémoille's capture came in 1415 at the battle of Agincourt, the greatest military disaster for the French in all the Hundred Years' War. The English lost four hundred men while the French lost eight thousand, including most of their noble knights. After, Trémoille became the voice of defeat: He counseled the king to retreat instead of fight.

Alençon's capture came in 1424 at the battle of Verneuil, another big loss for the French. He spent five years as an English prisoner before his ransom came through. His feudal lands in Normandy were firmly in English hands: Alençon wanted to fight.

When Joan arrived at Chinon in 1429, she was seventeen years old. Trémoille was forty-three. Alençon was twenty-five. The king himself, Charles VII, was twenty-six. He had become king seven years before on the death of his father, Charles the Mad. It was during the long reign of Charles the Mad, from 1380 to 1422, that most of France lost all hope of winning the Hundred Years' War.

Trémoille and the rest of the royal court advised the king to play it safe lest he lose all in fighting. Half of France was better than none: Let England and Burgundy take the rest. Alençon spoke for the army: They wanted to fight. Right away they wanted the king to send supplies and troops to save Orléans. But Trémoille won out. The king did nothing. Orléans was on its own.

Alençon's chief ally was the French commander at Orléans, Jean Dunois the Bastard. The Duke of Orléans was still a prisoner in England, from his capture at Agincourt seventeen years before. Dunois was his brother, a "bastard" son of their dead father. Dunois ruled in the duke's absence. The English held on to the duke because they thought him the only man able to rally the French against them. And he was: So a woman did it instead.

Rumors of Joan reached Dunois before she reached Chinon. So he sent a knight, Jamet du Tillay, who made it in time to see Joan enter the court. Tillay reports:

I was there in Chinon and at the castle when the Maid arrived and I saw when she presented herself before the King with a great humility and simplicity, this poor little shepherdess; and I heard the following words she said to the King: "Very noble lord Dauphin, I am come and sent by God to bring help to you and your kingdom."

"Dauphin" meant uncrowned king. The kings of France were crowned in the cathedral of Reims, northeast of Paris, now in English hands. The dauphin Charles had given up hope to ever gain his crown. Meanwhile, the English king claimed the crown of France by marriage. After all, the line of English kings went back to William the Conqueror, who invaded England from France in 1066. Dozens of marriage ties wove together the French and English nobles. By 1429, it was perfectly possible—or even likely—for England to swallow up France completely. In the future, France would become like Wales: once an independent country with its own language, now a province of England.

As for Alençon, he was not at Chinon when Joan arrived:

I was out shooting quail when a messenger came to tell me that there was come to the King a maid who affirmed that she was sent by God to drive out the English, and to raise the siege which was laid by the English to Orléans ... I went to the King who was in the town of Chinon and I found Joan talking with the King. When I drew near, Joan asked who I was and the King replied that I was the Duke of Alençon. Thereupon, Joan said: "You, be very welcome. The more they shall be together from the blood royal of France, the better will it be." ... And on

the morrow . . . the King took Joan into a chamber and I was
with him and the Lord of la Trémoille whom the King kept
with him, telling the others to withdraw.

Right away, the struggle begins: Joan and the king in a room
alone with Alençon and Trémoille. We know that Trémoille counseled the king to ignore Joan. Alençon wanted to hear her out.

Joan asked several things of the King, among others that he
give his kingdom to the King of Heaven, and that the King of
Heaven after that gift would do unto him as he had done to his
predecessors and would restore him to his original estate; and
many other things which I do not remember were said until
the time of the meal. And after the meal the King went out to
walk in the meadows and Joan galloped a-tilt with a lance,
and I seeing her behave in this manner, bearing a lance, and
tilting, I gave her a horse.

This was the start of a minor *coup d'oeil* on Alençon's part. He
saw Joan on a horse with a lance. She was young and strong, used
to hard work, so riding a horse while holding a lance was easy
enough for Joan to do. But most likely, Alençon and his fellow soldiers had never seen a woman do it. He gave her a horse, to ride as
a soldier, at the head of a column to save Orléans.

At this point, Alençon saw that Joan's success was making
others believe that France had a chance to win the war. People
believed in her, starting with the six men who took her from Vaucouleur to Chinon. The leader of the six, Jean de Metz, praised her
to the skies:

I had great confidence in the Maid's sayings, and I was fired by
her sayings and with love for her, divine as I believe. I believe
that she was sent by God.

Thanks to the rumors, soldiers arrived at Chinon every day to join up with Joan. Alençon saw a way to use the faith that Joan inspired, soldier to soldier, among the army of France. He made his case to the king to send Joan with troops and supplies to Orléans.

But Trémoille stalled. And then he brought in the priests. Alençon continues:

> Thereafter, the King came to the conclusion that Joan should be examined by some churchmen. To this end were deputed the bishop of Castres . . . the bishop of Senlis . . . those of Maguellone and Poitiers . . . Master Pierre of Versailles . . . Master Jean Morin and several others whose names I do not recall. They questioned Joan in my presence: why she was come and who had made her come to the King. She answered that she was come on the King of Heaven's behalf and that she had voices and a counsel that told her what she was to do.

Note that Alençon stayed by Joan's side. So Trémoille sent her away:

> Once he had heard the report of those delegated to examine her, it was the King's will that Joan go to the town of Poitiers and that there she be examined again. But I was not present at the examination . . . I only know that thereafter in the King's council it was reported that those who had examined her had said that they had found nothing in her contrary to the Catholic faith and that, considering his necessity, the King could make use of her to help him.

Poor Trémoille! Instead of denouncing Joan, the Poitiers priests end up telling the King that "considering his necessity" he "could make use of her to help him."

At this point, there are two accounts of what "help" exactly Joan offered. Simon Charles, a member of the dauphin's court at Chinon, reports:

> *She said that she had two commissions for which she had been sent by the King of Heaven: one to raise the siege of Orléans, the other to lead the King to Reims for his coronation.*

Pierre Seguin, a priest in the dauphin's court who took her to Poitiers, adds a third item:

> *First, she said . . . the town of Orléans would be freed of the English . . . Second . . . the King would be anointed at Reims . . . Third . . . the city of Paris would return to the King's rule.*

For the moment, though, only Orléans counted. According to Seguin, the Poitiers priests gave specific advice to the King:

> *And . . . they were of the opinion that, in view of the urgent need and the peril that there was to the city of Orléans, the King could be aided by her and to send her to Orléans.*

Seguin himself became one of Joan's greatest converts:

> *I believe that Joan was sent by God, considering that the King and his court had no hope, but that all believed in beating a retreat.*

After the Poitiers priests gave Joan their blessing, the last step was for ladies of the court to make sure she was really a "maid"—that is, a virgin. She was.

So the king had no choice but to send Joan to Orléans. Alençon had his way. He dressed Joan in white armor, with a full sword, mounted on his white horse. She had her own standard: a white

flag with angels. By then hundreds of troops had arrived to follow
her. Alençon commanded the column, with Joan riding at his side.
But first: the supplies.

> *The King sent me to the Queen of Sicily to get together the sup-*
> *plies to be taken to Orléans for moving the army there ... But*
> *there was need of money, and to have money for these supplies*
> *I returned to the King and notified him that the supplies were*
> *ready and that it remained only to give the money for these*
> *supplies and for the soldiers.*

The "Queen of Sicily" was the king's mother. She held the purse
strings of the kingdom. One of her close attendants, Marguerite la
Touroulde, reports on the state of the treasury:

> *At that time there was in his kingdom and in those parts loyal*
> *to the King, such calamity and such penury of money that it was*
> *piteous, and indeed those true to their allegiance to the King*
> *were in despair. I know because my husband was at the time*
> *Receiver General and, both of the King's money and his own,*
> *he had not four crowns. And the city of Orléans was besieged*
> *by the English and there was no means of going to its aid. And*
> *it was in the midst of this calamity that Joan came, and, I believe*
> *it firmly, she came from God and was sent to raise up the King*
> *and the people still within his allegiance, for at that time there*
> *was no hope but in God.*

Here the struggle between Trémoille and Alençon comes down
to money. The dauphin's court spent a fortune on clothing, food,
servants, and entertainment. The army wanted that money for
fighting. When Alençon found the regular treasury empty, he went
to the king and asked for money from the court account. That is,
from Trémoille.

Alençon continues:

Then the King sent someone to deliberate of the money needful to conclude all this, so that the supplies and the soldiers were ready to go to Orléans to attempt to raise the siege.

So again, Alençon got his way. The column set out for Orléans. It was all he wanted. His presence of mind made him ready for the unexpected: Joan. He saw her achievements in giving hope to soldiers and civilians alike. He turned those achievements into a way to bring reinforcements to Orléans. His resolution carried him through the king's doubt and the court's opposition, especially by Trémoille.

Alençon took the column halfway to Orléans, where it met up with other contingents at Blois. The total came to four thousand men—all come to follow Joan. At Blois, a more experienced general took over: La Hire, older than Alençon by more than a decade.

His work was done—or so he thought—so Alençon stayed behind.

The Friday following twenty-ninth of the same month (April), came into Orléans certain news that the King was sending . . . supplies, powder, cannon, and other equipment of war under the guidance of the Maid, who came from Our Lord to revictual and comfort the town and raise the siege—by which were those of Orléans much comforted.

So records the *Journal of the Siege*, by an unknown citizen of Orléans. It tells us further that Jean Dunois went out to meet the column. A "great skirmish" in "great strength" with "many dead" distracted the English enough for the column to enter the town.

She entered thus into Orléans, having on her left hand the

Bastard of Orléans very richly armed and mounted, and after came many other noble and valiant lords, esquires, captains and men of war . . . On the other hand came to receive her the other men of war, burgesses and matrons of Orléans, bearing great plenty of torches and making such rejoicing as if they had seen God descend in their midst.

And then—nothing.

Joan entered on Friday. The next day, according to Lois de Coutes, her page:

Joan went to see the Bastard of Orléans and spoke to him, and on her return she was in great anger; for, said she, he had decided that on that day they would not go out against the enemy.

Instead, Dunois went out again to lead more troops from Blois to the city. Sunday, Monday, Tuesday passed. Sometimes Joan rode around the city to cheering crowds. Once she came close enough to the English to speak to them: "If they would yield themselves to God their lives were safe." The English "answered basely, insulting her and calling her 'cow-girl,' shouting very loudly that they would have her burned if they could lay their hands on her."

Wednesday: Dunois came back with more troops from Blois. Joan's valet, Jean d'Aulon, reports:

As soon as she knew they were come . . . hastily the Maid sprang to horse and, with some of her men, went out to meet them . . . That same day, after dinner came my lord of Dunois to the Maid's lodging where she and I had dined together. And speaking to her his lord of Dunois told her that he knew it for true by trustworthy men, that one Falstaff, an enemy captain, would soon be coming to the besieger enemies, both to bring

them succor and reinforce the army and to supply them, and
that he was already at Janville. At these words the Maid was
right rejoiced, as it appeared to me, and she spoke to my lord
of Dunois these words, or similar ones: "Bastard, Bastard, in
God's name I command thee that, as soon as thou knowest
that Falstaff is come, thou shalt make it known to me, for if he
pass without my knowing of it, I promise thee I will have thy
head taken off!" To which answered the lord of Dunois that she
doubt not, for he would indeed make it known to her.

We see here that Joan really thought she was leading the army.
She gives Dunois orders and threatens to cut off his head. For his
part, Dunois throws her off the scent. He tells her the fighting will
start when Falstaff arrives, and Falstaff is at least a day's march
away at Janville. But the truth is: Falstaff is still in Paris, many days
from Orléans.

Aulon continues:

After these exchanges, I who was weary and fatigued cast
myself down on a mattress in the Maid's chamber, to rest a
little. And likewise did she, with her hostess, on another bed, to
sleep and rest.

While Joan sleeps, Dunois attacks the English.

We see that Dunois has no intention of letting Joan fight. She did
her job, to bring troops and supplies to Orléans. Now it is up to
those troops, under Dunois's command, to do their job in turn.
The English hold four forts outside the city: Saint Loup, Blanc,
Augustins, and Tourelles. Dunois attacks Saint Loup first, the
smallest of the four.

But then Joan wakes up.

She hears the battle.

Lois de Coutes recounts that she said to him: "Ah, bloody boy, you told me not that the blood of France was spilling!" Joan throws on her armor, mounts her horse, and takes up her standard. Off she goes to join the battle, with Coutes hurrying after.

He reports:

> *The English were preparing their defense when Joan came in haste at them, and as soon as the French saw Joan, they began to shout and the bastion and fortress of Saint-Loup were taken.*

That was it.

Coup d'oeil.

Dunois sees Joan's success in battle. She does not fight, but the French fight harder with Joan among them. So next time, he brings her along to battle.

For the English fort of Blanc, Dunois puts Joan on horseback alongside La Hire, the most experienced general present. La Hire directs part of the attack from a spot where all can see him but does not enter the actual fighting. There we see Joan at his side, lance in hand, watching over the troops like a guardian angel.

When the French reach Blanc fort, the English are gone. They had run away to the two remaining strongholds. So the French continue to Augustins and take it.

For the last fort, Tourelles, Joan joins the "council of war." She is there by the side of Dunois as the French make their plan of assault for the next day.

He recounts:

> *On 7 May, early in the morning, when the attack began . . . Joan was wounded by an arrow which penetrated her flesh between her neck and her shoulder, for a depth of half a foot. Nevertheless, her wound not restraining her, she did not*

*retreat from the conflict, nor did she take medication for her
wound.*

For the Tourelles attack, Joan moves closer to the fighting,
within range of English arrows. By the end of the day, despite her
wound, she moves even closer.

Dunois continues:

*The assault lasted from the morning until eight o'clock ... so
there was hardly hope of victory that day. So that I was
going to break off and wanted the army to withdraw
towards the city. Then the Maid came to me and required
me to wait yet a while. She ... mounted her horse and retired
alone into a vineyard ... And ... remained at prayer during
one half of a quarter of an hour. Then she came back from
that place, at once seized her standard in hand and placed
herself on the parapet of the trench, and the moment she
was there the English trembled and were terrified. And the
king's soldiers regained courage and began to go up,
charging against the stronghold without meeting the least
resistance.*

For the last fort, Joan gathers her courage for a few moments
and thrusts herself onto the front line, in full view of English
archers. It is an act of great courage, putting herself in the same
danger as an ordinary soldier. Still, she does not fight, but her ges-
ture has its effect on the English as well as the French.

The last fort falls.

Orléans is saved.

Jean Dunois had the presence of mind to expect the unexpected:
Joan threw herself into battle, and it rallied the French troops.
Based on her first success at the Saint Loup fort, he helped her do

it again, at Blanc, Augustins, and Tourelles. They freed Orléans in only four days.

After Orléans, Dunois took Joan to Alençon. Now Alençon saw it too: a great *coup d'oeil* to repeat the model of Orléans and win the Hundred Years' War.

Dunois:

> *After the deliverance of Orléans, the Maid, with me and the other captains of war, went to seek the King . . . to ask him for armed forces in order to recover the castles and towns situated on the river Loire . . . so as to clear the way and make it safe for him to go to Reims for his coronation. She urged the King eagerly and often to hasten and not to delay any longer. From that time he used all possible diligence, and he sent me, as likewise the Duke of Alençon and the other captains, with Joan, to recover the said towns and castles.*

As Dunois commanded at Orléans, Alençon took command of the Rheims campaign. They were brothers-in-law, and Orléans was a year older, but Alençon outranked him by far in noble blood. Together, they saw how best to use Joan. And she joined them not as a mascot, but as an equal.

Dunois again:

> *I remember that . . . the lords of the blood royal wanted the King to go into Normandy and not to Rheims, but the Maid was still of opinion that we should go to Rheims to consecrate the King . . . for . . . once the King should be crowned . . . the strength of his adversaries would go on declining and that at last they would not be able to harm him or his kingdom. All rallied to her opinion.*

Rheims had no military value. Normandy was the English base

in France, so that was where the "lords of the blood royal" wanted to aim for next. Again, Dunois and Alençon had the presence of mind to shift from the obvious plan to Joan's. In Orléans, she showed them that the way to beat the English was not through normal military means but by rallying France behind Joan herself. She promised the king his crown at Rheims, so she had to make good her word.

Rheims versus Normandy is the only military decision that comes from Joan. Dunois and Alençon endorse it. To get to Rheims, Alençon first chases the English out of the Loire valley towns of Jargeau, Meung, and Beaugency. It takes only a week. At each battle, Joan is among the fighting, holding her standard high for all to see.

Meanwhile, more French troops enlist. At Beaugency, a key general appears: Arthur Richemont. He is of La Hire's generation, a decade older than Alençon and Dunois. Richemont held the rank of king's chief counsel until a few months before Joan arrived on the scene. He counseled the king to fight. Trémoille pushed him out and took his place, and counseled the king to retreat. Now Richemont returns, first as a general, but soon to rival Trémoille again.

After the Loire, the French army heads north for Rheims. At Patay, they meet Falstaff's army. Dunois and Alençon ride in the front, with Joan and Richemont in the rear. The French hardly pause on their march: They win the battle in less than an hour. The English lose two thousand men. The French, only three.

It was now safe for the king to join the army. They marched the rest of the way to Rheims without any further battles. Letters went out to all of France calling nobles to the coronation. Joan even sent a letter to the Duke of Burgundy, asking him to abandon the English and come to Rheims. The duke never answered. At the coronation, the crowd cheered Joan even more than the king.

After Rheims, the way was clear to take Paris. Instead, Trémoille worked out a truce with Burgundy. It helped that Trémoille had a cousin in the Burgundy court. The truce gave the English time to send reinforcements to Paris. Then the king renewed the truce, giving up some of the land he had just won.

Thanks to Trémoille, the king was ready to let victory slip from his hands. In early September, the king finally gave permission to attack Paris, once again with Alençon leading and Joan by his side. But right in the middle of the battle, the king called it off—again, thanks to Trémoille. The king and his court retreated to the Loire.

That was the end of Joan's campaign. Alençon's official scribe, Perceval de Cagny, reports:

> *Messire Regnauld de Chartres, the lord de la Trémoille, the sire of Gaucourt, who at that time governed the King's council and matters of war, would never consent, nor permit, nor suffer that the Maid and the Duke of Alençon be together, and since then he has not been able to recover her.*

Of Dunois and the others we hear no more. The main army scatters to fight the English here and there instead of as a single force. Joan remains at court, and sometimes at Trémoille's castle at Sully in the Loire valley. She keeps urging the king to fight, so in October he lets her try for the town of Charité. To get there, she takes the lesser town of Moutiers, but her siege of Charité fails.

For a few weeks, she wanders with her band of soldiers, seeking battle. She finds it at Compiègne. The Burgundians have the town under siege. Joan slips in, just like at Orléans. Then she rides out to attack. The Burgundians beat her back. Her troops retreat across the drawbridge over the moat to the main gate of the town. The Compiègne garrison sees the Burgundians right at their heels, so they pull up the drawbridge. Most of the French make it inside. A few remain behind, cut off. The Burgundians capture them.

Among the captives: Joan.

From there, the Burgundians sell Joan to the English for a fabulous sum. The French court never lifts a finger to ransom her. By the rules of war, the English cannot execute a prisoner captured in battle. So instead, they give her to a court of French priests in Rouen, their main base in Normandy. Since England treats Normandy like English soil, the priests are on England's payroll. No surprise: They convict Joan of witchcraft and burn her at the stake.

But the damage is done. The French army fights on without the king. Right after Joan's capture, they arrive at Compiègne and beat back the Burgundians. While Joan awaits trial, La Hire sweeps through Normandy. Victories come hard, but the tide has turned. In 1433, two years after Joan's death, Richemont returns as chief counselor. Trémoille's reign is over.

So the generals are back in power. Two years later, the Duke of Burgundy gives up the fight. He turns on the English and joins the French. A year later, 1436, Richemont takes Paris. Still the war continues. Bit by bit, France retakes its land. When Dunois retakes the Bordeaux region in 1453, the English give up trying to conquer France. Their last bastion, Calais, falls in 1465. The war is over. It began in 1340, a hundred twenty-five years before.

So Joan did not win the Hundred Years' War: She saved France from defeat. She gave the army new life, and it went on to drive out the English.

Joan was only nineteen when she died. After Paris, it seemed she thought she knew how to fight on her own. So maybe she never understood how Dunois and Alençon used her after their *coups d'oeil* showed them how. But they never used her against her will. And they gave her all the credit.

Alençon:

In everything that she did, apart from the conduct of the war,

Joan was young and simple; but in the conduct of war she was most skilful, both in carrying a lance herself, in drawing up an army in battle order, and in placing the artillery. And everyone was astonished that she acted with such prudence and clearsightedness in military matters, as cleverly as some great captain with twenty or thirty years experience.

It seems that Joan learned quickly the skills of a soldier and general in the few short months of her great campaign. But not enough to command on her own. Under Dunois and Alençon, she won. Without them, she lost.

Dunois:

I believe that Joan was sent by God, and that her deeds in the war were the fruit of divine inspiration rather than of human agency.

Alençon and Dunois believed in Joan only after her first achievements. Alençon saw how she gave the French new spirit, so he used that to send relief to Orléans. Dunois saw her rally the troops to take Saint Loup, so he used her again to take the other three Orléans forts. Then together, Alençon and Dunois repeated the Orléans model all the way to Paris.

So, Alençon and Dunois showed presence of mind, their *coups d'oeil* came from past achievements, and their resolution overcame court opposition. They proved themselves masters of Napoleon's glance.

But what about Joan—did she have a *coup d'oeil* too?

Let's go back to her voices.

When I was thirteen years old, I had a voice from God to help me govern my conduct. And the first time I was very fearful.

And came this voice, about the hour of noon, in the summer-time, in my father's garden; I had not fasted on the eve preceding that day. I heard the voice on the right-hand side, towards the church; and rarely do I hear it without a brightness. This brightness comes from the same side as the voice is heard. It is usually a great light . . . This voice . . . told me that I should go to France and . . . I should raise the siege laid to the city of Orléans . . . And me, I answered it that I was a poor girl who knew not how to ride nor lead in war . . . Saint Michael, when he came to me, told me that Saint Catherine and Saint Margaret would come to me and that I should act by their advice, that they were bidden to lead me in what I had to do.

This is a *coup d'oeil* of some kind, for sure. It starts as a nagging voice in your head, over and over until you say, "I see the light!" when your path appears. So voices and brightness can mark a *coup d'oeil*. Because of the times and her tender age, Joan's *coup d'oeil* struck with a mystical, holy force wrapped up in ancient legends.

We know about her three saints: Joan saw herself fighting, like Michael, and dying a virgin at the hands of foreign rulers, like Catherine and Margaret. Popular legends made these saints real to the people of Joan's time. But there is another legend behind Joan's *coup d'oeil*. It never comes up in her speech or in any account of her life. Yet this missing legend was always there, surrounding Joan like the sea surrounds a fish, or following like a shadow.

The missing legend is the Holy Grail.

In Joan's day, the Holy Grail was fresh in the mind of every knight. There were versions of the tale in English, French, and German. An English knight, Thomas Malory, drew mostly from the French to write *Le Morte d'Arthur*. It brings together dozens of tales of King Arthur and his Knights of the Round Table. A few of those stories tell of the Grail. Malory died in 1471, and his book came out in 1485. After that, *Le Morte d'Arthur* became the leading source in all languages for the legend of the Holy Grail.

Malory fought against Joan. He served under the Earl of Warwick, a famous English general and Joan's captor at Rouen. Malory picked up French accounts of the Grail and brought them back to England. In Malory's tale, the Grail is the chalice that Christ used at the Last Supper before his death on the cross. Today, the "Holy Grail" is a common term for a great achievement just beyond your reach. So a low-cost fuel that causes no pollution is the Holy Grail for car makers. A treaty that all sides agree to is the Holy Grail for the Middle East. And so on. But in Joan's time, the Holy Grail was real. The Knights of the Round Table really saw it.

Malory drew mostly from *La Queste del Saint Graal,* written by an anonymous French monk sometime between 1215 and 1230. *La Queste* tells how on the feast of the Pentecost—when the Holy Ghost came down to the Apostles after Christ was dead—King Arthur and his knights partake of a similar event. The windows fly open, thunder sounds, light fills the hall, and the Grail appears. It gives off a wonderful fragrance and pours forth to every knight whatever and how much he wishes to eat. Then the Grail disappears. The knights set off to find it.

But the Grail was not always a chalice. Its original form comes through in *Parzival,* written by a German knight, Wolfram von Eschenbach, in 1210. Parzival, or "Perceval" in English, is the knight who finds the Grail. Richard Wagner used this version for his great opera, *Parsifal.* Wolfram describes the Grail:

> *. . . a precious stone . . .*
> *Amply wide and amply long*
> *Cut thin, for lightness' sake, but strong*
> *To make a table of it . . .*

Perceval and four hundred other knights eat and drink whatever and how much they wish from the "table." In earlier myths, this "table of plenty" also brings the dead back to life when you place them on it. And Wolfram's Grail was made of the "philosopher's stone:" Alchemists make a bowl of the stone, put in iron and lead, and they come out gold.

The original Grail was a magic cauldron that made wishes come true. We see a glimpse of this even in *La Queste,* where the Grail becomes a Christian relic. It fed King Arthur's knights, and when the Grail knight finally finds it again, he looks inside:

> *Now I see all openly what tongue cannot speak, neither heart conceive: the beginning and end of the great adventure.*

In other words: *coup d'oeil.*

In the legend of the Holy Grail, you see something, it vanishes, and you set off after it. You see the "beginning and end" together: that is, the whole path. Not in detail, but enough to follow through with resolution. Today, when your *coup d'oeil* and resolution are very strong, you might joke that you're on a "mission from God." In the Middle Ages, it was no joke: In everyone's mind, worthwhile missions came from God.

Perhaps in the Middle Ages, Napoleon's glance was a wondrous thing. No one knew how to explain it, so it took on a holy, magic cast. For Joan, saving Orléans and crowning the king was her mission from God. She saw it, and set off after it. And from the first she saw the end of the "great adventure:" death like Catherine and Margaret.

Joan was a knight of the Holy Grail.

✠ ✠ ✠

CONCLUSION:
A LESSON OF HISTORY

Those who cannot remember the past are condemned to repeat it.

George Santayana, an American philosopher, wrote these words around 1905. Half a century later, William Shirer made them famous as an opening quote for *The Rise and Fall of the Third Reich.* Shirer's book became the most popular source in English for the story of Nazi Germany. He uses the Santayana quote as a warning: Heed the lessons of history. Study what happened in Germany to make sure it never happens again, there or anywhere else.

But Santayana meant his quote as encouragement too, not just as a warning: He thought the past had good to offer as well as bad. His famous quote comes from his book *Reason and Common Sense* in a section he calls "Continuity Necessary to Progress." Here is more of the section:

> *Progress, far from consisting in change, depends on retentiveness. When change is absolute there remains no being to improve and no direction is set for possible improvement: and when experience is not retained, as among savages, infancy is perpetual. Those who cannot remember the past are condemned to repeat it. In the first stage of life the mind is frivolous and easily distracted; it misses progress by failing in consecutiveness and persistence. This is the condition of children and barbarians, in whom instinct has learned nothing from experience.*

This passage is a century out of date for its "savages" and "barbarians." Today, historians know that nonliterate societies made "progress" too—just slower and harder to trace. So Santayana's view of progress applies to those societies too. For him, progress requires "retentiveness." Those who cannot remember the past are condemned to repeat it *exactly*, while those who can remember the past are free to repeat it *partly*. They carry forward the parts of the past most worth retaining. That is, they learn "from experience."

Napoleon's glance offers a way to describe how progress comes from experience. Santayana proclaims, "Continuity Necessary to Progress," but not complete continuity. You try to carry forward achievements and leave mistakes behind. And the "experience" you learn from is human experience, not just your own.

As Santayana says: "Civilization is cumulative." We can update this to "social progress is cumulative," and see that it applies throughout the world. As von Clausewitz says, "Strategy . . . turns to experience, and directs its attention on those combinations which military history can furnish." History is the sum of human experience. In Napoleon's glance, you draw from it "combinations" to suit the new situation. Like Shirer's warning, this is a lesson of history too.

Yet Nazi Germany taught us well that history can also go terribly wrong. Progress might be cumulative, but it's never a sure thing. So, too, with Napoleon's glance: You see a battle you know you can win, but that does not mean you will win it. Our ten stories show how strategists drew from history to make history: That improved their chances, yet never guaranteed their success. The drama of history remains. You can never know how the story ends before the story is over.

There is another common saying about missing the lessons of history: "Generals always fight the last war."

The recent war in Afghanistan looked very different from war two centuries ago, when Napoleon won his first victories. Does Napoleon's glance still apply? If you draw from history to make history, do you risk fighting the last war and so miss winning the next one? And above all: Does modern technology make obsolete the commander's *coup d'oeil*?

The notion that generals "fight the last war" comes from World War II, where the French and British expected a repeat of World War I. The Germans drove right around them. Yet that hardly argues for junking the past: The Germans and Patton drew from Napoleon and von Clausewitz to make successful modern war. More often, generals make the opposite mistake, when they think the next war will be completely different, thanks to new technology.

We recall Colonel Maude, in his introduction to the 1905 edition of *On War* by von Clausewitz: Maude thought that technical advances in long-range artillery made battlefield strategy obsolete. Bombard the enemy, and they will surrender. World War I proved him wrong. Yet right afterward, in 1921, *The Command of the Air* by an Italian officer, Giulio Doucet, promised the world an end to war on land and sea. Thanks to the latest technical marvel, the airplane, from now on all wars would be fought from the air.

The Germans pioneered the new method in April 1937 during the Spanish Civil War. They bombed the town of Guernica. Three months later, Picasso unveiled his masterpiece of the scene. During World War II, the cities of Europe and Japan suffered "strategic bombing" to stop their war machines, just like Doucet advised. It did not work: except for the nuclear attacks on Hiroshima and Nagasaki. From World War II, generals drew the lesson that airplanes best support the age-old movement of troops, and that nuclear weapons were far too dangerous to use again.

In recent decades, a new technological marvel has captured the eye of generals: PGM, or "precision-guided munitions." A satellite tells you the target's exact position, or if it's moving a laser beam locks onto it. Then a computer makes all the adjustments to guide the shot home. So computers link missiles on airplanes, ships, tanks, trucks, and even held by hand—in one big "digital battlefield."

The idea of the digital battlefield dates from the 1960s. In 1969, at the height of the Vietnam War, the American commander William Westmoreland gave this speech to a Washington audience:

On the battlefield of the future, enemy forces will be located, tracked and targeted almost instantaneously through the use of data-links, computer-assisted intelligence evaluation and automated fire control. With first-round kill probabilities approaching certainty, and with surveillance devices that can continuously track the enemy, the need for large forces to fix the opposition physically will be less important. I see battlefields that are under 24-hour real or near-real time surveillance of all types. I see battlefields on which we can destroy anything we can locate through instant communications and almost instantaneous application of highly lethal firepower.

In 2000, more than thirty years later, we find the same idea in a book by Admiral William Owens, *Lifting the Fog of War:*

The commander will know the precise location and activity of enemy units . . . enabling him to direct nearly instantaneous air strikes, artillery fire, and infantry assaults . . .

For Westmoreland and Owens, the commander is far from the battle, in a computer command center. Satellites beam information up and commands back down. There may be troops in the mix, but not "large forces," according to Westmoreland. Above all, command comes from the commander who sits at the screen, not from a commander on the ground.

So, is this the end of Napoleon's glance? Can generals now "lift the fog of war," as Owens declares? Do we no longer need a commander's *coup d'oeil* to cut through it? Jomini told you to make war "on the map" by plotting out your "objective points" and marching your troops to take them. Do we finally have maps that are good enough, and weapons that "march" fast enough, that Jomini wins over von Clausewitz?

Let's take a look at a digital battlefield, and see for ourselves.

In the spring of 1994, the army invited politicians, the press, and civilian experts to see its first digital brigade in action. Among the experts was James Der Derian, a military scholar, who wrote an article for *Wired* magazine on what he saw.

The action took place at the U.S. army's National Training Center in the Mojave Desert of California. Der Derian reports:

> *Combining real-time airborne and satellite surveillance, digitized battlefield communications, helmet-mounted displays, a 486 computer for every warrior, and an array of other high-tech weaponry, the brigade had come wired to move faster, kill better, and live longer than the enemy. If the old nuclear deterrent was to depend on the frightful force of mass destruction, the new digital strategy is to win the total information war.*

Sure enough, Der Derian sees Napoleon's glance at stake:

> *Back when messages traveled at the speed of a horse, and overhead surveillance meant a view from a hilltop, Prussian strategist Carl von Clausewitz warned in* On War *against the arrogance of leaders who thought scripted battles would resemble the actual thing: "All action must, to a certain extent, be planned in a mere twilight, which in addition not infrequently—like the effect of fog or moonlight—gives to things exaggerated dimensions and an unnatural appearance." Would digitization render von Clausewitz's famous dictum obsolete? Would today's commanders be able to use satellite tracking and computer-equipped soldiers to dispel the fog of war?*

In the war games he watched, Der Derian saw that the equipment mostly worked as promised. For such a staged event, that was no surprise. But would it work in actual war?

The Army has always prided itself on being grounded in reality.

*Now . . . the Army is leaping into a realm of hyperreality, where
the enemy disappeared as flesh and blood, and reappeared, pix-
ilated and digitized on computer screens in kill zones, as icons of
opportunity. Was there a paradox operating here, that the closer
the war game was able to technically reproduce the reality of
war, the greater the danger of confusing one for the other?*

So for Der Derian, the digital battlefield replaces the "fog of war"
with the "fog of war games." An overload of information gives the
simulated battlefield "exaggerated dimensions and an unnatural
appearance," just like a lack of information did for Napoleon. Der
Derian doubts that modern war will look much like the simulation.

The first real test of the digital battlefield came five years later,
in 1999, during the Kosovo war. For this we have a book by Wesley
Clark, the commanding general: *Waging Modern War.*

After the fall of its communist regime, the Serb government of
Yugoslavia fought a series of wars to keep all its provinces from
becoming independent countries. In the province of Kosovo, the
war became a campaign of "ethnic cleansing" to kill or drive out
non-Serbs. NATO, led by the United States, attacked Yugoslavia to
make them stop.

Clark tells us about the military education that guided his
command:

*Napoleonic strategy was part of our instruction in military
art in 1965 at West Point . . . The strategic art was to bring
the enemy to battle at the time and place of your choosing,
where you had the advantage and you could finish him.*

Yet Clark entered the war without seeing clearly a battle he
knew he could win. His "experiences and insights" from his "full
thirty-seven years of military service" told him he needed
ground troops to follow an air assault, while the civilian authorities back in Washington hoped that the digital battlefield could

win the war from the air alone. Clark argued his case, but then gave in:

> *There was an important distinction between keeping the final requirements in view and pushing so hard that the initial options couldn't be executed. I couldn't be sure that an air campaign wouldn't work; it might. More important, it certainly didn't preclude a later decision to deploy a ground force. But if we pushed too hard for an immediate commitment to go in on the ground, we jeopardized our ability to take action at all . . . In Clausewitz's* On War, *there is a crucial passage in which Clausewitz writes that "No one in his right mind would, or ought to, begin a war if he didn't know how to finish it." This had been one of the favorite Vietnam critiques . . . at the Army Command and Staff College . . . But in practice, this proved to be an unreasonable standard.*

There is another way to interpret this passage from von Clausewitz: Before you start, you must see a way to finish—but not exactly. A *coup d'oeil* shows the path, but often it lacks many details. Clark did see a way to finish: By a classic ground assault. He did not see a way to gain approval for it back in Washington—yet. So he began the air war, and day by day he figured out how to win the political battle to authorize a ground assault.

How? By mobilizing NATO troops elsewhere in Europe. Then he made his case at all levels of the civilian and military hierarchies that made up NATO's nineteen-country alliance. In the end, Clark won his authorization. The Yugoslav government gave up. After seventy-eight days, the war ended in victory. Afterward, independent studies by the Brookings Institution and RAND confirmed that the threat of a ground assault had won the day.

Like Patton, Clark obeyed orders but still found a way to follow his own *coup d'oeil*:

> *I was torn between the guidance and perspective gained from*

NATO, heavily influenced by the Department of State and the White House, and what I would hear in my U.S. military chain reporting to the Pentagon . . . Many times, I had to set my own compass and follow it.

Clark inherited in Europe the position, the office, and even the desk of General Eisenhower from World War II. Yet his alliance included far more nations, who wanted a "surgical" war as different from World War II as possible. Here's how Clark handled it: "I had to use my leverage with the Americans to gain influence with the Europeans and vice versa." And then, in preparing the ground assault, he came up against another problem: the Jomini planners within his own ranks. They insisted on a fully "coordinated" plan:

A year or two to produce one of these fully coordinated plans is not unusual. In a crisis, short-term, more limited plans can also be produced, and relatively quickly . . . but in the case of Kosovo, there simply was no detailed planning. There was no strategic consensus in Washington . . . Planning for a ground force could be seen as an admission that the air campaign might not work . . . We have been schooled on planning by using big matrices, with every cell to be filled before moving forward. We have learned a passion for detail, but not necessarily how to compromise for the sake of urgency.

To plan, you start with your "objective points." For ground troops, Washington would never agree on what those objective points were. So Clark went ahead anyway, without a plan. He would move in troops and win battles as they arose. And like Patton, he studied the path ahead with his own expert eye:

I had a final opportunity to visit Albania, and see again the routes and forbidding terrain over which I had recommended we proceed. I just had to confirm it, again. As we circled the helicopter above the steep mountain slopes and the dark green lakes, I measured with my eye the widths of the road, and imagined the wide-eyed concern of the young soldiers who would be driving their trucks, self-propelled guns, and infantry fighting vehicles up this road. They could do it, I thought. "Walt, Senator, what do you think?" I asked. "Doable, doable," Senator Warner said. He had fought as a Marine in the Korean War. He knew rough countryside.

The victory in Kosovo gave the army its model for the next war: in Afghanistan, less than two years later. It followed the same strategy as Clark, except this time the enemy did not give up before the ground assault. That assault followed not a "coordinated" plan but "compromise for the sake of urgency," to win battles as they arose.

Clark's book came out a few months before the attack on the World Trade Center provoked the Afghan war. His advice on the future of combat seems eerily accurate:

. . . High technology air power . . . has given some the clever idea that it is within our grasp to know everything about any given 200 kilometer square, and that by so doing, we can dominate the outcome of a battle with minimal risk and central control, with a couple of smart people making the key calls . . . Even with the best-intentioned efforts, "precision strike" will need augmentation by "precision acquisition and identification" of targets. We will need specific information, in real time . . . We will want to know whether the men on the tractors and inside the buses are soldiers or civilians. We will want to know whether trucks are carrying food or weapons . . . Neither the specific information nor the range of actions can yet be done from a distance. Instead, we will need to place people on the ground to observe and listen. They may have to come close, even face-close, with those we oppose. No doubt they will have fabulously powerful communications and other

technologies. But they will also require physical courage and a
willingness to take physical risks . . .

There are simply tasks that can't be done from the air. Flex-
ible, agile ground forces are required, along with strategic
transport to deploy them and sustain them. And, in the final
analysis, "boots on the ground" are more likely to be decisive in
the long term. This means having the required ground capa-
bilities and the will to use them if necessary.

In the end, Clark combined the *coup d'oeil* of Patton with the
political skill of Eisenhower—at least until the Kosovo war was
over. Six weeks later, Washington fired him.

So much for the future of war: Napoleon's glance lives on. Yet our
ten stories covered other domains of human endeavor as well: In
those, too, Napoleon's glance helps you draw from history to make
history in whatever field you're in.

For despite great prosperity in much of the world, enormous
problems remain: of poverty, disease, pollution, oppression, and
violence. There is no guarantee we can solve any one of them. But
now we know how to improve our chances. You look for success to
build on, to carry forward, to combine in new ways to suit the situation at hand. Maybe you will have the good fortune to hit on the
right combination yourself. More likely, you will find that someone
has found it before you. Then you will gladly join in.

Our cases show that *coup d'oeil* can strike at any age, in any
place, at any time. After reading these cases, you know what to look
for: a sudden truth, new but familiar, of past success emerging
from the shadows to show the path ahead.

Such is the lesson of Napoleon's glance.

A NOTE ON SOURCES

NAPOLEON

Thousands of books tell the tale of Napoleon's rise and fall, mostly from the political or social side. For the military side, see especially *The Campaigns of Napoleon* (1966) by David Chandler; and *The Age of Napoleon* (1963) by J. C. Herold. Quotes by Napoleon in the text come from Herold's *The Mind of Napoleon* (1955) and a compilation, *L'art de la guerre* (1965), by the *Club de l'honnête homme* in Paris.

For the influence of von Clausewitz on military strategy, see *The Art of War* (2000) by Martin van Crefeld; and *Clausewitz in English* (1994) by Christopher Bassford.

Here are other sources cited in the text: Carl von Clausewitz, *On War* (1832); Antoine Jomini, *Summary of the Art of War* (1838); Leo Tolstoy, *War and Peace* (1865); J. M. Barrie, *Peter Pan* (1911); Paul Johnson, *Napoleon* (2002); Frank McLynn, *Napoleon* (2002); and Mark Mazower, "The Little Corporal Who Could," *New York Times Book Review* (June 23, 2002).

PICASSO

The chapter draws from two standard works: *A Life of Picasso* (1991, 1996) by John Richardson; and *Picasso—Life and Art* (1987) by Pierre Daix. For Matisse's influence on Picasso, see *The Unknown Matisse* (1998) by Hilary Spurling; and *Matisse and Picasso* (1999) by Yves-Alain Bois. Quotes by Matisse come from *Matisse on Art* (1973) by Jack Flam. And in *Creativity: Beyond the Myth of Genius* (1993), Robert Weisberg provides a psychologist's view of Picasso's style as mix of previous elements.

The text also cites *If I Told Him: A Completed Portrait of Picasso* (1923) by Gertrude Stein.

ST. PAUL THE APOSTLE

For the basic story of early Christianity, see *A History of the Early Church* (1937) by Hans Lietzman and various entries in the *Catholic Encyclopedia*, especially: Acts of the Apostles, Antioch, Cornelius, Luke, New

Testament, Old Testament, Pharisees, Sadducees, St. Paul, St. Peter, and St. Stephen. Quotes from the Bible come from the King James version.

For Paul himself, see *The Genius of Paul* (1958) by Samuel Sandmel; *The Mythmaker: Paul and the Invention of Christianity* (1986) by Hyam Maccoby; and *Paul: A Critical Life* (1996) by Jerome Murphy-O'Connor.

LION KING

The single best source on the founding of Mali remains *Sundiata: An Epic of Old Mali* (1965) by D. T. Niane. The quotations here from G. D. Pickett's translation simplify some names: the various versions of Balla Fasséké become "Balla the Griot"; and Soumaoro's son, Balla, becomes "Soumaoro's son."

For the history of Mali and other medieval empires of West Africa, see *A History of Islam in West Africa* (1962) by J. Trimingham; *The Golden Trade of the Moors* (1968) by E. W. Bovill; and *Ancient Ghana and Mali* (1973) by Nehemiah Levtzion.

ELLA BAKER

Joanne Grant has produced three vivid portraits of Ella Baker: a book, *Ella Baker: Freedom Bound* (1998); an article, "Ella Baker," in *Portraits of American Women* (1991) by G. J. Barker-Benfield and Catherine Clinton; and a documentary film, *Fundi: The Story of Ella Baker* (1991). See also an interview with Ella Baker by Eugene Walker for the Southern Oral History Program, University of North Carolina (September 4, 1974).

For the Southern Christian Leadership Conference, see *Parting the Waters* (1998) by Taylor Branch; *To Redeem the Soul* (1987) by Adam Fairclough; *Bearing the Cross* (1988) by David Garrow; and *Keeping the Dream Alive* (1987) by Thomas Peake.

For the Student Non-Violent Coordinating Committee, see *SNCC: The New Abolitionists* (1964) by Howard Zinn; and *In Struggle: SNCC and the Black Awakening of the 1960s* (1981) by Clayborne Carson; "The story of the Greensboro sit-ins," by Jim Schlosser, in *Greensboro News and Record* (1998) (online: *www.sitins.com*).

For Bayard Rustin, see *Bayard Rustin: Troubles I've Seen*, (1997) by Jervis Anderson; and *Bayard Rustin and the Civil Rights Movement* (2000) by Daniel Levine.

The text also cites *War Without Violence* (1939) by Krishnalal Shridharani.

ALICE PAUL

The most complete modern study on Alice Paul is *From Equal Suffrage to Equal Rights: Alice Paul and the National Woman's Party* (1986) by Christine Lunardini. The most complete eyewitness account is *The Story of Alice Paul and the National Women's Party* (1921) by Inez Hayes Irwin. See also Lunardini's article, "Alice Paul," in *Portraits of American Women* (1991) by G. J. Barker-Benfield and Catherine Clinton; and interviews with Alice Paul by Amelia Fry for the Suffragists Oral History Project, University of California at Berkeley (1972–73).

Other eyewitness accounts are *Jailed for Freedom* (1920) by Doris Stevens; and *Challenging Years* (1940) by Harriot Stanton Blatch and Alma Lutz. Stevens's book includes photographs of all the women jailed.

For Carrie Chapman Catt, see *Woman Suffrage and Politics: The Inner Story of the Suffrage Movement* (1923) by Catt and Nettie Shuler; and *Carrie Chapman Catt: A Public Life* (1987) by Jacqueline van Voris. For other views of the rift between NAWSA and the Women's Party, see *Southern Strategies: Southern Women and the Woman Suffrage Question* (1997) by Elna Green; and *A History of the American Suffragist Movement* (1998) by Doris Weatherford.

For the Pankhursts, see *The Story of Emmeline Pankhurst* (1961) by Josephine Kamm; and *The Fighting Pankhursts*, (1967) by David Mitchell.

PATTON

The most complete study of Patton is *Patton: A Genius for War* (1995) by Carlo D'Este. In two volumes of *The Patton Papers* (1972), Martin Blumenson provides insightful commentary as well as exhaustive sources. In *The Patton Mind* (1993), Roger Nye takes us on a tour of the books Patton gave to West Point. See also Patton's own memoirs, *War As I Knew It* (1947). Like von Clausewitz's *On War*, it was heavily edited by the author's wife after his death.

For accounts by soldiers who served with Patton, see especially *A Soldier's Story* (1951) by Omar Bradley; "Fourth Armored Division Spearhead at Bastogne," by Alvin Irzyk, in *World War II Magazine* (14, 1999); and *G-2: Intelligence for Patton* (1999) by Oscar Koch.

See also the film script *Patton* (1970) by Edmund North and Francis Coppola. Bradley served as adviser to the movie: Note how he seems to take credit for the Avranches breakout and Patton's first moves in the Battle of the Bulge.

GRAMEEN BANK

The best source on Grameen's origin is Yunus's autobiography, *Banker to the Poor* (1998). For Grameen in operation, see *The Price of a Dream* (1996) by David Bornstein; *Give Us Credit* (1996) by Alex Counts; *Women at the Center* (1996) by Helen Todd; and *Grameen As I See It* (1994) by Yunus again.

For a negative view of Grameen, see *Women and Microcredit in Rural Bangladesh* (1999) by Aminur Rahman.

For the spread of Grameen to other countries, see *The Microfinance Revolution* (2001) by Marguerite Robinson.

MEIJI REVOLUTION

Fukuzawa Yukichi's *Autobiography* (1898) remains the best source on his own life and one of the best on the Meiji era. For scholarly studies of the era, see *The Meiji Restoration* (1972) by W. G. Beasley; *Japan in Transition: Thought and Action in the Meiji Era,* (1984) by H. Conroy, Sandra Davis, and Wayne Patterson; and *Essays on Japanese Economy* (1958) by Shigeto Tsuru.

For Tsuda Umeko, see *Tsuda Umeko and Women's Education* in Japan (1992) by Barbara Rose.

The text also cites *The Book of Five Rings* (1645) by Miyamoto Musashi.

JOAN OF ARC

Régine Pernoud stands out as the leading scholar on Joan: See especially *The Re-Trial of Joan of Arc* (1955); *Joan of Arc* (1962); and *La liberation d'Orléans* (1969). The contemporary quotes come from Pernoud's work. For more on the military side, see *Joan of Arc* (1981) by Frances Gies; and *Joan of Arc: A Military Leader* (1999) by Kelly Devries.

For Margaret and Catherine, see *Lives of the Saints* (1759) by Alban Butler; and their entries in the *Catholic Encyclopedia*.

For the legend of the Grail, including the quote from the Grial knight, see *Creative Mythology* (1968) by Joseph Campbell. The Wolfram quote comes from *Wolfram von Eschenbach's Parzival* (1951) by Edwin Zeidel.

CONCLUSION

The text cites *The Command of the Air* (1921) by Giulio Doucet. The Westmoreland quote comes from *The Electronic Battlefield* (1976) by Paul Dickson. The text also quotes from *Lifting the Fog of War* (2000) by William Owens; "Cyber-Deterrence" by James Der Derian, in *Wired* (September 1994); and *Waging Modern War* (2001) by Wesley Clark.

The studies cited are Ivo Daalder and Michael O'Hanlon, *Winning Ugly: NATO's War to Save Kosovo*, Brookings Institution (2000); and Benjamin Lambeth, *NATO's Air War for Kosovo*, RAND (2001). For a similar view on Clark's strategy, see Michael Ignatieff, "Chains of Command," *New York Review of Books* (July 19, 2001).

PHOTO CREDITS

Pages 7, 29, 117 *Hulton/Archive by Getty Images*

Page 43 *Christie's Images/Corbis*

Page 61 *Illustration from* SUNDIATA: Lion King of Mali *by David Wisniewski. Copyright © 1992 by David Wisniewski. Reprinted by permission of Clarion Books/Houghton Mifflin Company. All rights reserved.*

Page 85 *AP Photo*

Pages 145, 189 *Corbis*

Page 221 *Courtesy Columbia University Press*

Page 243 *Archivo Iconografico, S.A./Corbis*

INDEX